STAR WARS®

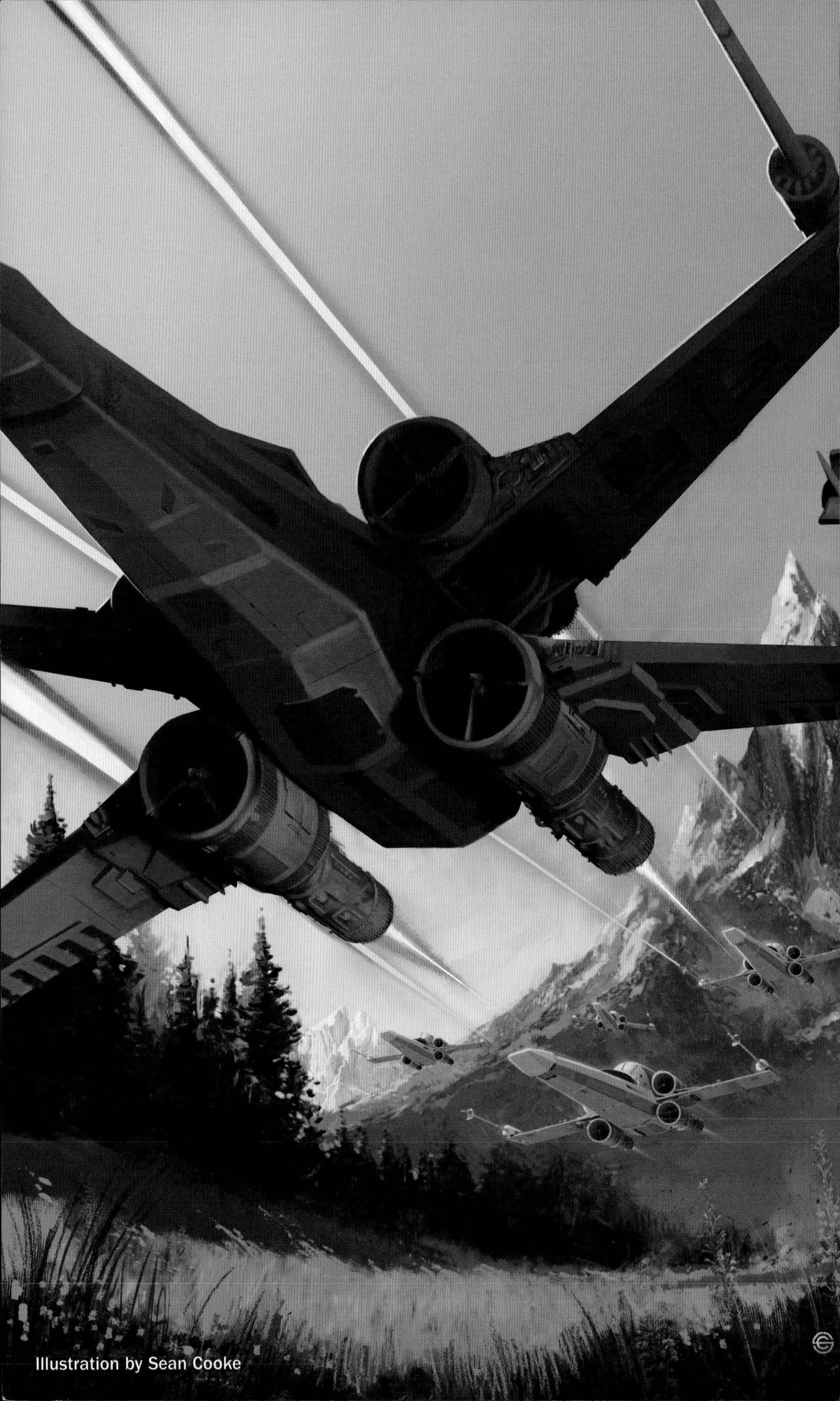

Illustration by Sean Cooke

THE REBELLION

FROM THE BATTLE OF YAVIN TO FIVE YEARS AFTER

Open resistance begins to spread across the galaxy in protest of the Empire's tyranny. Rebel groups unite, and the Galactic Civil War begins. This era starts with the Rebel victory that secured the Death Star plans, and ends a year after the death of the Emperor high over the forest moon of Endor. This is the era in which the events in *A New Hope*, *The Empire Strikes Back*, and *Return of the Jedi* take place.

The events in this story take place shortly after the events in *Star Wars: Episode IV—A New Hope*.

VOLUME THREE | REBEL GIRL

Script
BRIAN WOOD

Pencils
STÉPHANE CRÉTY

Inks
JULIEN HUGONNARD-BERT

Colors
GABE ELTAEB

Lettering
MICHAEL HEISLER

Front Cover Art
VÍCTOR MANUEL LEZA

DARK HORSE BOOKS

LUCAS BOOKS

President and Publisher
MIKE RICHARDSON

Collection Designer
RICK DeLUCCO

Editor
RANDY STRADLEY

Assistant Editor
FREDDYE LINS

Special thanks to Jennifer Heddle, Leland Chee, Troy Alders, Carol Roeder, Jann Moorhead, and David Anderman at Lucas Licensing.

STAR WARS® VOLUME 3: REBEL GIRL

This volume collects issues #15–#18 of the Dark Horse comic-book series *Star Wars*.

Published by Dark Horse Books
A division of Dark Horse Comics, Inc.
10956 SE Main Street
Milwaukie, OR 97222

DarkHorse.com StarWars.com

International Licensing: (503) 905-2377
To find a comics shop in your area, call the Comic Shop Locator Service toll-free at 1-888-266-4226

Library of Congress Cataloging-in-Publication Data

Wood, Brian, 1972-
  Star wars. Volume three, Rebel girl / script, Brian Wood ; pencils, Stéphane Créty ; inks, Julien Hugonnard-Bert ; colors, Gabe Eltaeb ; lettering, Michael Heisler ; front cover art, Víctor Manuel Leza. – First edition.
     pages cm
  Summary: ""Princess Leia agrees to marry the prince of a remote planet, gaining for the Rebellion a new base–a safe haven from the evil Empire"– Provided by publisher.
  "This volume collects issues #15-#18 of the Dark Horse comic-book series Star Wars"–T.p. verso.
  ISBN 978-1-61655-483-5
  1. Graphic novels. [1. Graphic novels. 2. Science fiction.] I. Créty, Stéphane, illustrator. II. Title. III. Title: Rebel girl.
  PZ7.7.W65Ste 2014
  741.5'973–dc23
                                      2014020044

First edition: October 2014
ISBN 978-1-61655-483-5

10 9 8 7 6 5 4 3 2 1
Printed in China

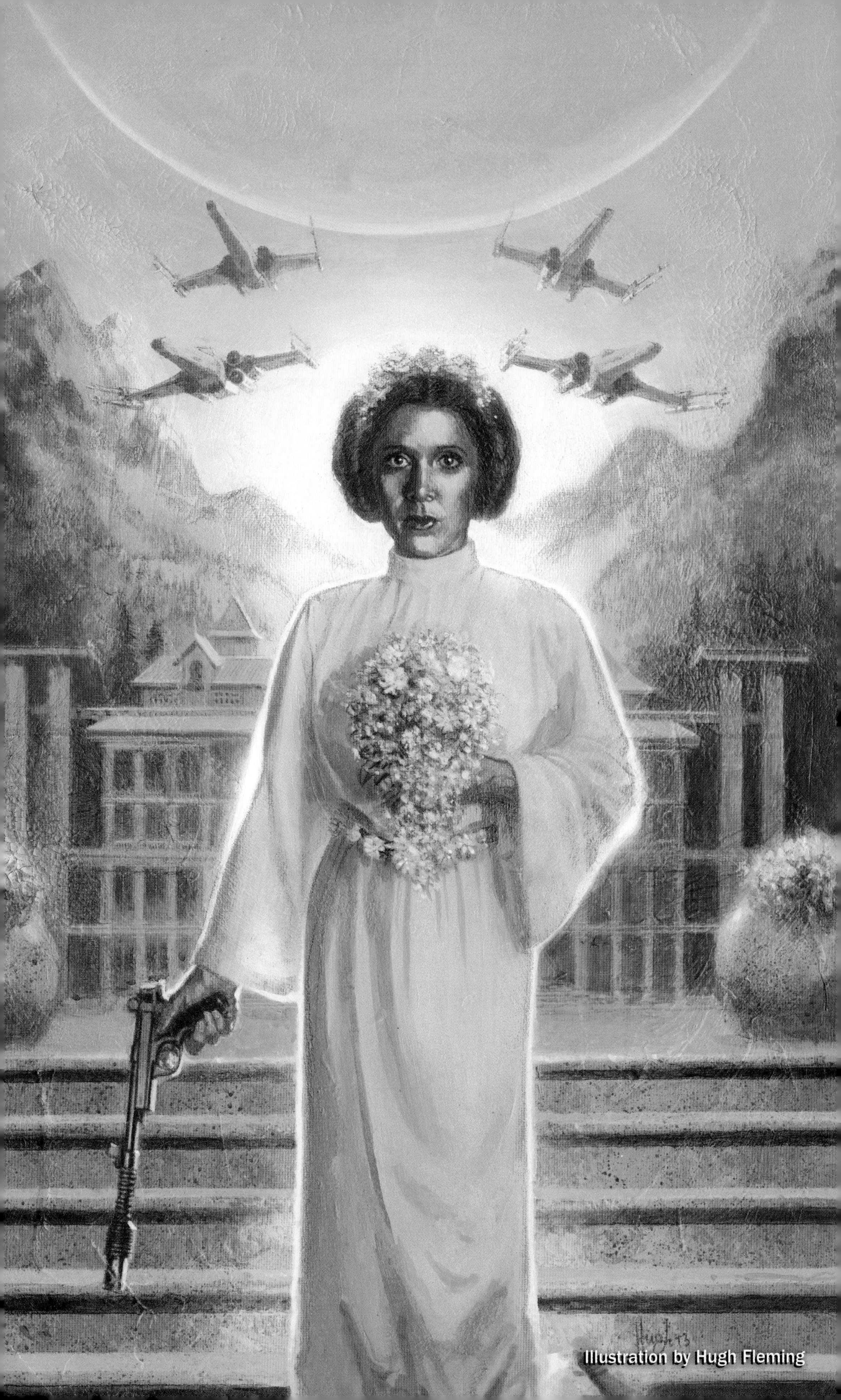

Illustration by Hugh Fleming

REBEL GIRL

Since abandoning its base on Yavin 4, the Rebel fleet has been without a sure destination or a home, constantly pursued and harassed by Imperial forces. But in the aftermath of a victorious skirmish with the Empire, Princess Leia—recently returned from a prolonged solo mission—makes the stunning announcement that she has located a safe haven for a new base: the planet Arrochar.

Even more stunning is the news of how the agreement with the government of Arrochar was reached and how the pact will be sealed: Leia is to marry the planet's prince.

As the Rebels scurry to build a new home and prepare for the upcoming nuptials, some have conflicting feelings about the impending wedding—and none more than Princess Leia herself . . .

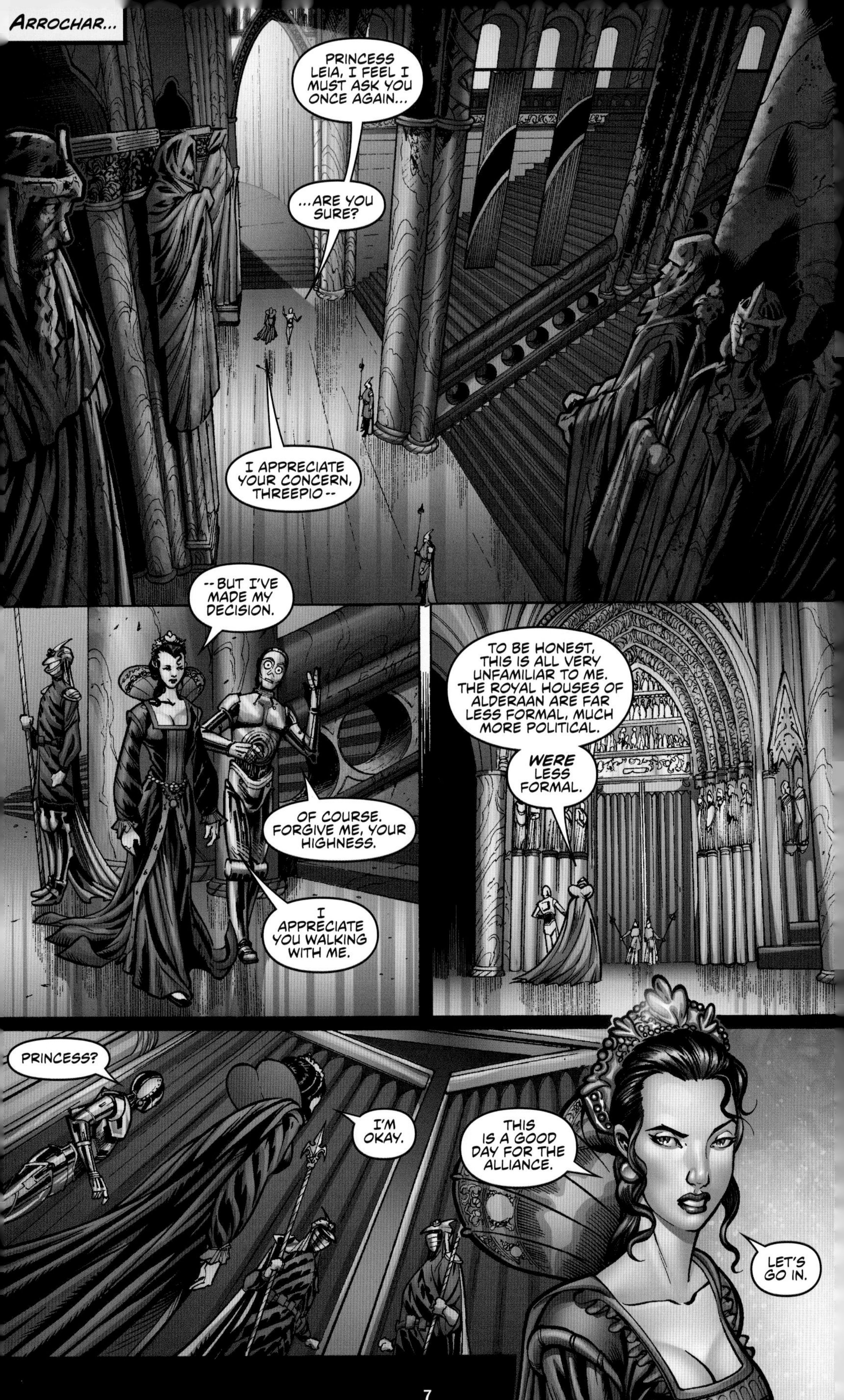
ARROCHAR...
PRINCESS LEIA, I FEEL I MUST ASK YOU ONCE AGAIN...
...ARE YOU SURE?
I APPRECIATE YOUR CONCERN, THREEPIO--
--BUT I'VE MADE MY DECISION.
OF COURSE. FORGIVE ME, YOUR HIGHNESS.
I APPRECIATE YOU WALKING WITH ME.
TO BE HONEST, THIS IS ALL VERY UNFAMILIAR TO ME. THE ROYAL HOUSES OF ALDERAAN ARE FAR LESS FORMAL, MUCH MORE POLITICAL.
WERE LESS FORMAL.
PRINCESS?
I'M OKAY.
THIS IS A GOOD DAY FOR THE ALLIANCE.
LET'S GO IN.

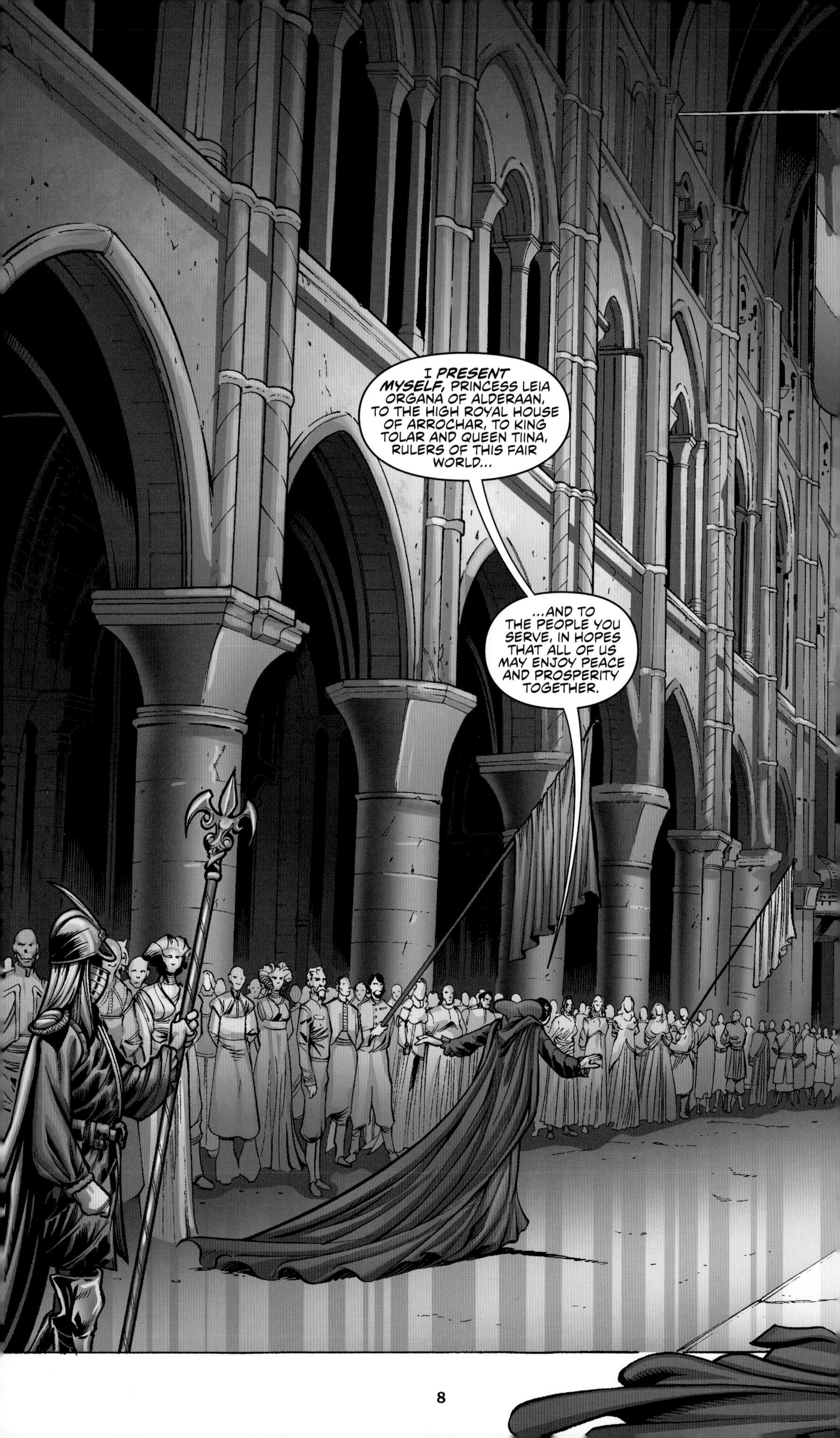
I PRESENT MYSELF, PRINCESS LEIA ORGANA OF ALDERAAN, TO THE HIGH ROYAL HOUSE OF ARROCHAR, TO KING TOLAR AND QUEEN TIINA, RULERS OF THIS FAIR WORLD...
...AND TO THE PEOPLE YOU SERVE, IN HOPES THAT ALL OF US MAY ENJOY PEACE AND PROSPERITY TOGETHER.

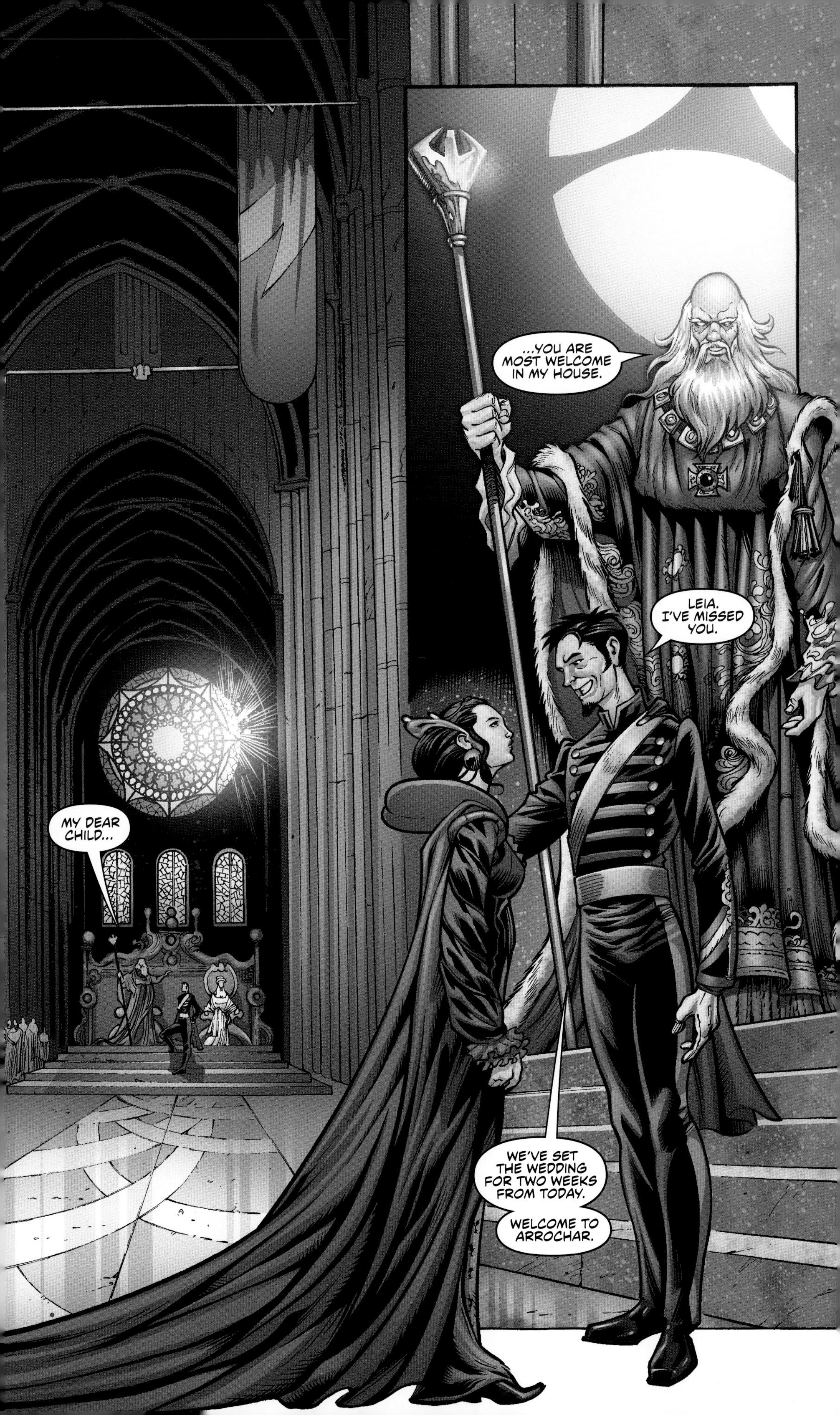
...YOU ARE MOST WELCOME IN MY HOUSE.
LEIA. I'VE MISSED YOU.
MY DEAR CHILD...
WE'VE SET THE WEDDING FOR TWO WEEKS FROM TODAY.
WELCOME TO ARROCHAR.

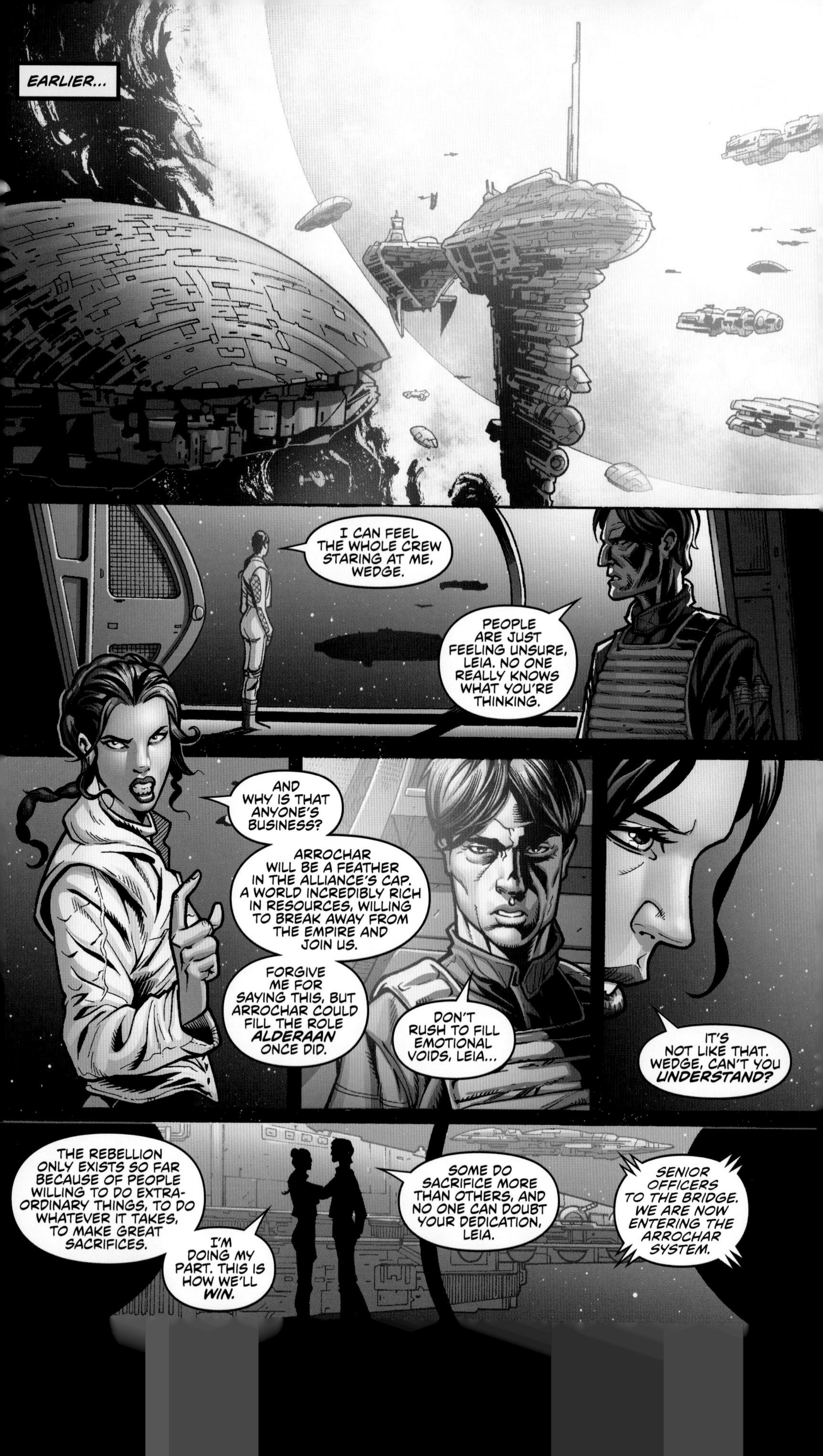
EARLIER...
I CAN FEEL THE WHOLE CREW STARING AT ME, WEDGE.
PEOPLE ARE JUST FEELING UNSURE, LEIA. NO ONE REALLY KNOWS WHAT YOU'RE THINKING.
AND WHY IS THAT ANYONE'S BUSINESS?
ARROCHAR WILL BE A FEATHER IN THE ALLIANCE'S CAP. A WORLD INCREDIBLY RICH IN RESOURCES, WILLING TO BREAK AWAY FROM THE EMPIRE AND JOIN US.
FORGIVE ME FOR SAYING THIS, BUT ARROCHAR COULD FILL THE ROLE ALDERAAN ONCE DID.
DON'T RUSH TO FILL EMOTIONAL VOIDS, LEIA...
IT'S NOT LIKE THAT. WEDGE, CAN'T YOU UNDERSTAND?
THE REBELLION ONLY EXISTS SO FAR BECAUSE OF PEOPLE WILLING TO DO EXTRAORDINARY THINGS, TO DO WHATEVER IT TAKES, TO MAKE GREAT SACRIFICES.
I'M DOING MY PART. THIS IS HOW WE'LL WIN.
SOME DO SACRIFICE MORE THAN OTHERS, AND NO ONE CAN DOUBT YOUR DEDICATION, LEIA.
SENIOR OFFICERS TO THE BRIDGE. WE ARE NOW ENTERING THE ARROCHAR SYSTEM.

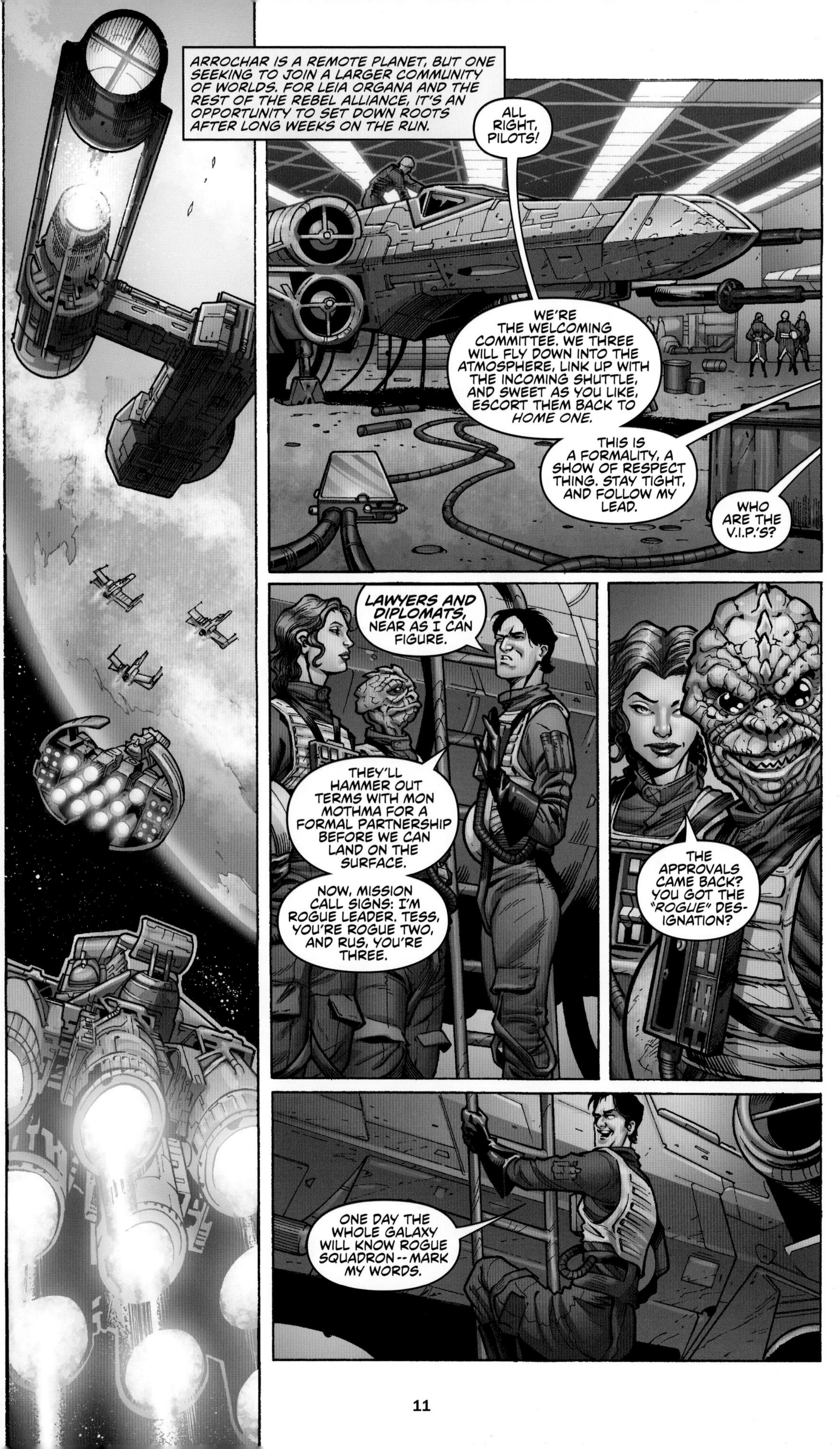
ARROCHAR IS A REMOTE PLANET, BUT ONE SEEKING TO JOIN A LARGER COMMUNITY OF WORLDS. FOR LEIA ORGANA AND THE REST OF THE REBEL ALLIANCE, IT'S AN OPPORTUNITY TO SET DOWN ROOTS AFTER LONG WEEKS ON THE RUN.
ALL RIGHT, PILOTS!
WE'RE THE WELCOMING COMMITTEE. WE THREE WILL FLY DOWN INTO THE ATMOSPHERE, LINK UP WITH THE INCOMING SHUTTLE, AND SWEET AS YOU LIKE, ESCORT THEM BACK TO *HOME ONE*.
THIS IS A FORMALITY, A SHOW OF RESPECT THING. STAY TIGHT, AND FOLLOW MY LEAD.
WHO ARE THE V.I.P.'S?
LAWYERS AND DIPLOMATS, NEAR AS I CAN FIGURE.
THEY'LL HAMMER OUT TERMS WITH MON MOTHMA FOR A FORMAL PARTNERSHIP BEFORE WE CAN LAND ON THE SURFACE.
NOW, MISSION CALL SIGNS: I'M ROGUE LEADER. TESS, YOU'RE ROGUE TWO, AND RUS, YOU'RE THREE.
THE APPROVALS CAME BACK? YOU GOT THE "ROGUE" DES-IGNATION?
ONE DAY THE WHOLE GALAXY WILL KNOW ROGUE SQUADRON--MARK MY WORDS.

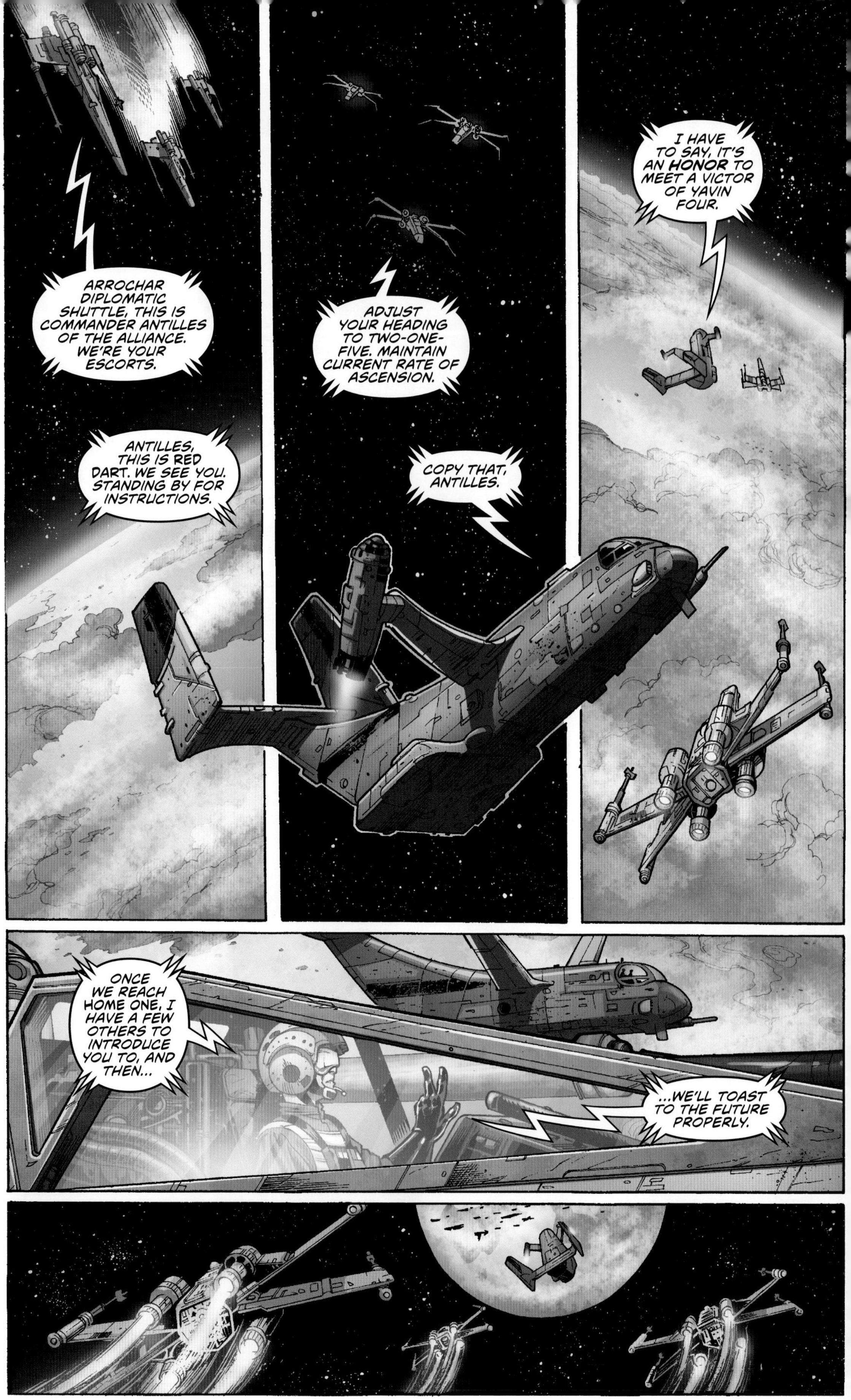
ARROCHAR DIPLOMATIC SHUTTLE, THIS IS COMMANDER ANTILLES OF THE ALLIANCE. WE'RE YOUR ESCORTS.
ANTILLES, THIS IS RED DART. WE SEE YOU. STANDING BY FOR INSTRUCTIONS.
ADJUST YOUR HEADING TO TWO-ONE-FIVE. MAINTAIN CURRENT RATE OF ASCENSION.
COPY THAT, ANTILLES.
I HAVE TO SAY, IT'S AN HONOR TO MEET A VICTOR OF YAVIN FOUR.
ONCE WE REACH HOME ONE, I HAVE A FEW OTHERS TO INTRODUCE YOU TO, AND THEN...
...WE'LL TOAST TO THE FUTURE PROPERLY.

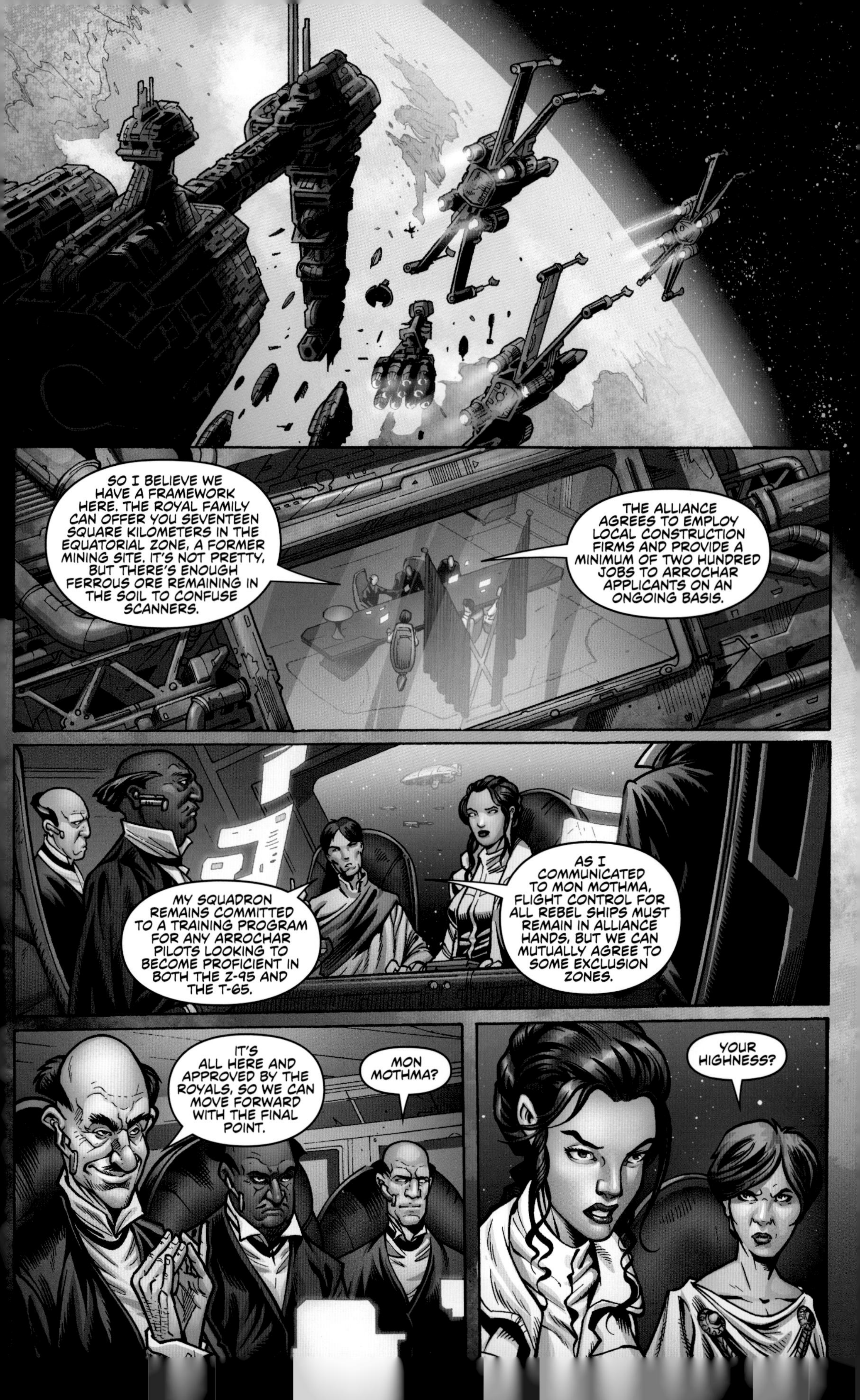
SO I BELIEVE WE HAVE A FRAMEWORK HERE. THE ROYAL FAMILY CAN OFFER YOU SEVENTEEN SQUARE KILOMETERS IN THE EQUATORIAL ZONE, A FORMER MINING SITE. IT'S NOT PRETTY, BUT THERE'S ENOUGH FERROUS ORE REMAINING IN THE SOIL TO CONFUSE SCANNERS.
THE ALLIANCE AGREES TO EMPLOY LOCAL CONSTRUCTION FIRMS AND PROVIDE A MINIMUM OF TWO HUNDRED JOBS TO ARROCHAR APPLICANTS ON AN ONGOING BASIS.
MY SQUADRON REMAINS COMMITTED TO A TRAINING PROGRAM FOR ANY ARROCHAR PILOTS LOOKING TO BECOME PROFICIENT IN BOTH THE Z-95 AND THE T-65.
AS I COMMUNICATED TO MON MOTHMA, FLIGHT CONTROL FOR ALL REBEL SHIPS MUST REMAIN IN ALLIANCE HANDS, BUT WE CAN MUTUALLY AGREE TO SOME EXCLUSION ZONES.
IT'S ALL HERE AND APPROVED BY THE ROYALS, SO WE CAN MOVE FORWARD WITH THE FINAL POINT.
MON MOTHMA?
YOUR HIGHNESS?

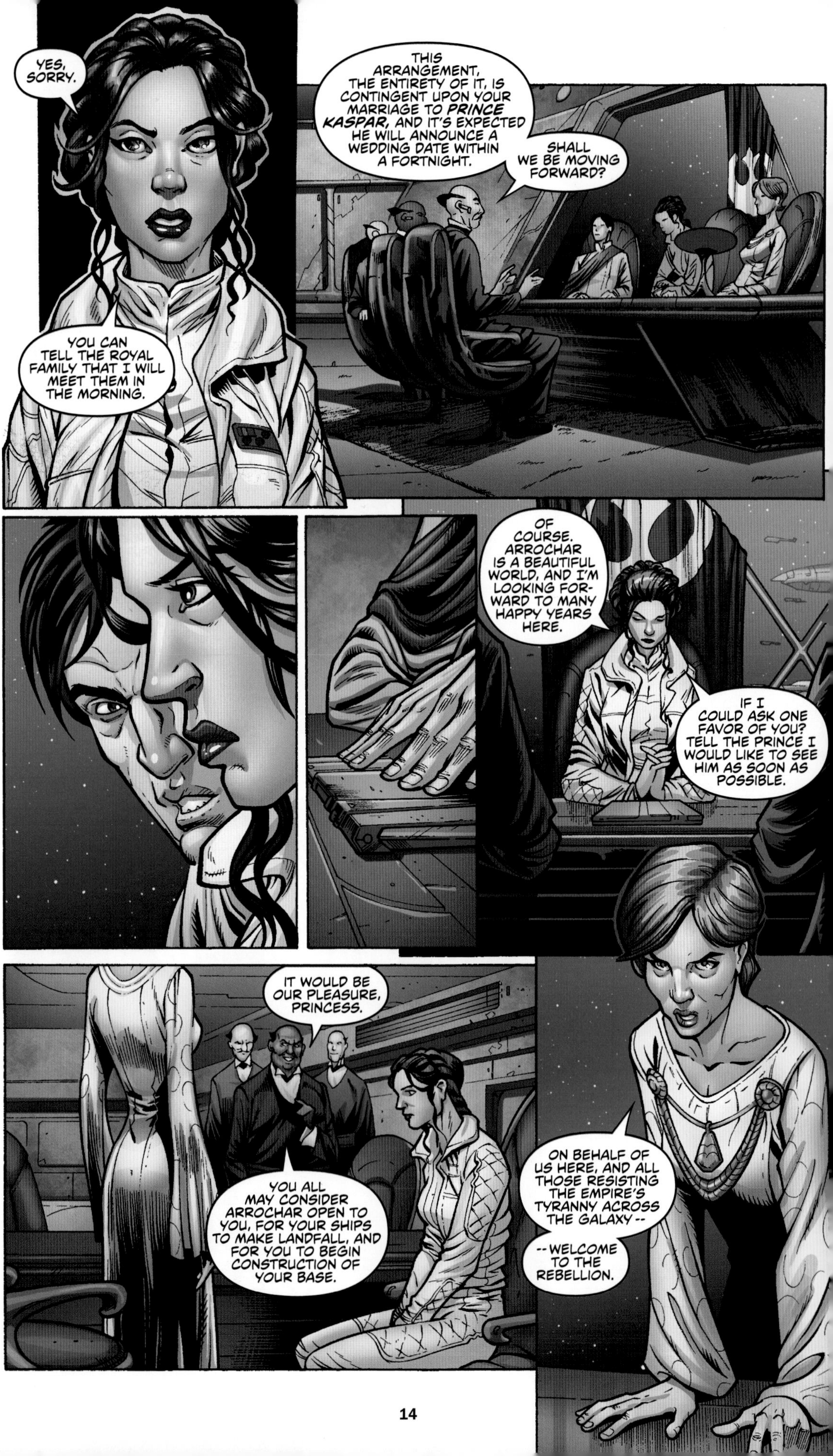
YES, SORRY.
YOU CAN TELL THE ROYAL FAMILY THAT I WILL MEET THEM IN THE MORNING.
THIS ARRANGEMENT, THE ENTIRETY OF IT, IS CONTINGENT UPON YOUR MARRIAGE TO PRINCE KASPAR, AND IT'S EXPECTED HE WILL ANNOUNCE A WEDDING DATE WITHIN A FORTNIGHT.
SHALL WE BE MOVING FORWARD?
OF COURSE. ARROCHAR IS A BEAUTIFUL WORLD, AND I'M LOOKING FOR-WARD TO MANY HAPPY YEARS HERE.
IF I COULD ASK ONE FAVOR OF YOU? TELL THE PRINCE I WOULD LIKE TO SEE HIM AS SOON AS POSSIBLE.
IT WOULD BE OUR PLEASURE, PRINCESS.
YOU ALL MAY CONSIDER ARROCHAR OPEN TO YOU, FOR YOUR SHIPS TO MAKE LANDFALL, AND FOR YOU TO BEGIN CONSTRUCTION OF YOUR BASE.
ON BEHALF OF US HERE, AND ALL THOSE RESISTING THE EMPIRE'S TYRANNY ACROSS THE GALAXY --
--WELCOME TO THE REBELLION.

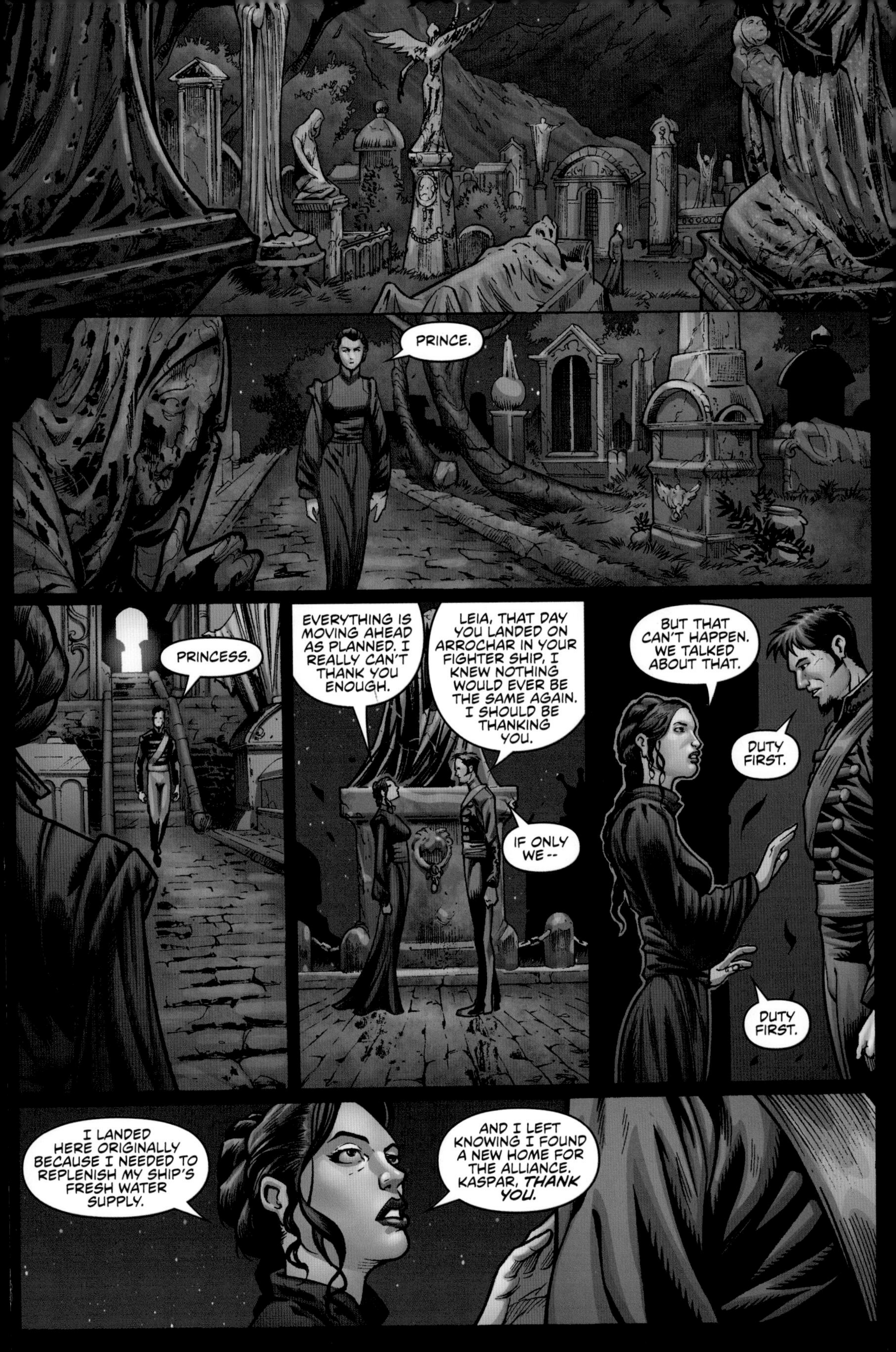

PRINCE.
PRINCESS.
EVERYTHING IS MOVING AHEAD AS PLANNED. I REALLY CAN'T THANK YOU ENOUGH.
LEIA, THAT DAY YOU LANDED ON ARROCHAR IN YOUR FIGHTER SHIP, I KNEW NOTHING WOULD EVER BE THE SAME AGAIN. I SHOULD BE THANKING YOU.
IF ONLY WE --
BUT THAT CAN'T HAPPEN. WE TALKED ABOUT THAT.
DUTY FIRST.
DUTY FIRST.
I LANDED HERE ORIGINALLY BECAUSE I NEEDED TO REPLENISH MY SHIP'S FRESH WATER SUPPLY.
AND I LEFT KNOWING I FOUND A NEW HOME FOR THE ALLIANCE. KASPAR, *THANK YOU.*

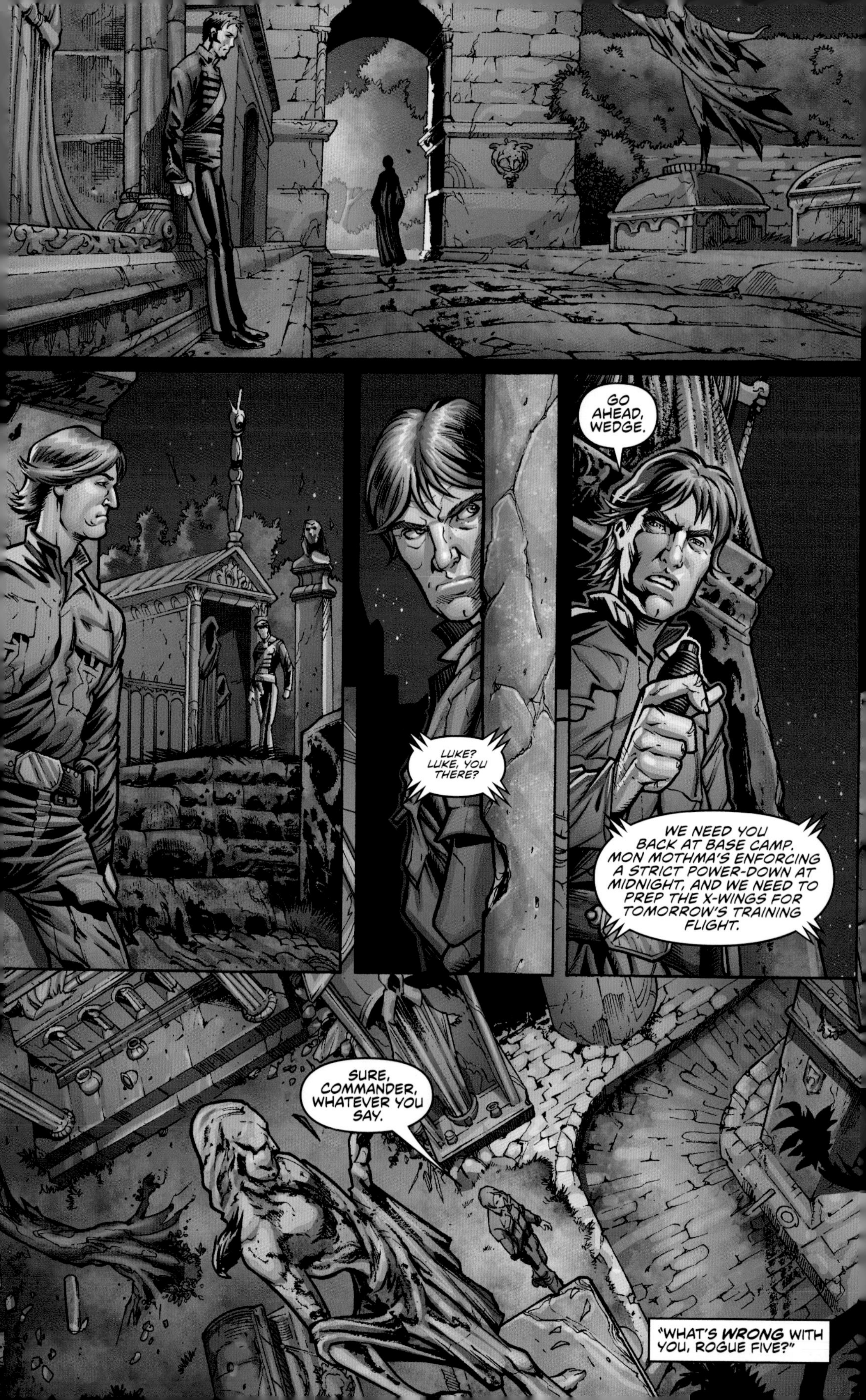
GO AHEAD, WEDGE.
LUKE? LUKE, YOU THERE?
WE NEED YOU BACK AT BASE CAMP. MON MOTHMA'S ENFORCING A STRICT POWER-DOWN AT MIDNIGHT, AND WE NEED TO PREP THE X-WINGS FOR TOMORROW'S TRAINING FLIGHT.
SURE, COMMANDER, WHATEVER YOU SAY.
"WHAT'S WRONG WITH YOU, ROGUE FIVE?"

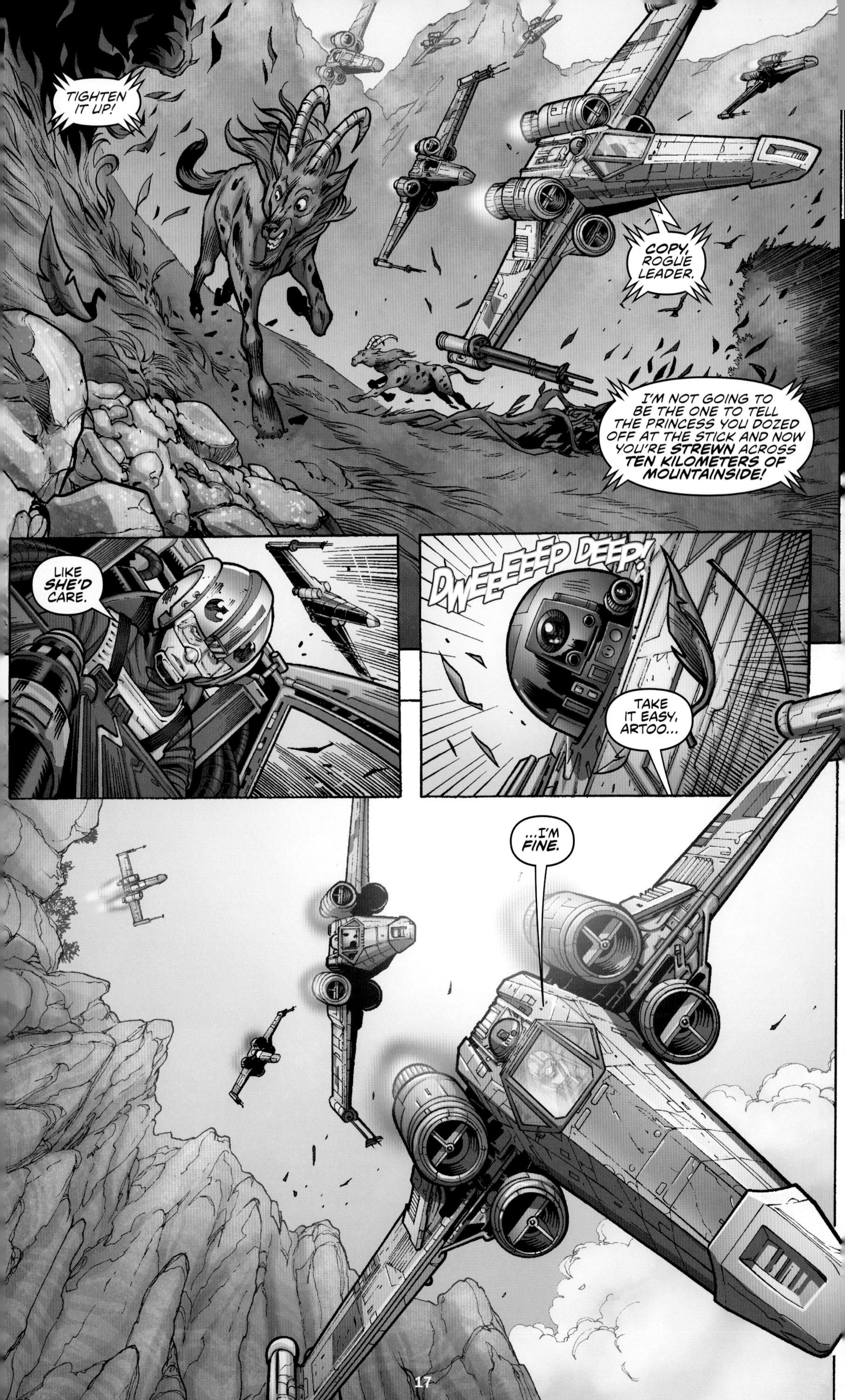
TIGHTEN IT UP!
COPY, ROGUE LEADER.
I'M NOT GOING TO BE THE ONE TO TELL THE PRINCESS YOU DOZED OFF AT THE STICK AND NOW YOU'RE **STREWN** ACROSS **TEN KILOMETERS OF MOUNTAINSIDE!**
LIKE **SHE'D** CARE.
DWEEEEEP DEEP!
TAKE IT EASY, ARTOO...
...I'M **FINE.**

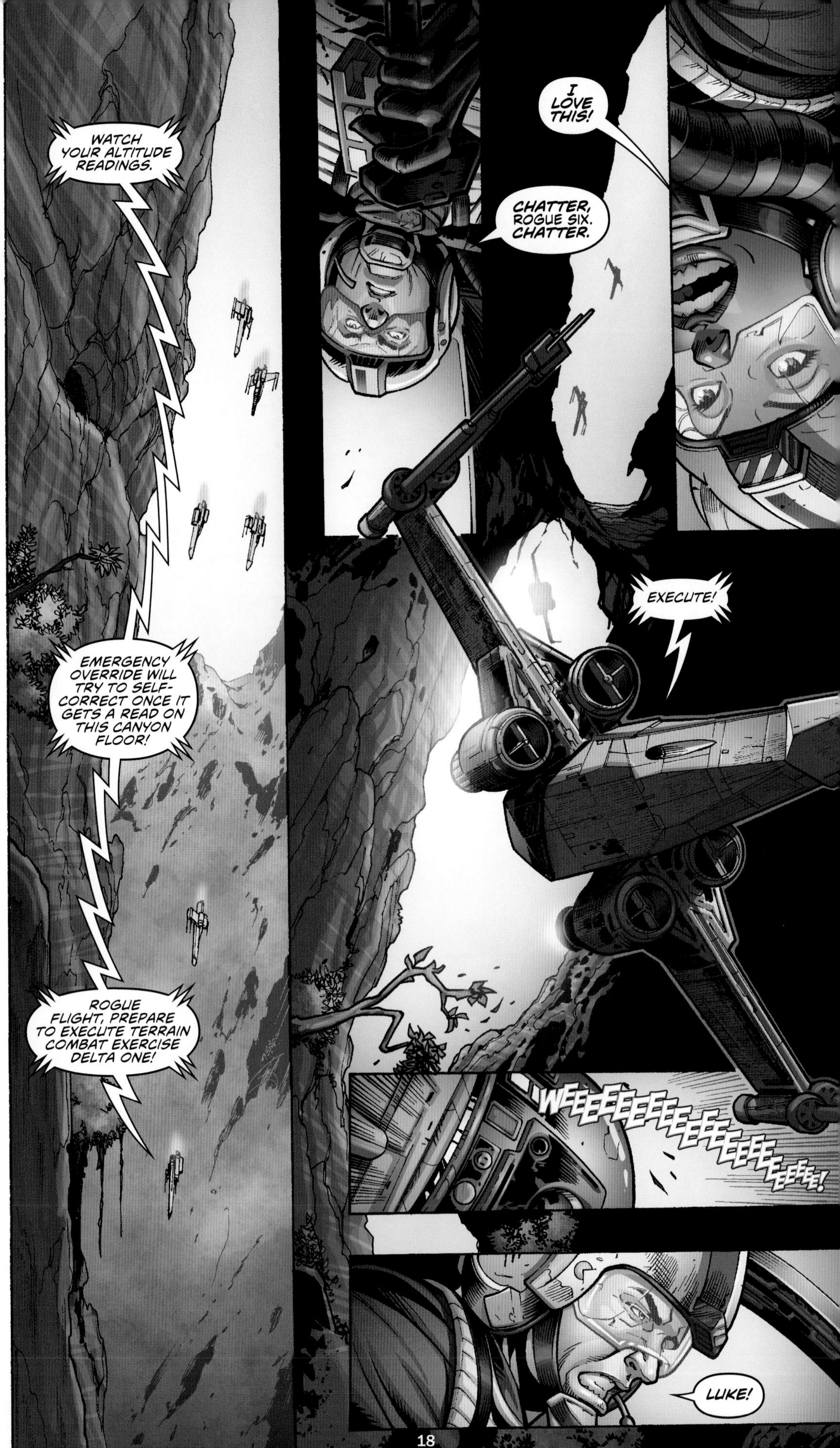
WATCH YOUR ALTITUDE READINGS.
EMERGENCY OVERRIDE WILL TRY TO SELF-CORRECT ONCE IT GETS A READ ON THIS CANYON FLOOR!
ROGUE FLIGHT, PREPARE TO EXECUTE TERRAIN COMBAT EXERCISE DELTA ONE!
CHATTER, ROGUE SIX. CHATTER.
I LOVE THIS!
EXECUTE!
WEEEEEEEEEEEEEEEEEEEEEEEE!
LUKE!

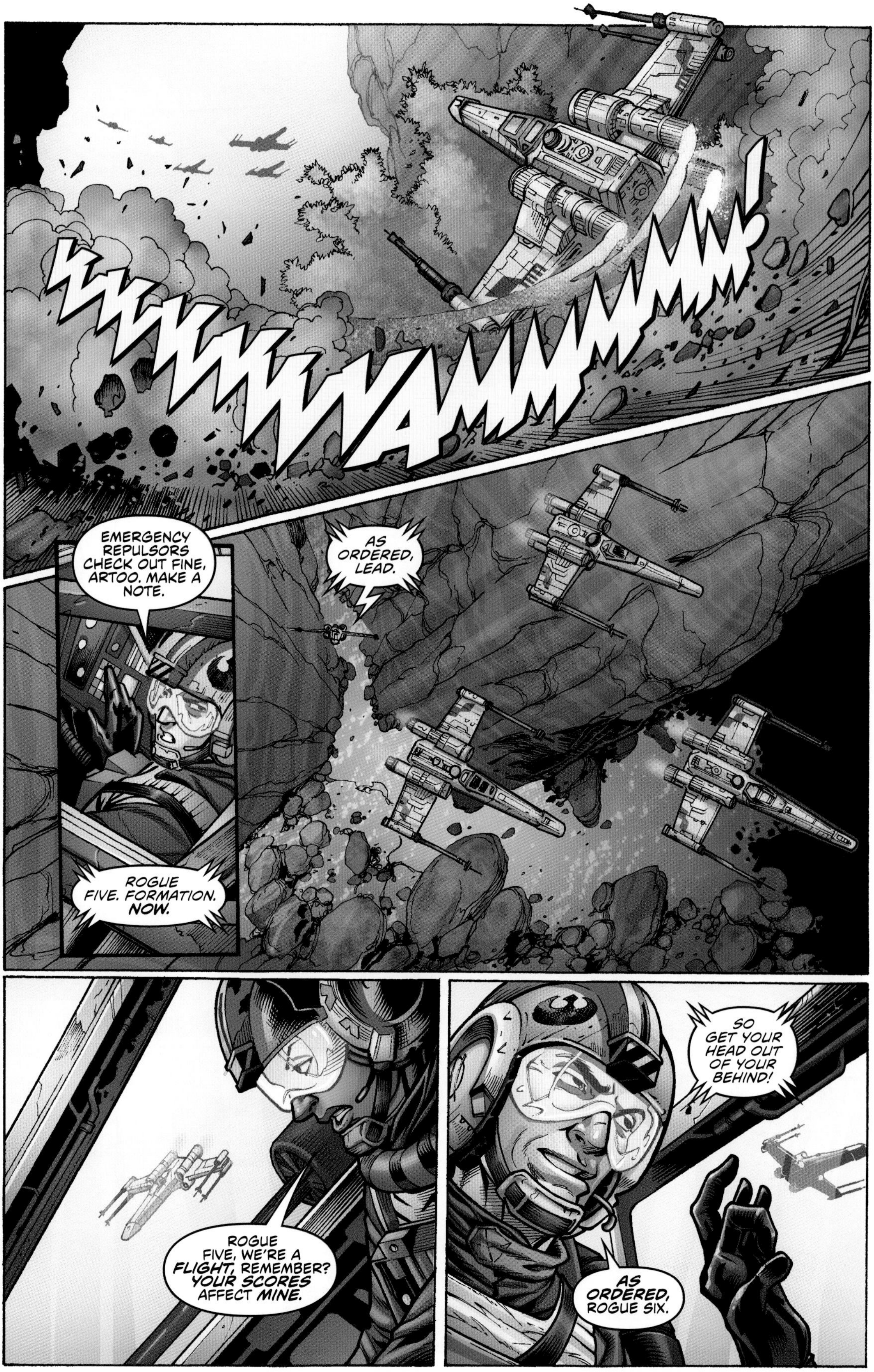
KKKWWAMMMMM!
EMERGENCY REPULSORS CHECK OUT FINE, ARTOO. MAKE A NOTE.
AS ORDERED, LEAD.
ROGUE FIVE. FORMATION. NOW.
ROGUE FIVE, WE'RE A FLIGHT, REMEMBER? YOUR SCORES AFFECT MINE.
SO GET YOUR HEAD OUT OF YOUR BEHIND!
AS ORDERED, ROGUE SIX.

WE'RE OVERSHOT FOR DELTA ONE, SO I'LL IMPROVISE.

THIS CANYON IS ROUGHLY FOURTEEN KLICKS IN LENGTH. I'M RECORDING YOUR TELEMETRY STRAIGHT INTO MY COMPUTER. RUN THE COURSE. I WANT TO SEE ACCURACY, CONSISTENCY...

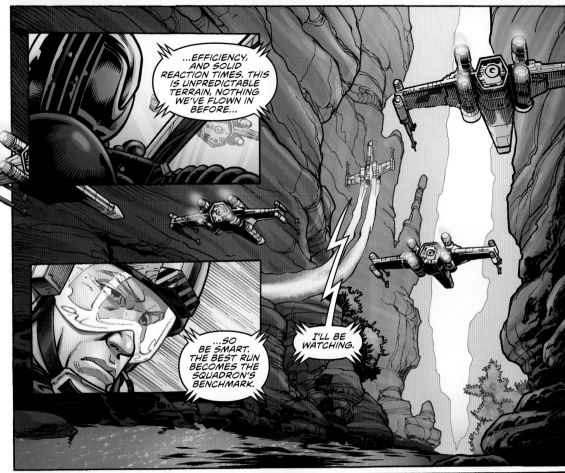

...EFFICIENCY, AND SOLID REACTION TIMES. THIS IS UNPREDICTABLE TERRAIN, NOTHING WE'VE FLOWN IN BEFORE...

...SO BE SMART. THE BEST RUN BECOMES THE SQUADRON'S BENCHMARK.

I'LL BE WATCHING.

FIVE, WHAT DO YOU SAY--SHOULD WE MAKE THE RUN TOGETHER--?

ROARR!

FIVE?

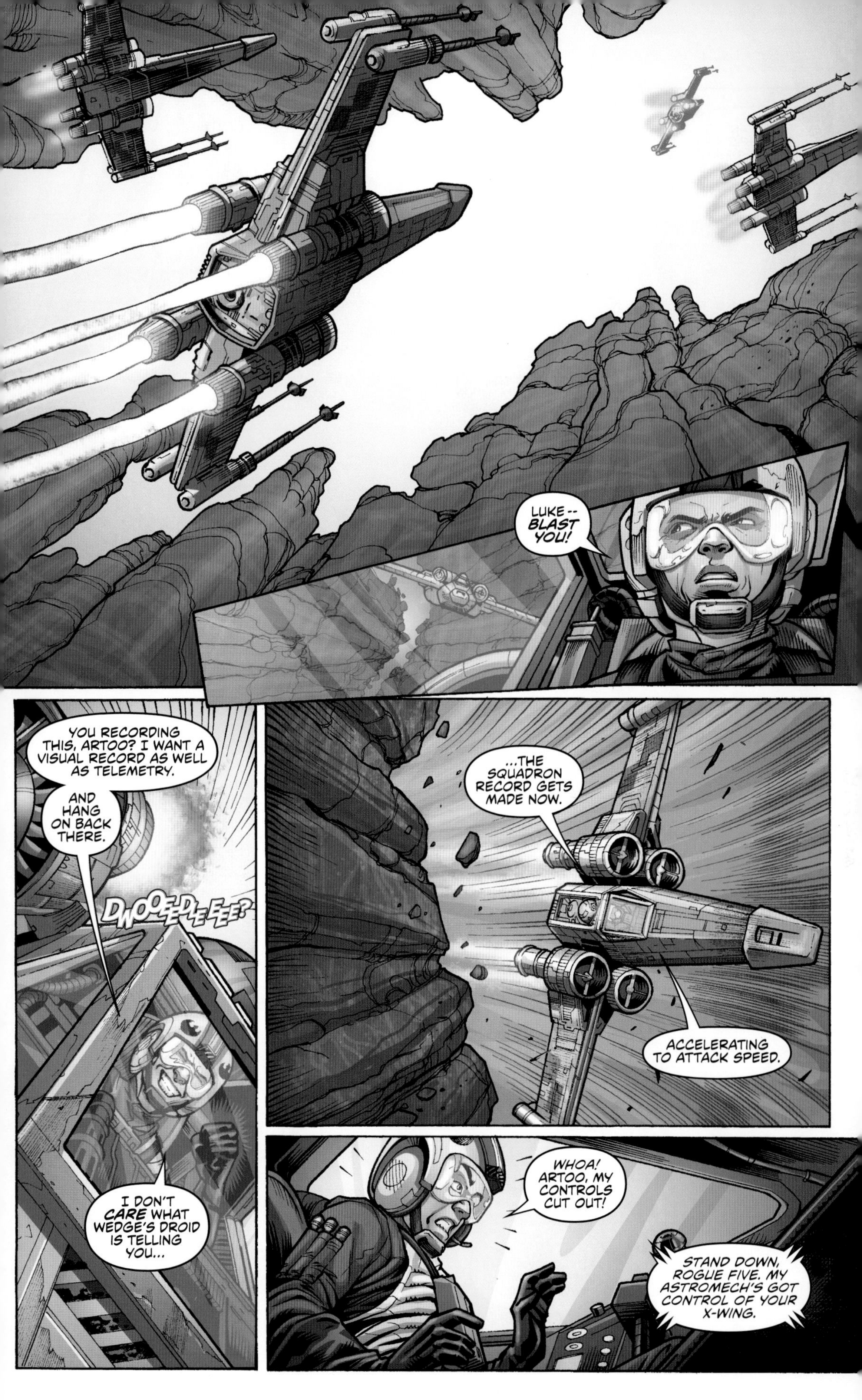
LUKE -- BLAST YOU!
YOU RECORDING THIS, ARTOO? I WANT A VISUAL RECORD AS WELL AS TELEMETRY.
AND HANG ON BACK THERE.
DWOOEEDLEEEE?
I DON'T CARE WHAT WEDGE'S DROID IS TELLING YOU...
...THE SQUADRON RECORD GETS MADE NOW.
ACCELERATING TO ATTACK SPEED.
WHOA! ARTOO, MY CONTROLS CUT OUT!
STAND DOWN, ROGUE FIVE. MY ASTROMECH'S GOT CONTROL OF YOUR X-WING.

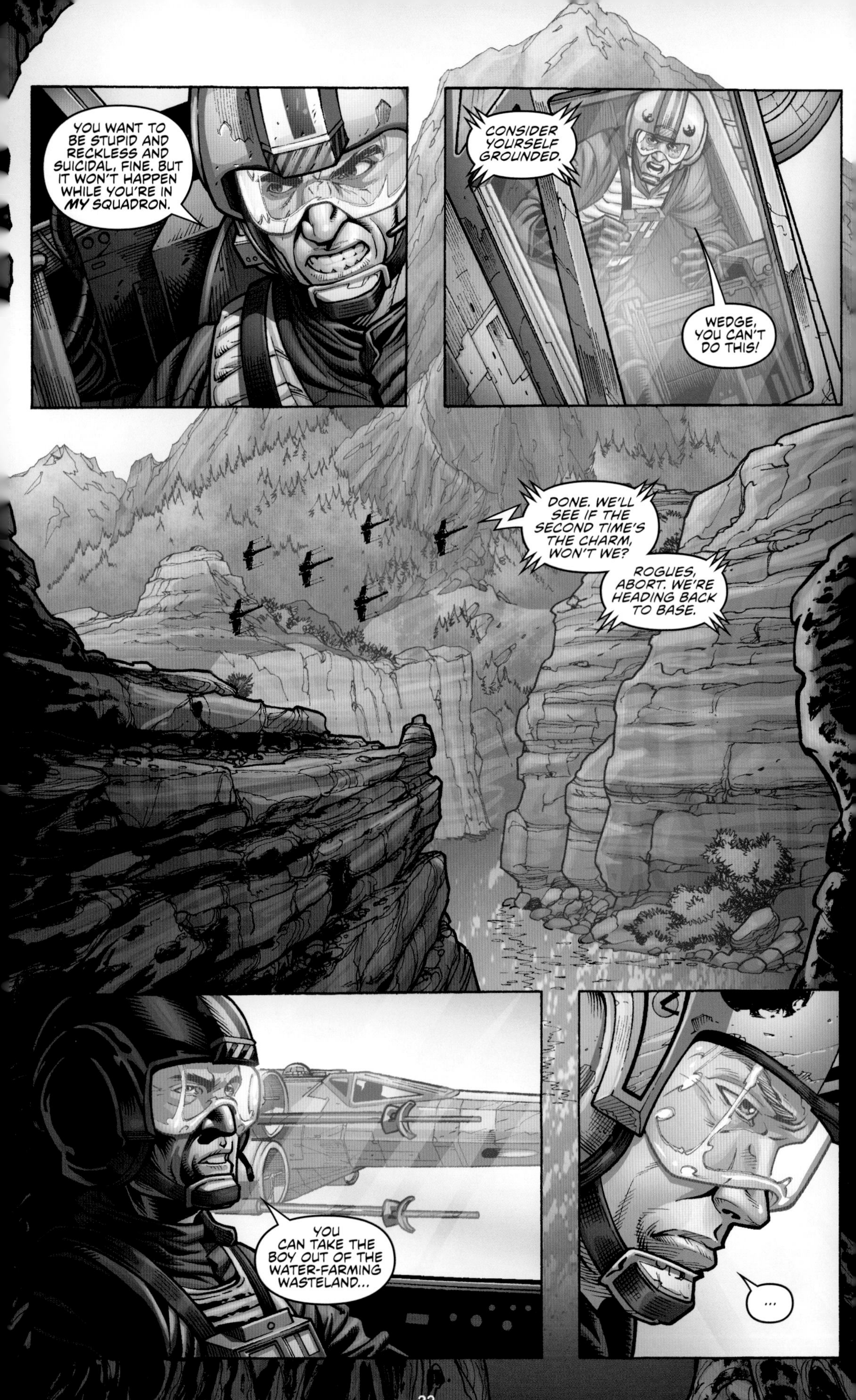
YOU WANT TO BE STUPID AND RECKLESS AND SUICIDAL, FINE. BUT IT WON'T HAPPEN WHILE YOU'RE IN *MY* SQUADRON.
CONSIDER YOURSELF GROUNDED.
WEDGE, YOU CAN'T DO THIS!
DONE. WE'LL SEE IF THE SECOND TIME'S THE CHARM, WON'T WE?
ROGUES, ABORT. WE'RE HEADING BACK TO BASE.
YOU CAN TAKE THE BOY OUT OF THE WATER-FARMING WASTELAND...
...

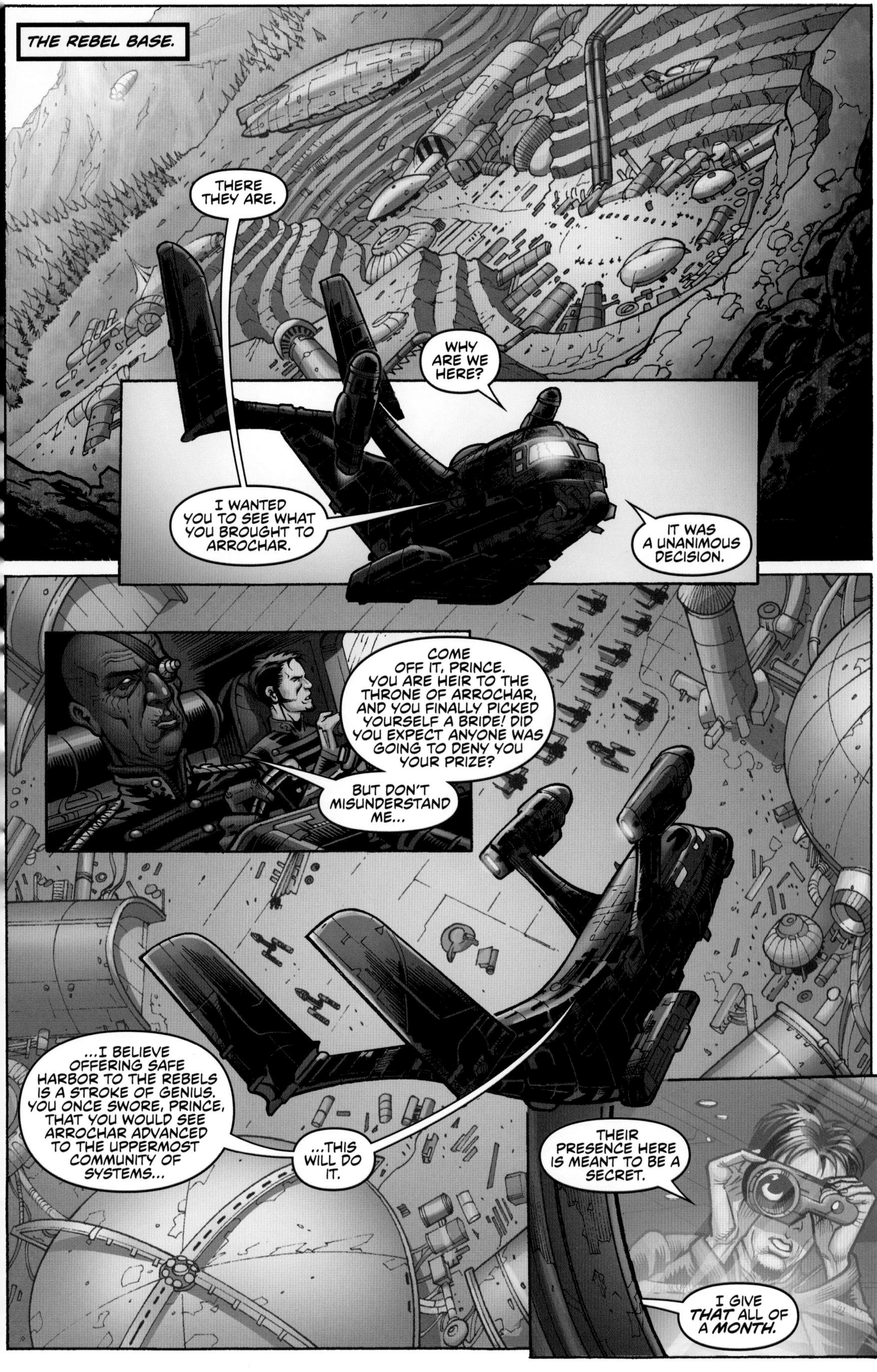
THE REBEL BASE.
THERE THEY ARE.
WHY ARE WE HERE?
I WANTED YOU TO SEE WHAT YOU BROUGHT TO ARROCHAR.
IT WAS A UNANIMOUS DECISION.
COME OFF IT, PRINCE. YOU ARE HEIR TO THE THRONE OF ARROCHAR, AND YOU FINALLY PICKED YOURSELF A BRIDE! DID YOU EXPECT ANYONE WAS GOING TO DENY YOU YOUR PRIZE?
BUT DON'T MISUNDERSTAND ME...
...I BELIEVE OFFERING SAFE HARBOR TO THE REBELS IS A STROKE OF GENIUS. YOU ONCE SWORE, PRINCE, THAT YOU WOULD SEE ARROCHAR ADVANCED TO THE UPPERMOST COMMUNITY OF SYSTEMS...
...THIS WILL DO IT.
THEIR PRESENCE HERE IS MEANT TO BE A SECRET.
I GIVE *THAT* ALL OF A *MONTH*.

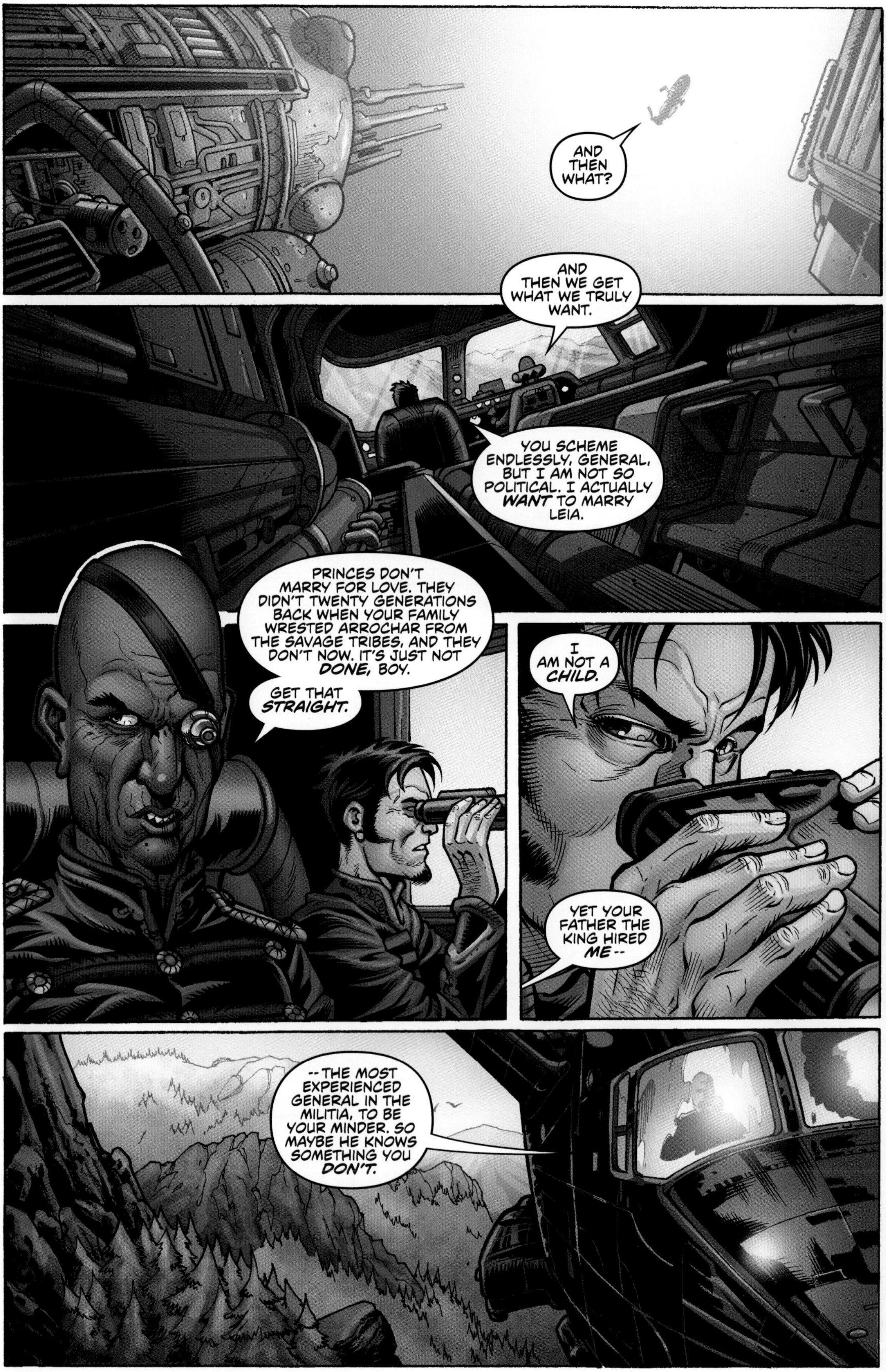
AND THEN WHAT?
AND THEN WE GET WHAT WE TRULY WANT.
YOU SCHEME ENDLESSLY, GENERAL, BUT I AM NOT SO POLITICAL. I ACTUALLY WANT TO MARRY LEIA.
PRINCES DON'T MARRY FOR LOVE. THEY DIDN'T TWENTY GENERATIONS BACK WHEN YOUR FAMILY WRESTED ARROCHAR FROM THE SAVAGE TRIBES, AND THEY DON'T NOW. IT'S JUST NOT DONE, BOY.
GET THAT STRAIGHT.
I AM NOT A CHILD.
YET YOUR FATHER THE KING HIRED ME --
-- THE MOST EXPERIENCED GENERAL IN THE MILITIA, TO BE YOUR MINDER. SO MAYBE HE KNOWS SOMETHING YOU DON'T.

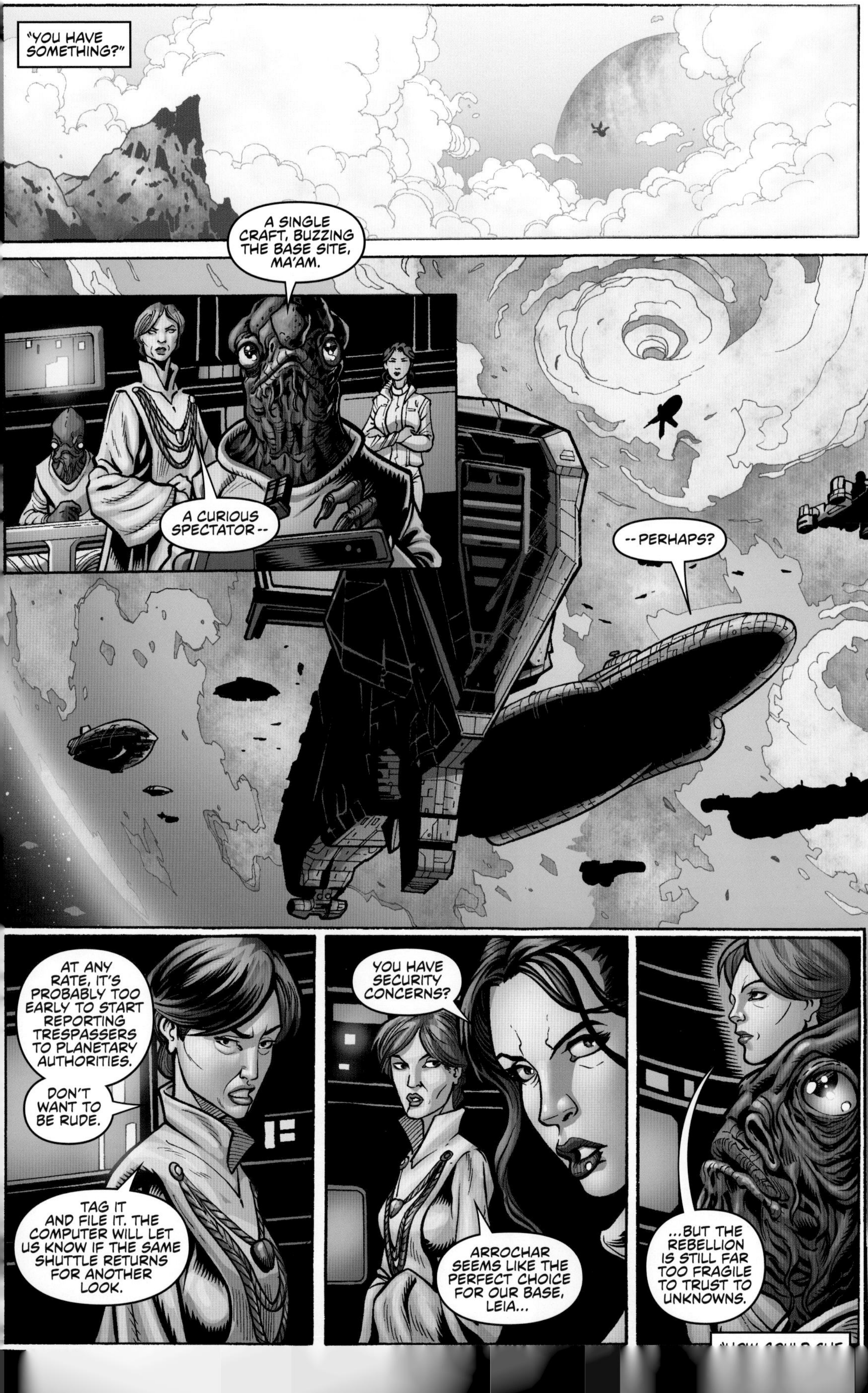
"YOU HAVE SOMETHING?"
A SINGLE CRAFT, BUZZING THE BASE SITE, MA'AM.
A CURIOUS SPECTATOR--
--PERHAPS?
AT ANY RATE, IT'S PROBABLY TOO EARLY TO START REPORTING TRESPASSERS TO PLANETARY AUTHORITIES.
DON'T WANT TO BE RUDE.
TAG IT AND FILE IT. THE COMPUTER WILL LET US KNOW IF THE SAME SHUTTLE RETURNS FOR ANOTHER LOOK.
YOU HAVE SECURITY CONCERNS?
ARROCHAR SEEMS LIKE THE PERFECT CHOICE FOR OUR BASE, LEIA...
...BUT THE REBELLION IS STILL FAR TOO FRAGILE TO TRUST TO UNKNOWNS.

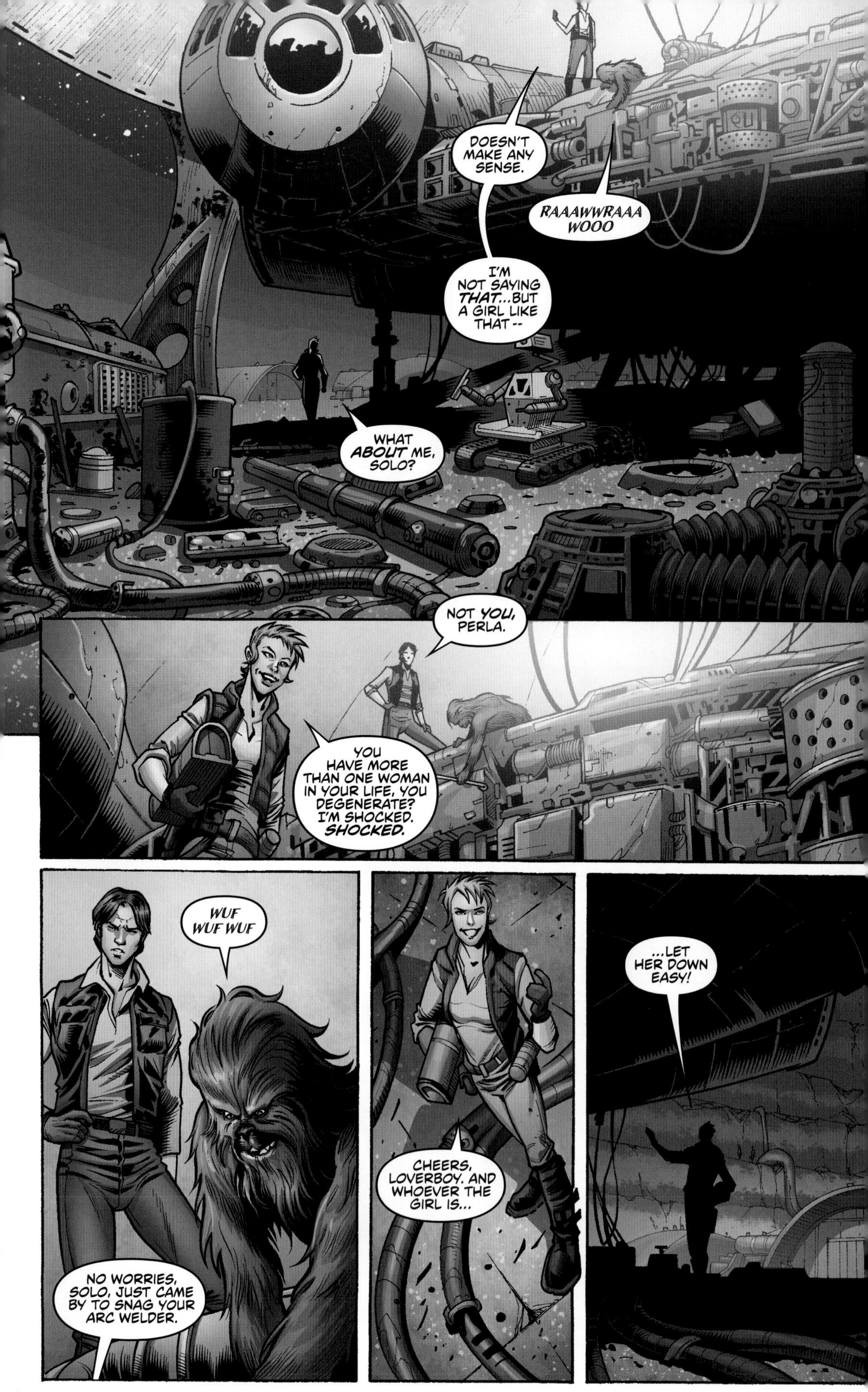
DOESN'T MAKE ANY SENSE.
RAAAWWRAAA WOOO
I'M NOT SAYING THAT...BUT A GIRL LIKE THAT --
WHAT ABOUT ME, SOLO?
NOT YOU, PERLA.
YOU HAVE MORE THAN ONE WOMAN IN YOUR LIFE, YOU DEGENERATE? I'M SHOCKED. SHOCKED.
WUF WUF WUF
NO WORRIES, SOLO, JUST CAME BY TO SNAG YOUR ARC WELDER.
CHEERS, LOVERBOY. AND WHOEVER THE GIRL IS...
...LET HER DOWN EASY!

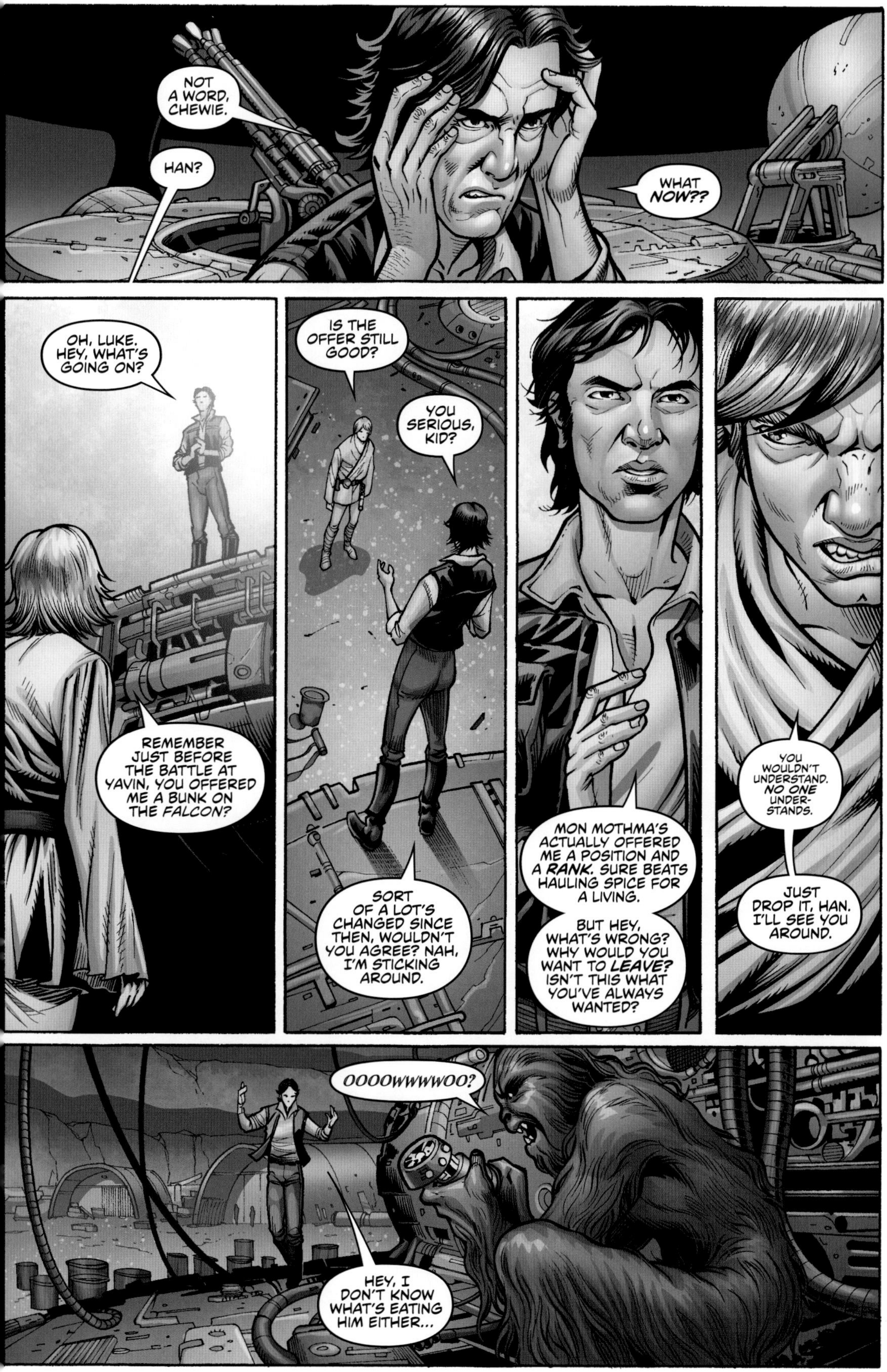
NOT A WORD, CHEWIE.
HAN?
WHAT *NOW??*
OH, LUKE. HEY, WHAT'S GOING ON?
REMEMBER JUST BEFORE THE BATTLE AT YAVIN, YOU OFFERED ME A BUNK ON THE *FALCON?*
IS THE OFFER STILL GOOD?
YOU SERIOUS, KID?
SORT OF A LOT'S CHANGED SINCE THEN, WOULDN'T YOU AGREE? NAH, I'M STICKING AROUND.
MON MOTHMA'S ACTUALLY OFFERED ME A POSITION AND A *RANK.* SURE BEATS HAULING SPICE FOR A LIVING.
BUT HEY, WHAT'S WRONG? WHY WOULD YOU WANT TO *LEAVE?* ISN'T THIS WHAT YOU'VE ALWAYS WANTED?
YOU WOULDN'T UNDERSTAND. *NO ONE* UNDER-STANDS.
JUST DROP IT, HAN. I'LL SEE YOU AROUND.
OOOOWWWWOO?
HEY, I DON'T KNOW WHAT'S EATING HIM EITHER...

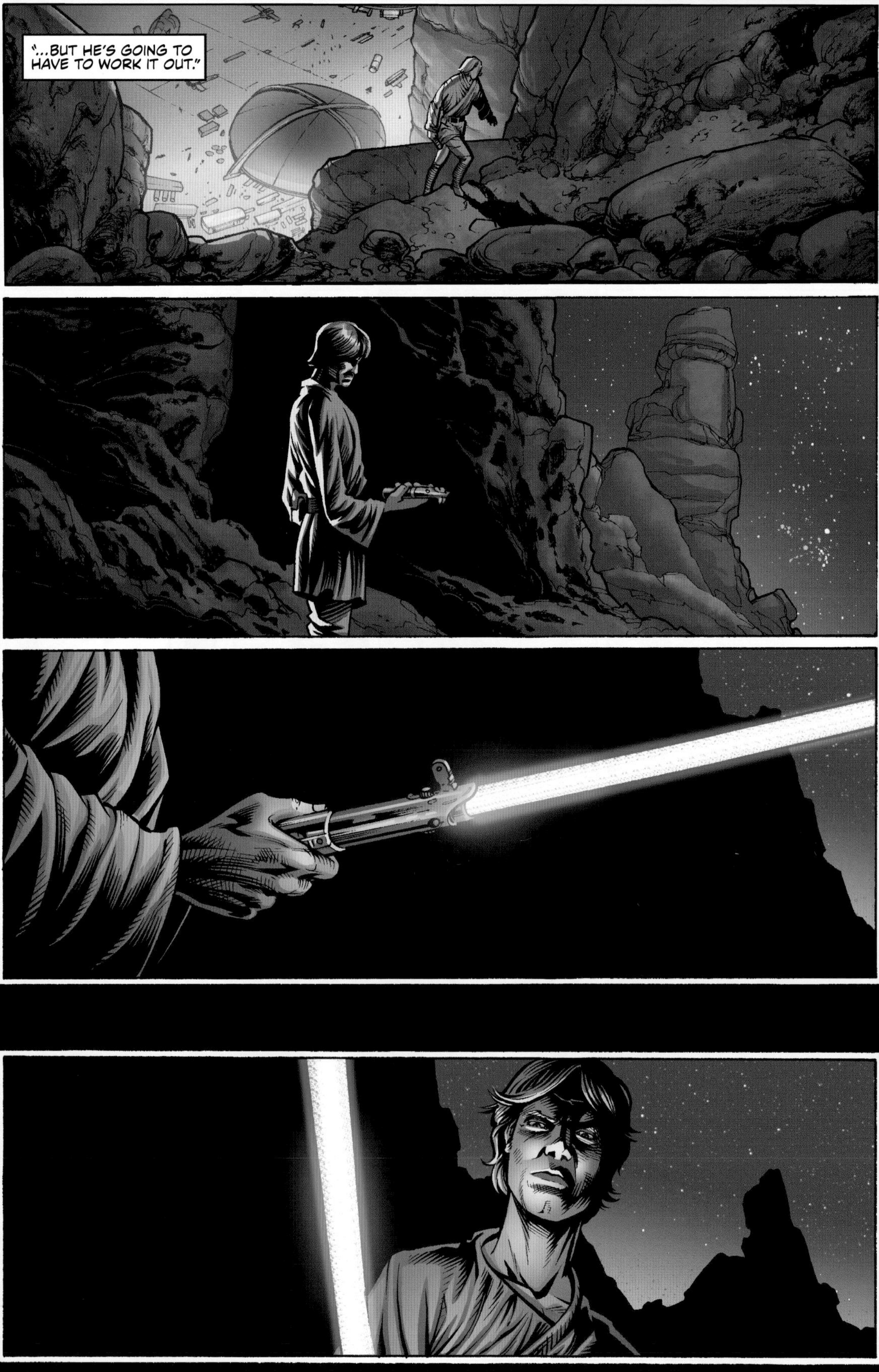
"...BUT HE'S GOING TO HAVE TO WORK IT OUT."

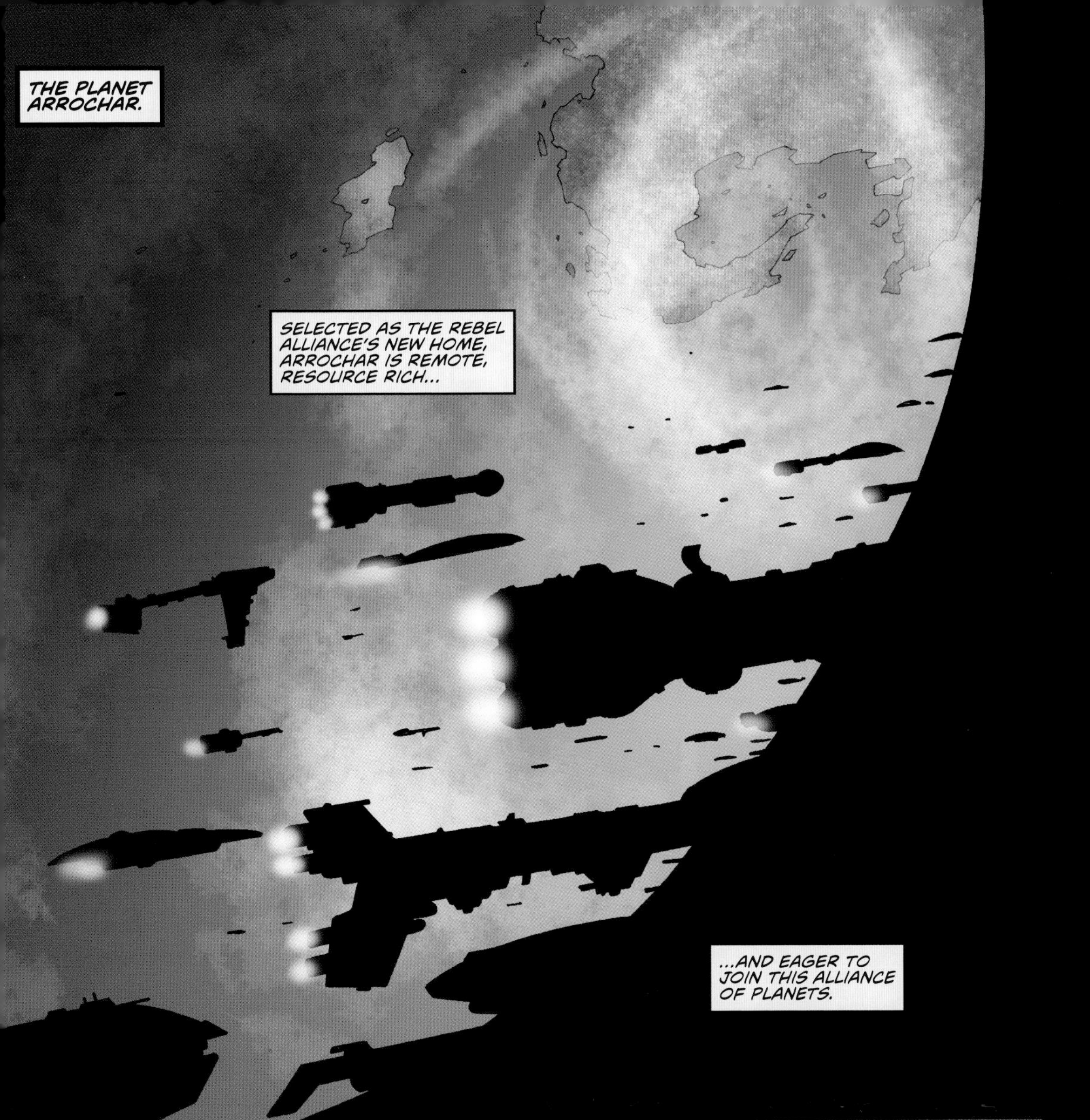
THE PLANET ARROCHAR.
SELECTED AS THE REBEL ALLIANCE'S NEW HOME, ARROCHAR IS REMOTE, RESOURCE RICH...
...AND EAGER TO JOIN THIS ALLIANCE OF PLANETS.

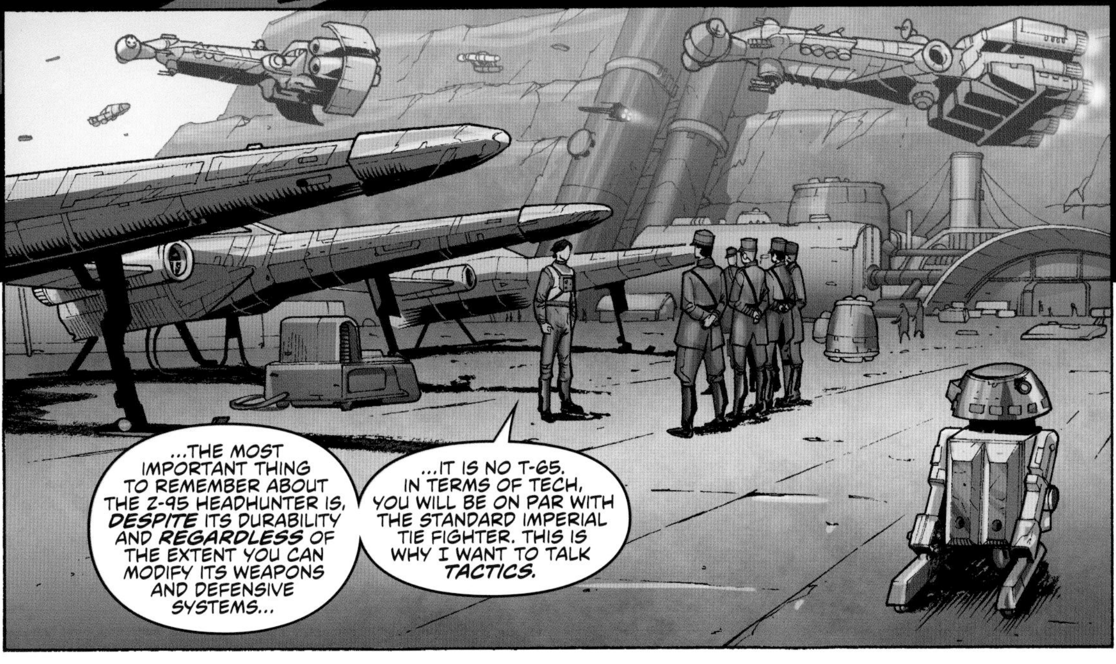
...THE MOST IMPORTANT THING TO REMEMBER ABOUT THE Z-95 HEADHUNTER IS, DESPITE ITS DURABILITY AND REGARDLESS OF THE EXTENT YOU CAN MODIFY ITS WEAPONS AND DEFENSIVE SYSTEMS...
...IT IS NO T-65. IN TERMS OF TECH, YOU WILL BE ON PAR WITH THE STANDARD IMPERIAL TIE FIGHTER. THIS IS WHY I WANT TO TALK TACTICS.

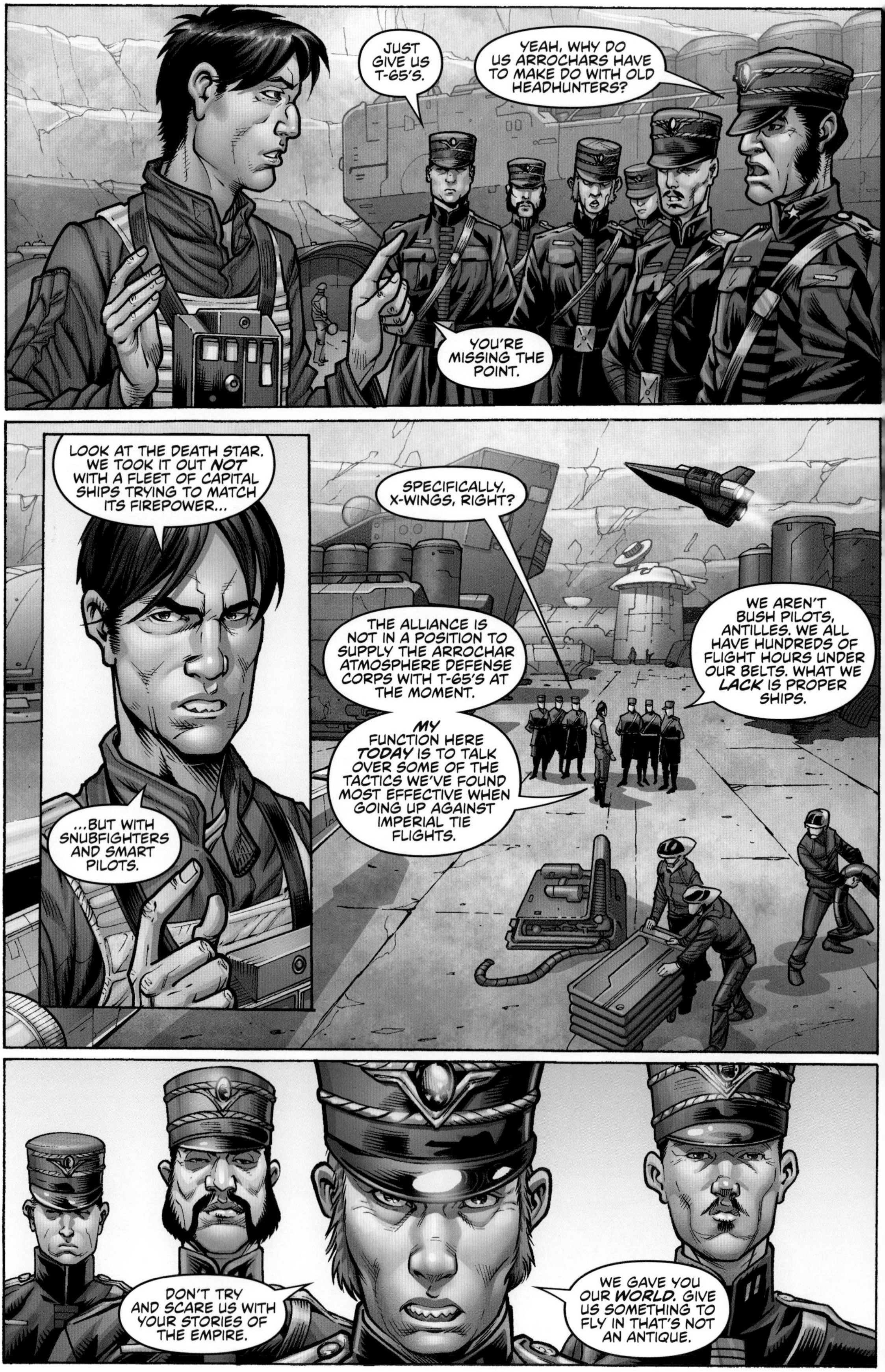
JUST GIVE US T-65'S.
YEAH, WHY DO US ARROCHARS HAVE TO MAKE DO WITH OLD HEADHUNTERS?
YOU'RE MISSING THE POINT.
LOOK AT THE DEATH STAR. WE TOOK IT OUT NOT WITH A FLEET OF CAPITAL SHIPS TRYING TO MATCH ITS FIREPOWER...
...BUT WITH SNUBFIGHTERS AND SMART PILOTS.
SPECIFICALLY, X-WINGS, RIGHT?
THE ALLIANCE IS NOT IN A POSITION TO SUPPLY THE ARROCHAR ATMOSPHERE DEFENSE CORPS WITH T-65'S AT THE MOMENT.
MY FUNCTION HERE TODAY IS TO TALK OVER SOME OF THE TACTICS WE'VE FOUND MOST EFFECTIVE WHEN GOING UP AGAINST IMPERIAL TIE FLIGHTS.
WE AREN'T BUSH PILOTS, ANTILLES. WE ALL HAVE HUNDREDS OF FLIGHT HOURS UNDER OUR BELTS. WHAT WE LACK IS PROPER SHIPS.
DON'T TRY AND SCARE US WITH YOUR STORIES OF THE EMPIRE.
WE GAVE YOU OUR WORLD. GIVE US SOMETHING TO FLY IN THAT'S NOT AN ANTIQUE.

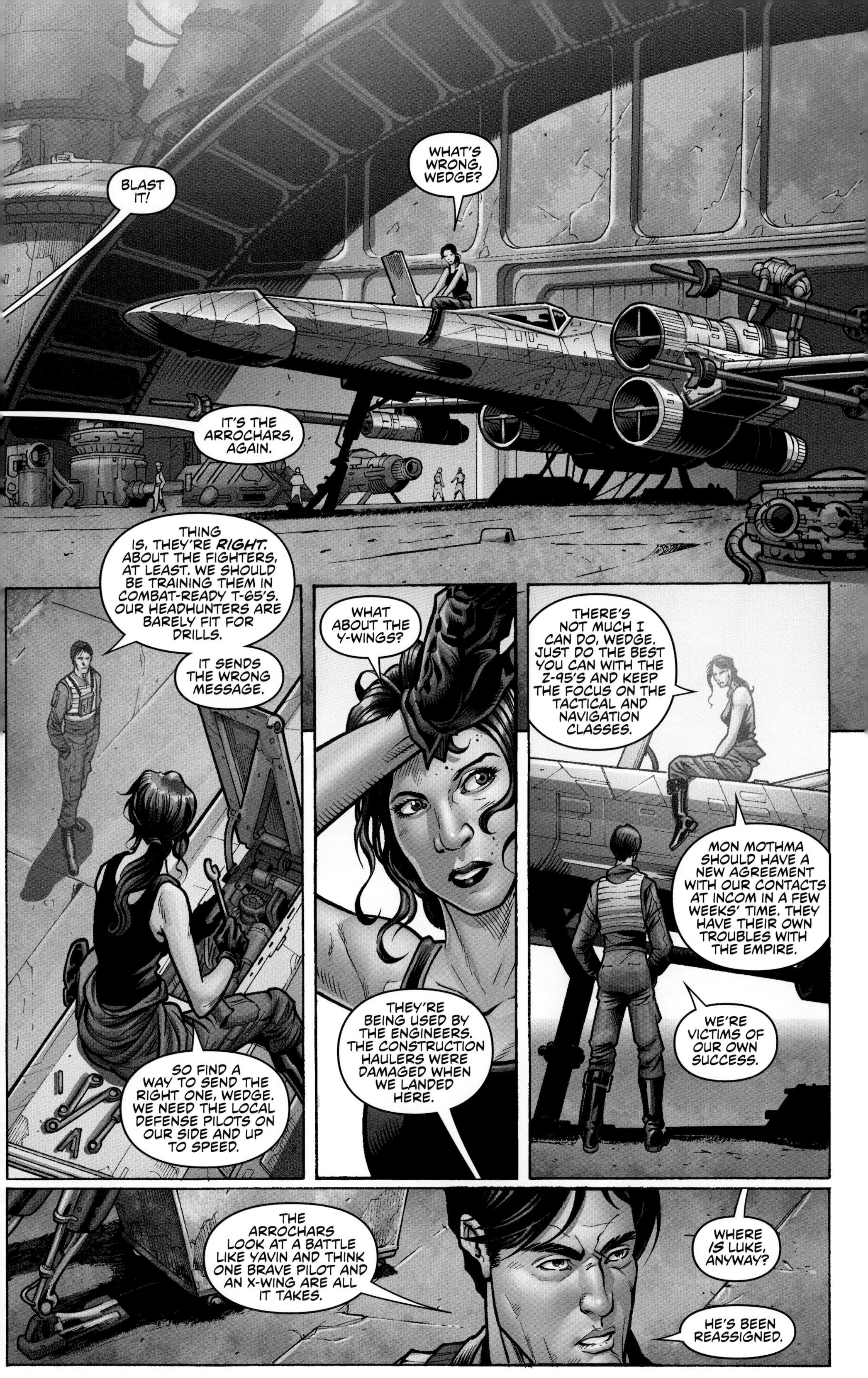

BLAST IT!
WHAT'S WRONG, WEDGE?
IT'S THE ARROCHARS, AGAIN.
THING IS, THEY'RE *RIGHT.* ABOUT THE FIGHTERS, AT LEAST. WE SHOULD BE TRAINING THEM IN COMBAT-READY T-65'S. OUR HEADHUNTERS ARE BARELY FIT FOR DRILLS.
IT SENDS THE WRONG MESSAGE.
SO FIND A WAY TO SEND THE RIGHT ONE, WEDGE. WE NEED THE LOCAL DEFENSE PILOTS ON OUR SIDE AND UP TO SPEED.
WHAT ABOUT THE Y-WINGS?
THEY'RE BEING USED BY THE ENGINEERS. THE CONSTRUCTION HAULERS WERE DAMAGED WHEN WE LANDED HERE.
THERE'S NOT MUCH I CAN DO, WEDGE. JUST DO THE BEST YOU CAN WITH THE Z-95'S AND KEEP THE FOCUS ON THE TACTICAL AND NAVIGATION CLASSES.
MON MOTHMA SHOULD HAVE A NEW AGREEMENT WITH OUR CONTACTS AT INCOM IN A FEW WEEKS' TIME. THEY HAVE THEIR OWN TROUBLES WITH THE EMPIRE.
WE'RE VICTIMS OF OUR OWN SUCCESS.
THE ARROCHARS LOOK AT A BATTLE LIKE YAVIN AND THINK ONE BRAVE PILOT AND AN X-WING ARE ALL IT TAKES.
WHERE *IS* LUKE, ANYWAY?
HE'S BEEN REASSIGNED.

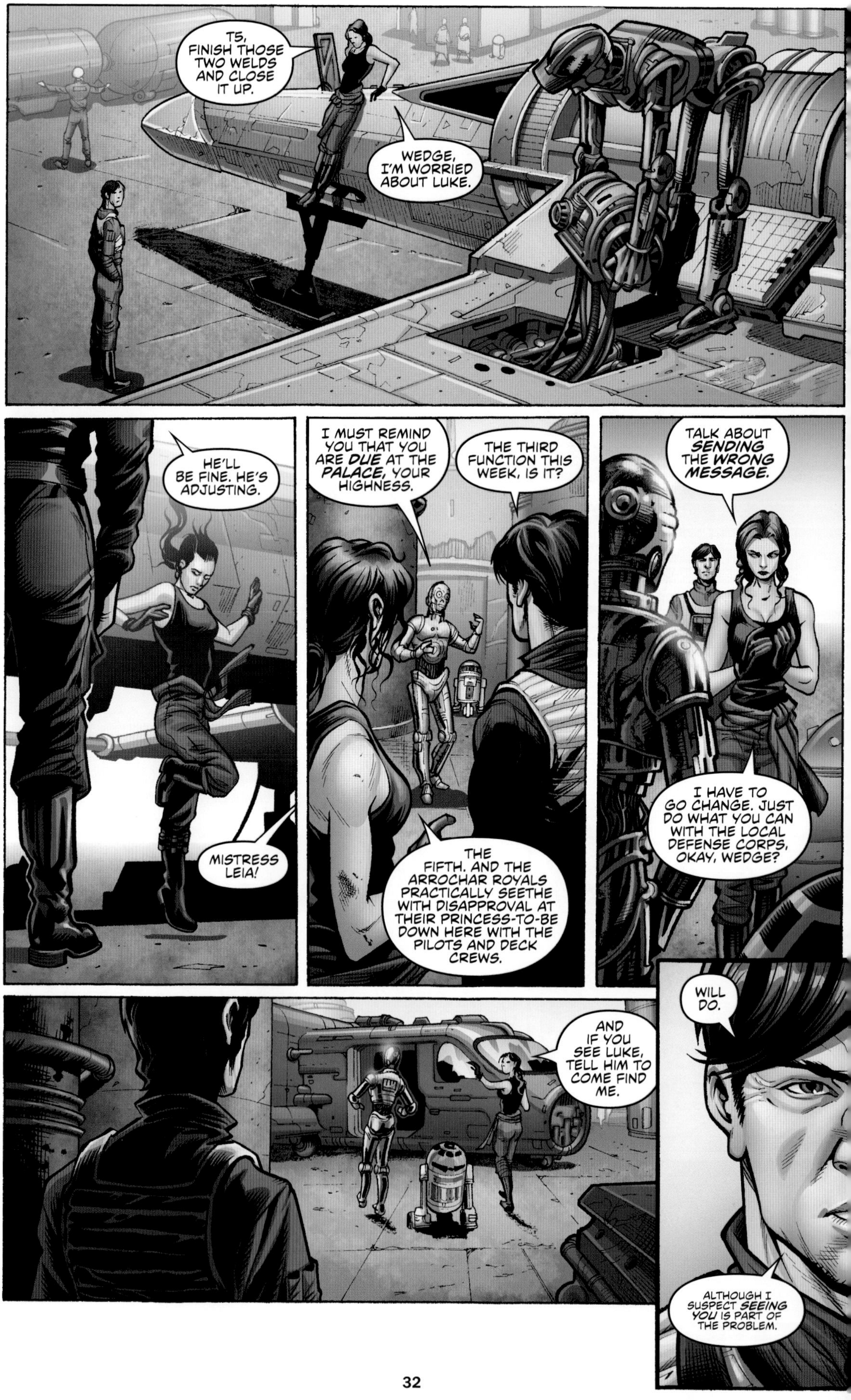
T5, FINISH THOSE TWO WELDS AND CLOSE IT UP.
WEDGE, I'M WORRIED ABOUT LUKE.
HE'LL BE FINE. HE'S ADJUSTING.
MISTRESS LEIA!
I MUST REMIND YOU THAT YOU ARE *DUE* AT THE *PALACE,* YOUR HIGHNESS.
THE THIRD FUNCTION THIS WEEK, IS IT?
THE FIFTH. AND THE ARROCHAR ROYALS PRACTICALLY SEETHE WITH DISAPPROVAL AT THEIR PRINCESS-TO-BE DOWN HERE WITH THE PILOTS AND DECK CREWS.
TALK ABOUT *SENDING* THE *WRONG MESSAGE.*
I HAVE TO GO CHANGE. JUST DO WHAT YOU CAN WITH THE LOCAL DEFENSE CORPS, OKAY, WEDGE?
AND IF YOU SEE LUKE, TELL HIM TO COME FIND ME.
WILL DO.
ALTHOUGH I SUSPECT *SEEING YOU* IS PART OF THE PROBLEM.

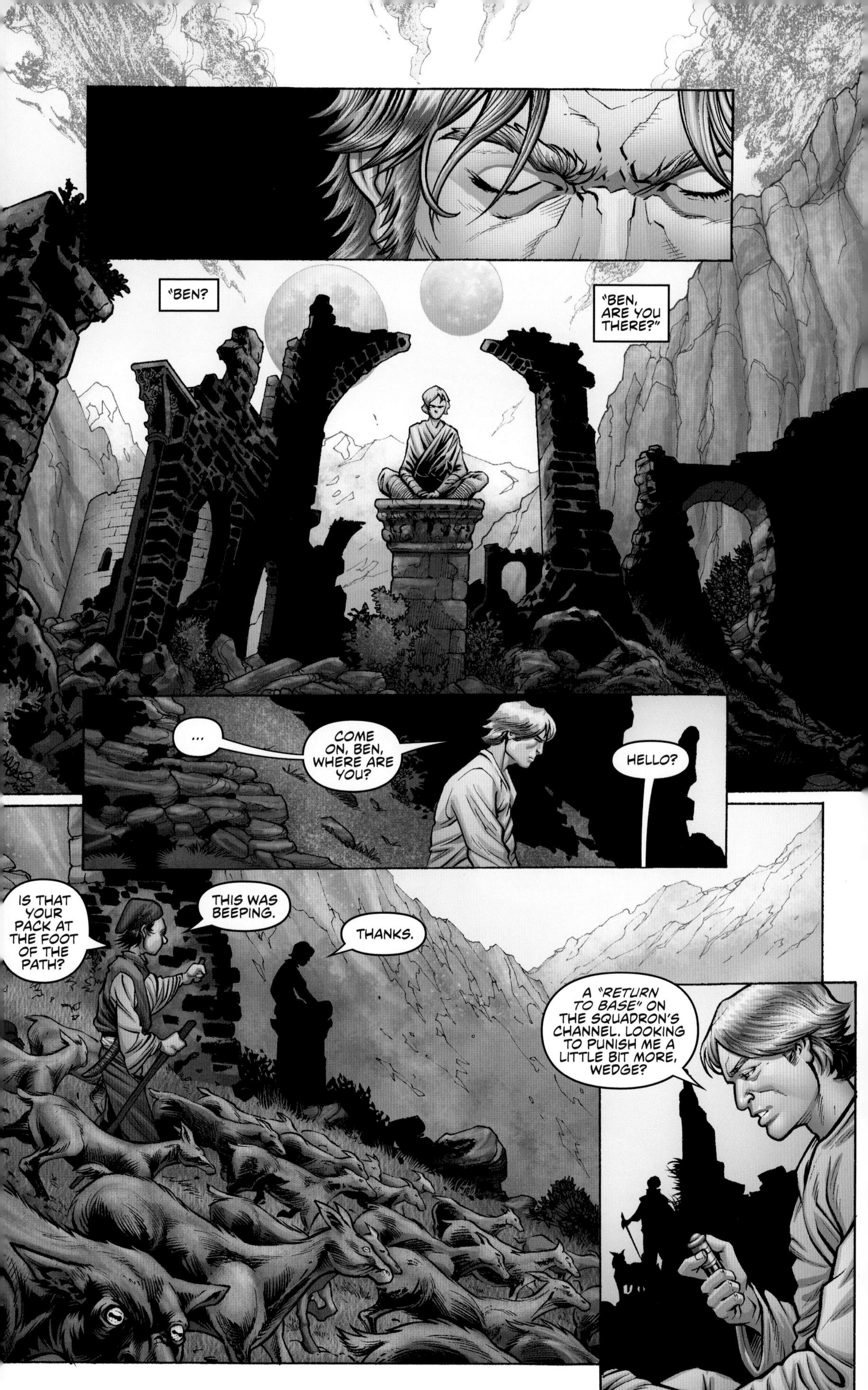
"BEN?
"BEN, ARE YOU THERE?"
...
COME ON, BEN, WHERE ARE YOU?
HELLO?
IS THAT YOUR PACK AT THE FOOT OF THE PATH?
THIS WAS BEEPING.
THANKS.
A "RETURN TO BASE" ON THE SQUADRON'S CHANNEL. LOOKING TO PUNISH ME A LITTLE BIT MORE, WEDGE?

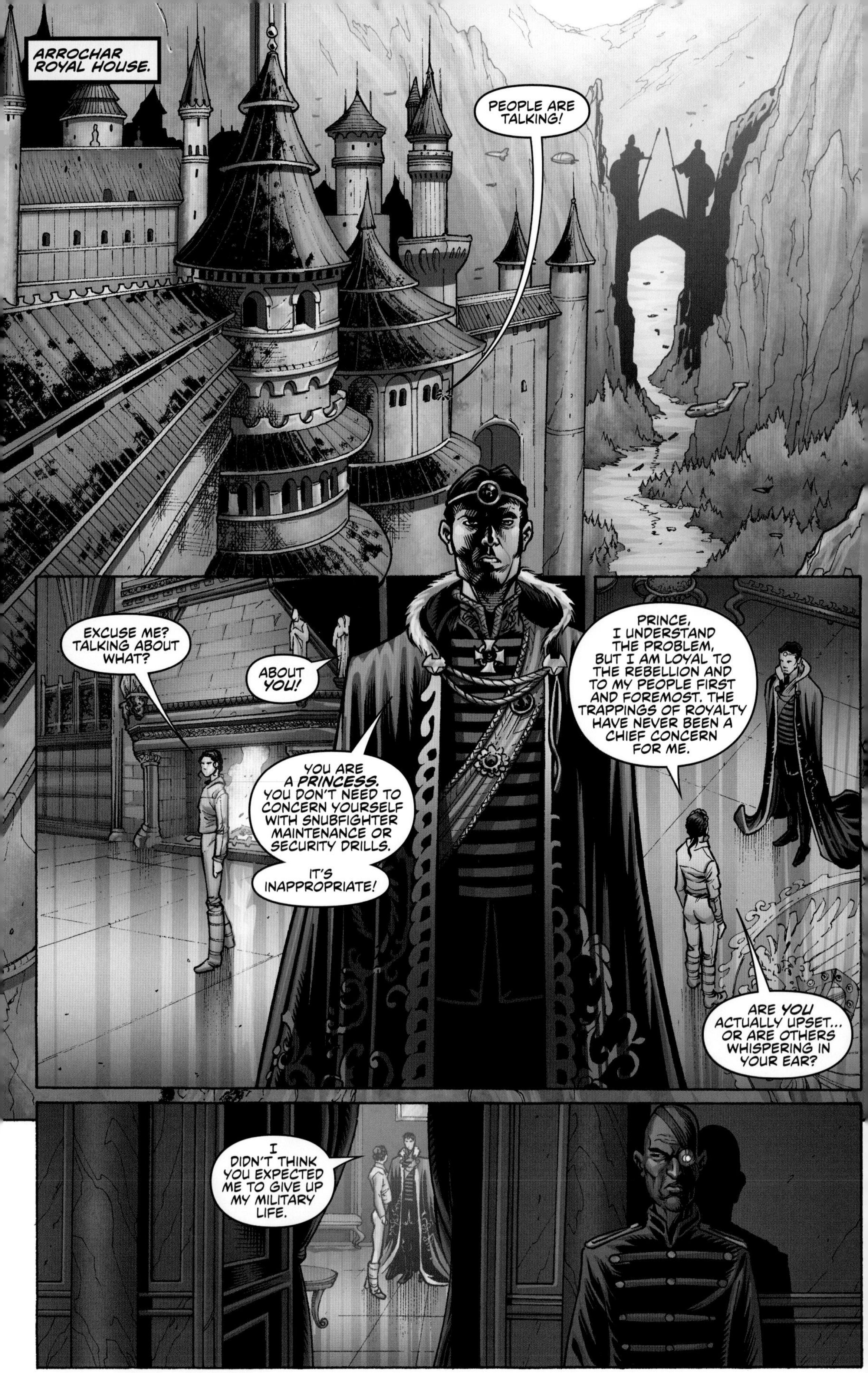

ARROCHAR ROYAL HOUSE.
PEOPLE ARE TALKING!
EXCUSE ME? TALKING ABOUT WHAT?
ABOUT YOU!
YOU ARE A PRINCESS. YOU DON'T NEED TO CONCERN YOURSELF WITH SNUBFIGHTER MAINTENANCE OR SECURITY DRILLS.
IT'S INAPPROPRIATE!
PRINCE, I UNDERSTAND THE PROBLEM, BUT I AM LOYAL TO THE REBELLION AND TO MY PEOPLE FIRST AND FOREMOST. THE TRAPPINGS OF ROYALTY HAVE NEVER BEEN A CHIEF CONCERN FOR ME.
ARE YOU ACTUALLY UPSET... OR ARE OTHERS WHISPERING IN YOUR EAR?
I DIDN'T THINK YOU EXPECTED ME TO GIVE UP MY MILITARY LIFE.

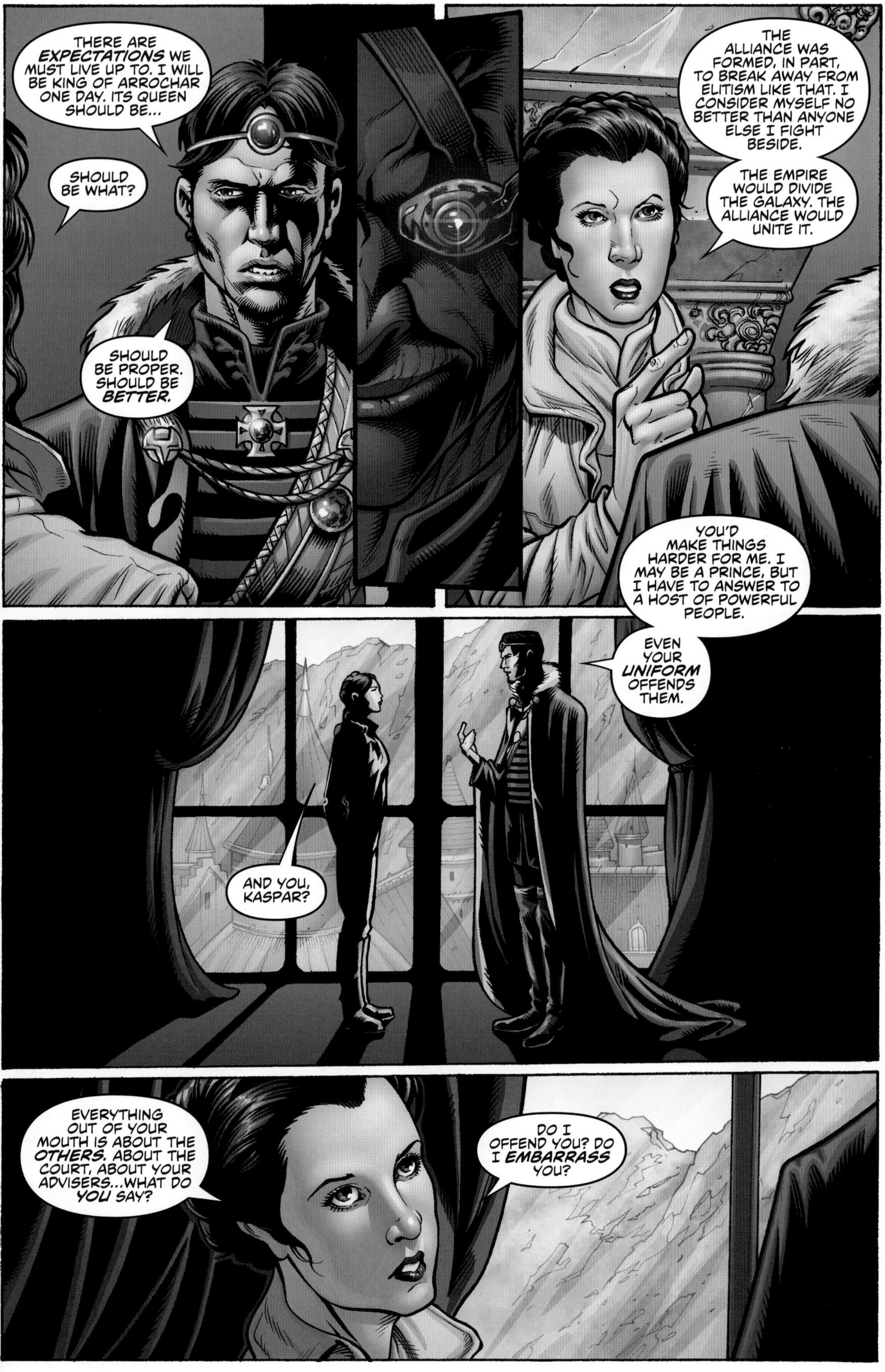
THERE ARE EXPECTATIONS WE MUST LIVE UP TO. I WILL BE KING OF ARROCHAR ONE DAY. ITS QUEEN SHOULD BE...
SHOULD BE WHAT?
SHOULD BE PROPER. SHOULD BE BETTER.
THE ALLIANCE WAS FORMED, IN PART, TO BREAK AWAY FROM ELITISM LIKE THAT. I CONSIDER MYSELF NO BETTER THAN ANYONE ELSE I FIGHT BESIDE.
THE EMPIRE WOULD DIVIDE THE GALAXY. THE ALLIANCE WOULD UNITE IT.
YOU'D MAKE THINGS HARDER FOR ME. I MAY BE A PRINCE, BUT I HAVE TO ANSWER TO A HOST OF POWERFUL PEOPLE.
EVEN YOUR UNIFORM OFFENDS THEM.
AND YOU, KASPAR?
EVERYTHING OUT OF YOUR MOUTH IS ABOUT THE OTHERS. ABOUT THE COURT, ABOUT YOUR ADVISERS...WHAT DO YOU SAY?
DO I OFFEND YOU? DO I EMBARRASS YOU?

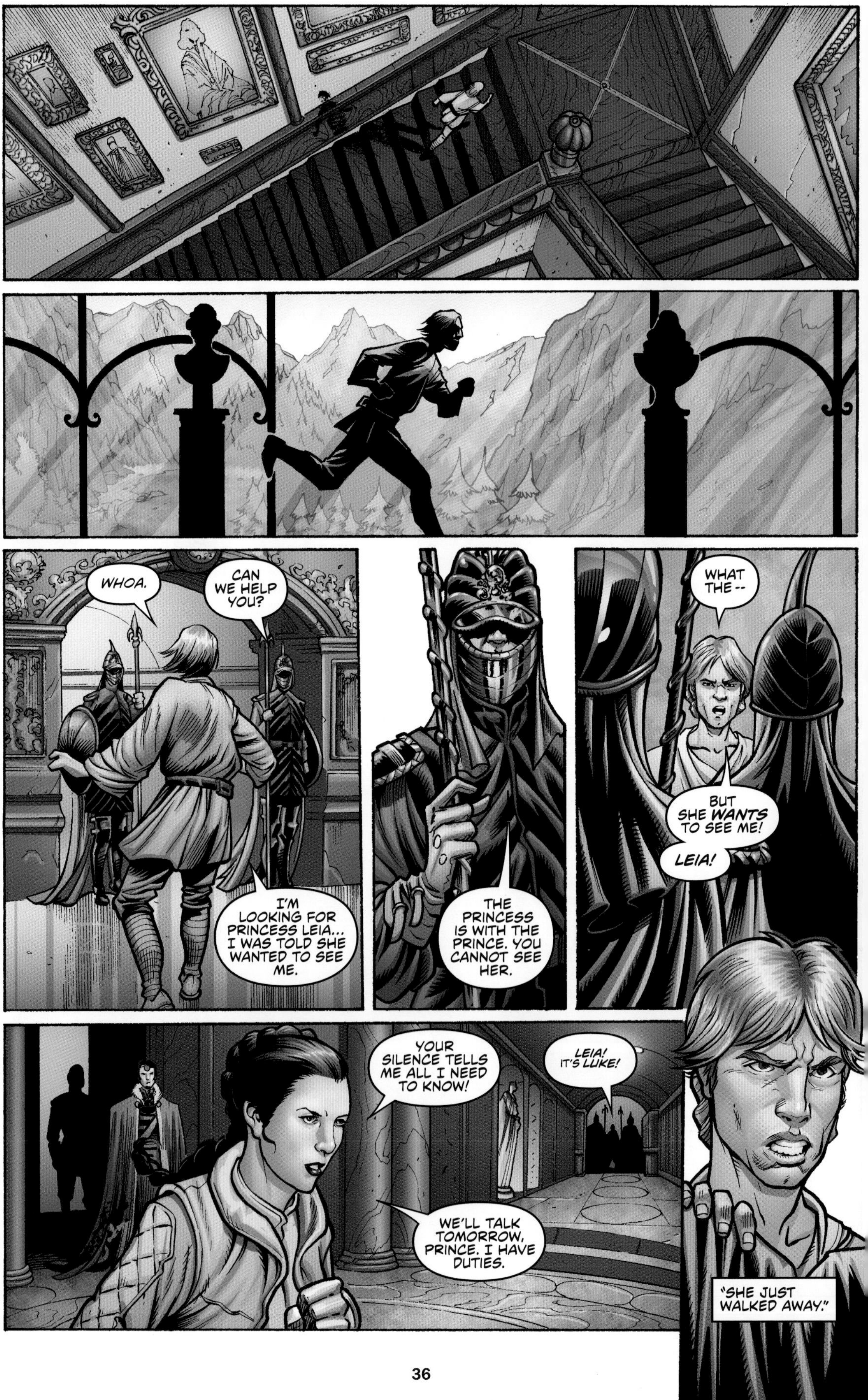
WHOA.
CAN WE HELP YOU?
I'M LOOKING FOR PRINCESS LEIA... I WAS TOLD SHE WANTED TO SEE ME.
THE PRINCESS IS WITH THE PRINCE. YOU CANNOT SEE HER.
WHAT THE --
BUT SHE *WANTS* TO SEE ME!
LEIA!
YOUR SILENCE TELLS ME ALL I NEED TO KNOW!
LEIA! IT'S *LUKE!*
WE'LL TALK TOMORROW, PRINCE. I HAVE DUTIES.
"SHE JUST WALKED AWAY."

THE PRINCESS IS A BUSY PERSON, SKYWALKER. WHAT CAN I DO FOR YOU?

REPORTING FOR DUTY, MA'AM.

WEDGE MAY HAVE GROUNDED ME, BUT I CAN STILL CONTRIBUTE. I CAN DO SOMETHING.

COMMANDER, I --

IF I MAY, MON MOTHMA...

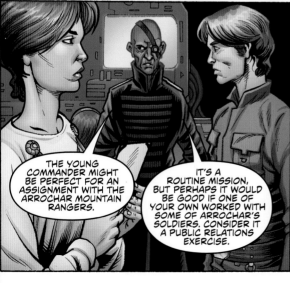

THE YOUNG COMMANDER MIGHT BE PERFECT FOR AN ASSIGNMENT WITH THE ARROCHAR MOUNTAIN RANGERS.

IT'S A ROUTINE MISSION, BUT PERHAPS IT WOULD BE GOOD IF ONE OF YOUR OWN WORKED WITH SOME OF ARROCHAR'S SOLDIERS. CONSIDER IT A PUBLIC RELATIONS EXERCISE.

I'D BE HONORED, GENERAL.

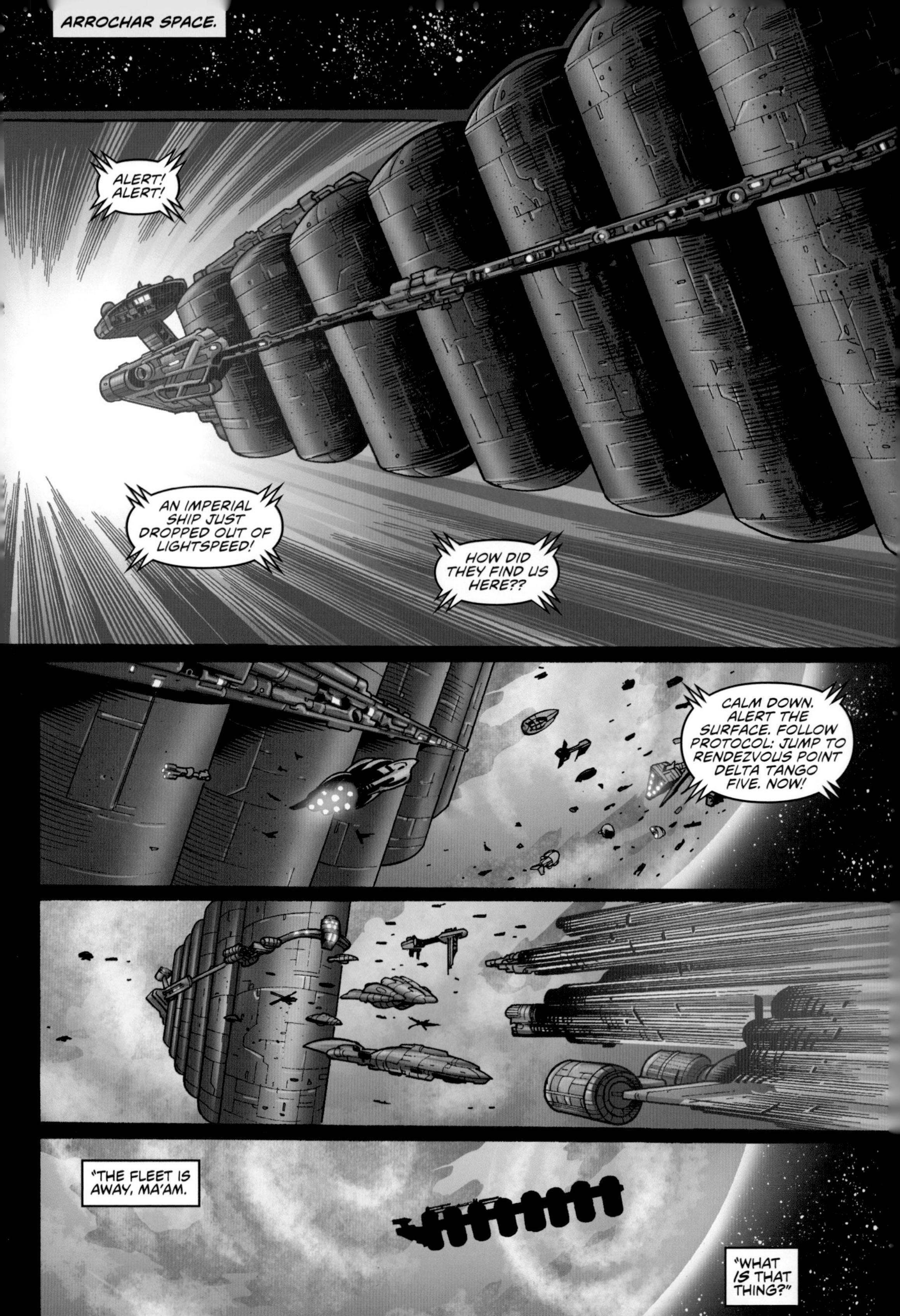
ARROCHAR SPACE.
ALERT! ALERT!
AN IMPERIAL SHIP JUST DROPPED OUT OF LIGHTSPEED!
HOW DID THEY FIND US HERE??
CALM DOWN. ALERT THE SURFACE. FOLLOW PROTOCOL: JUMP TO RENDEZVOUS POINT DELTA TANGO FIVE. NOW!
"THE FLEET IS AWAY, MA'AM.
"WHAT IS THAT THING?"

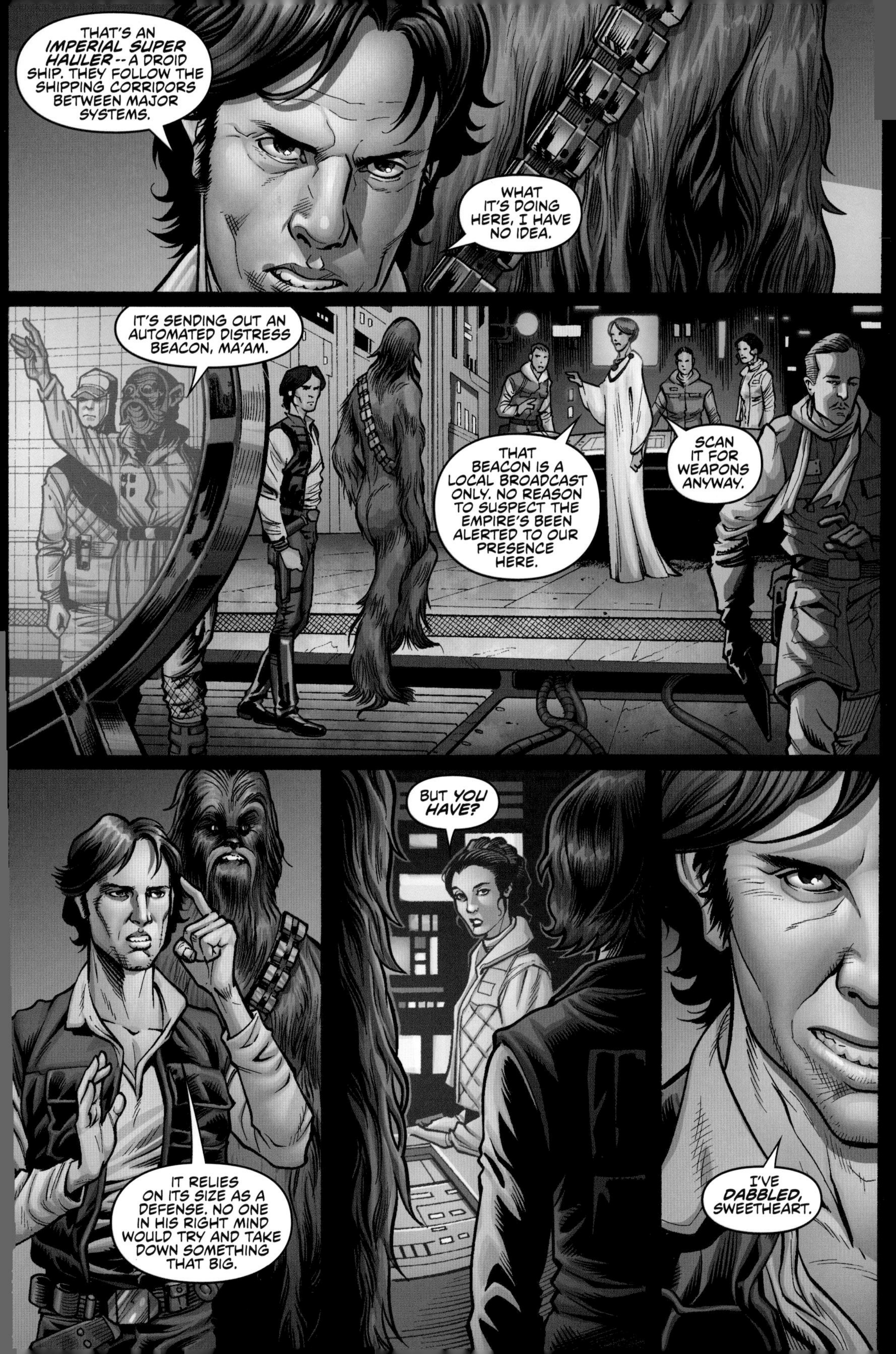
THAT'S AN IMPERIAL SUPER HAULER--A DROID SHIP. THEY FOLLOW THE SHIPPING CORRIDORS BETWEEN MAJOR SYSTEMS.
WHAT IT'S DOING HERE, I HAVE NO IDEA.
IT'S SENDING OUT AN AUTOMATED DISTRESS BEACON, MA'AM.
THAT BEACON IS A LOCAL BROADCAST ONLY. NO REASON TO SUSPECT THE EMPIRE'S BEEN ALERTED TO OUR PRESENCE HERE.
SCAN IT FOR WEAPONS ANYWAY.
IT RELIES ON ITS SIZE AS A DEFENSE. NO ONE IN HIS RIGHT MIND WOULD TRY AND TAKE DOWN SOMETHING THAT BIG.
BUT YOU HAVE?
I'VE DABBLED, SWEETHEART.

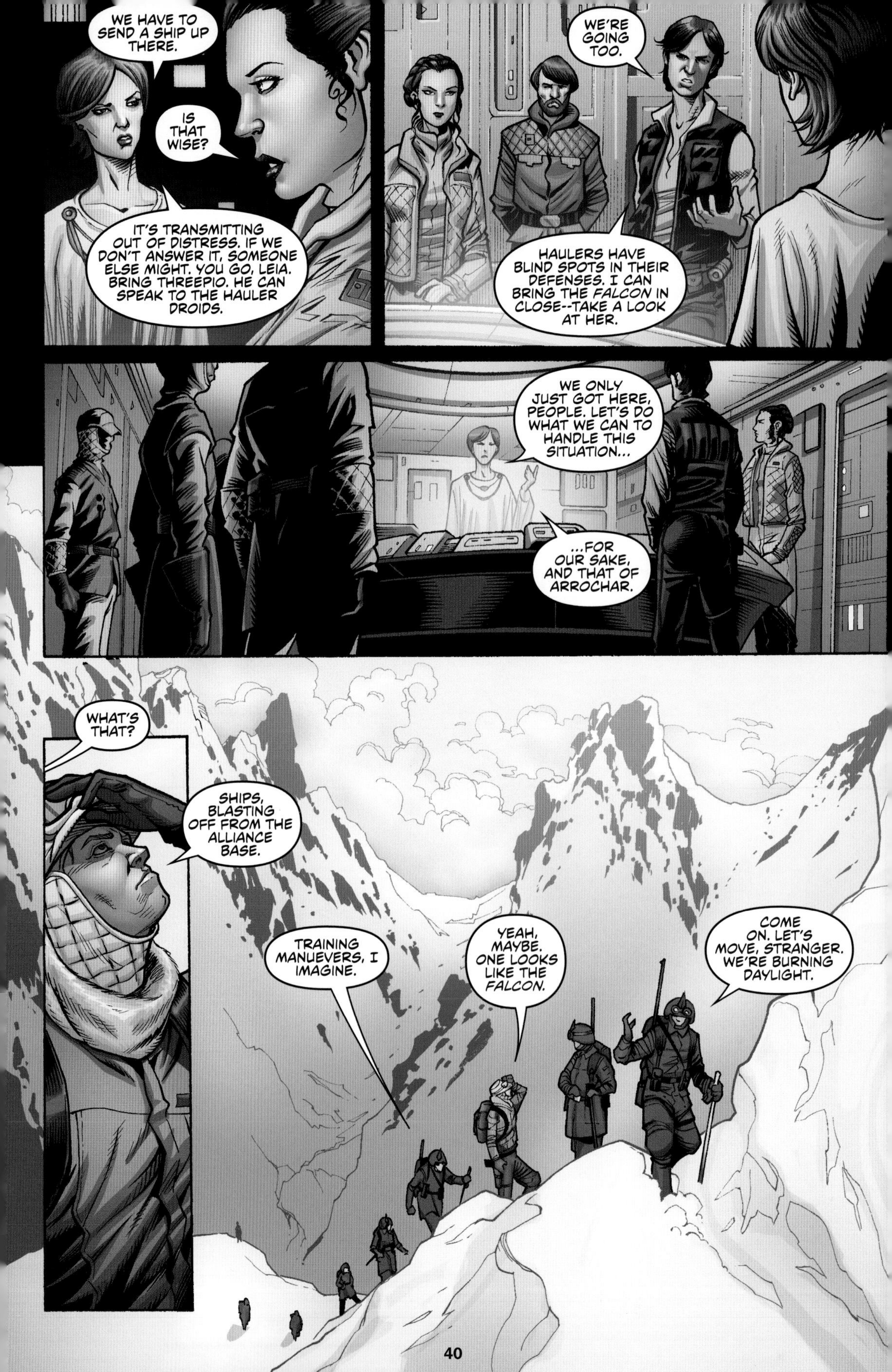
WE HAVE TO SEND A SHIP UP THERE.
IS THAT WISE?
IT'S TRANSMITTING OUT OF DISTRESS. IF WE DON'T ANSWER IT, SOMEONE ELSE MIGHT. YOU GO, LEIA. BRING THREEPIO. HE CAN SPEAK TO THE HAULER DROIDS.
WE'RE GOING TOO.
HAULERS HAVE BLIND SPOTS IN THEIR DEFENSES. I CAN BRING THE *FALCON* IN CLOSE--TAKE A LOOK AT HER.
WE ONLY JUST GOT HERE, PEOPLE. LET'S DO WHAT WE CAN TO HANDLE THIS SITUATION...
...FOR OUR SAKE, AND THAT OF ARROCHAR.
WHAT'S THAT?
SHIPS, BLASTING OFF FROM THE ALLIANCE BASE.
TRAINING MANUEVERS, I IMAGINE.
YEAH, MAYBE. ONE LOOKS LIKE THE *FALCON*.
COME ON. LET'S MOVE, STRANGER. WE'RE BURNING DAYLIGHT.

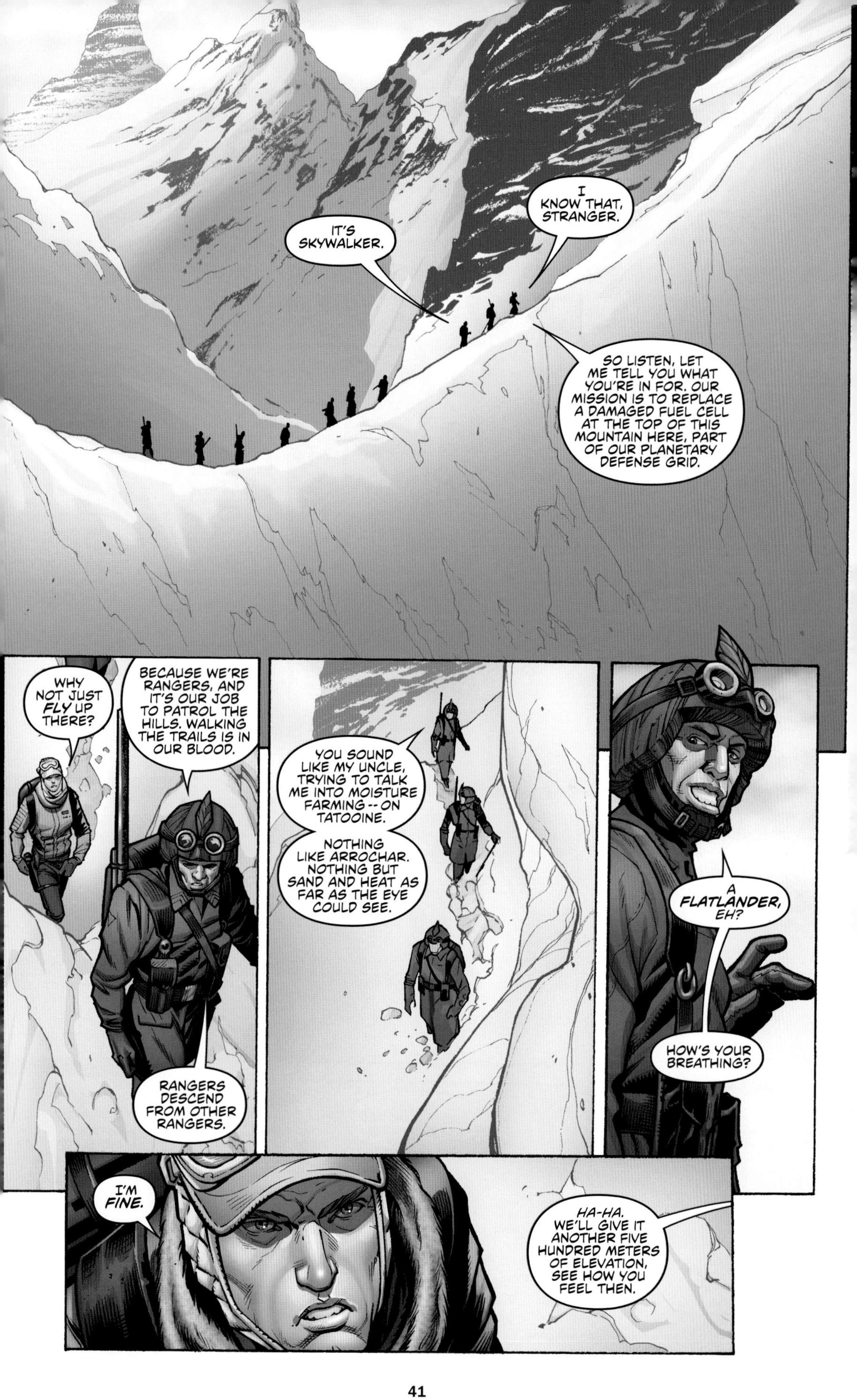
IT'S SKYWALKER.
I KNOW THAT, STRANGER.
SO LISTEN, LET ME TELL YOU WHAT YOU'RE IN FOR. OUR MISSION IS TO REPLACE A DAMAGED FUEL CELL AT THE TOP OF THIS MOUNTAIN HERE, PART OF OUR PLANETARY DEFENSE GRID.
WHY NOT JUST *FLY* UP THERE?
BECAUSE WE'RE RANGERS, AND IT'S OUR JOB TO PATROL THE HILLS. WALKING THE TRAILS IS IN OUR BLOOD.
RANGERS DESCEND FROM OTHER RANGERS.
YOU SOUND LIKE MY UNCLE, TRYING TO TALK ME INTO MOISTURE FARMING--ON TATOOINE.
NOTHING LIKE ARROCHAR. NOTHING BUT SAND AND HEAT AS FAR AS THE EYE COULD SEE.
A *FLATLANDER*, EH?
HOW'S YOUR BREATHING?
I'M *FINE*.
HA-HA. WE'LL GIVE IT ANOTHER FIVE HUNDRED METERS OF ELEVATION, SEE HOW YOU FEEL THEN.

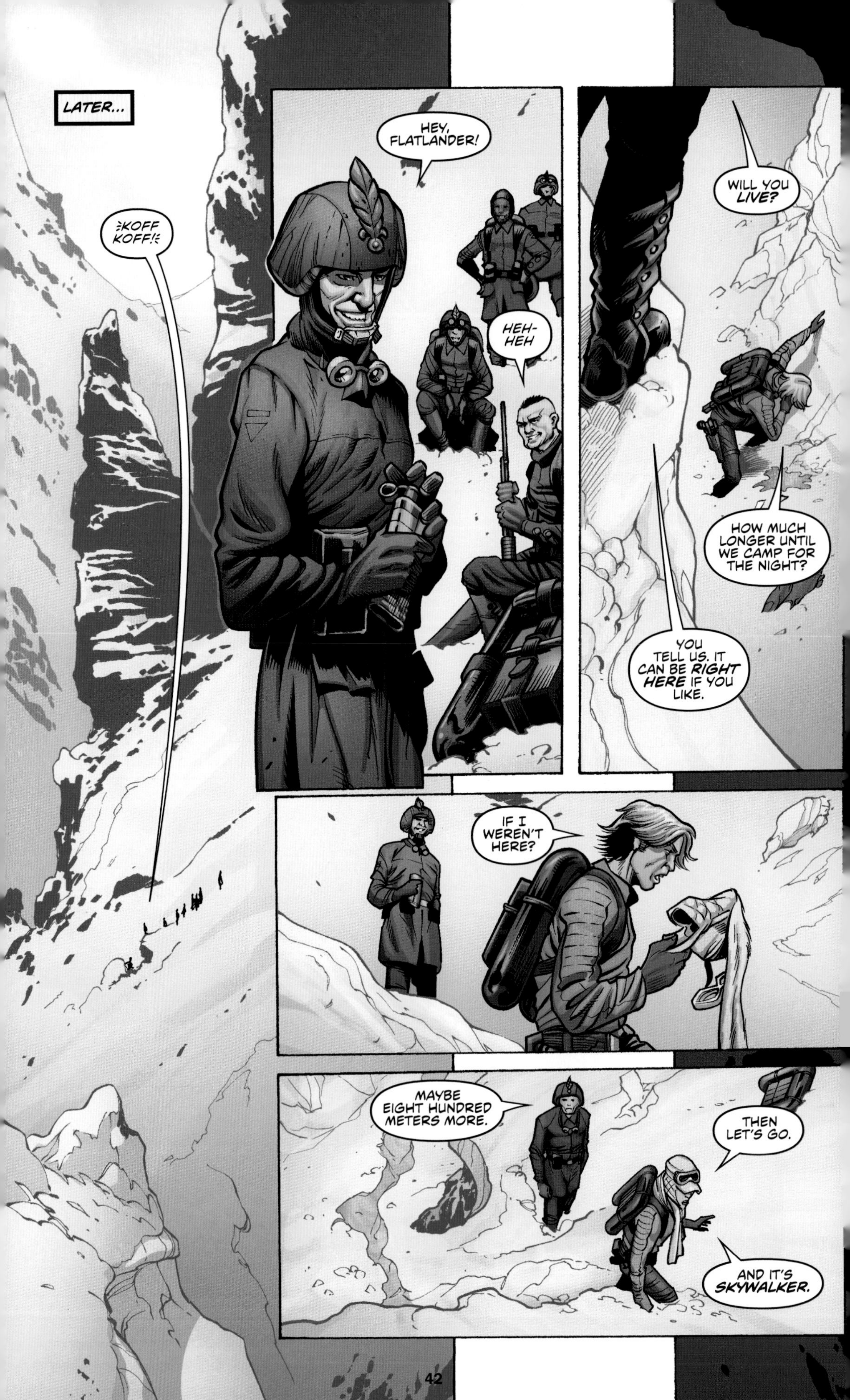
LATER...
HEY, FLATLANDER!
HEH-HEH
WILL YOU LIVE?
⁝KOFF KOFF!⁝
HOW MUCH LONGER UNTIL WE CAMP FOR THE NIGHT?
YOU TELL US. IT CAN BE RIGHT HERE IF YOU LIKE.
IF I WEREN'T HERE?
MAYBE EIGHT HUNDRED METERS MORE.
THEN LET'S GO.
AND IT'S SKYWALKER.

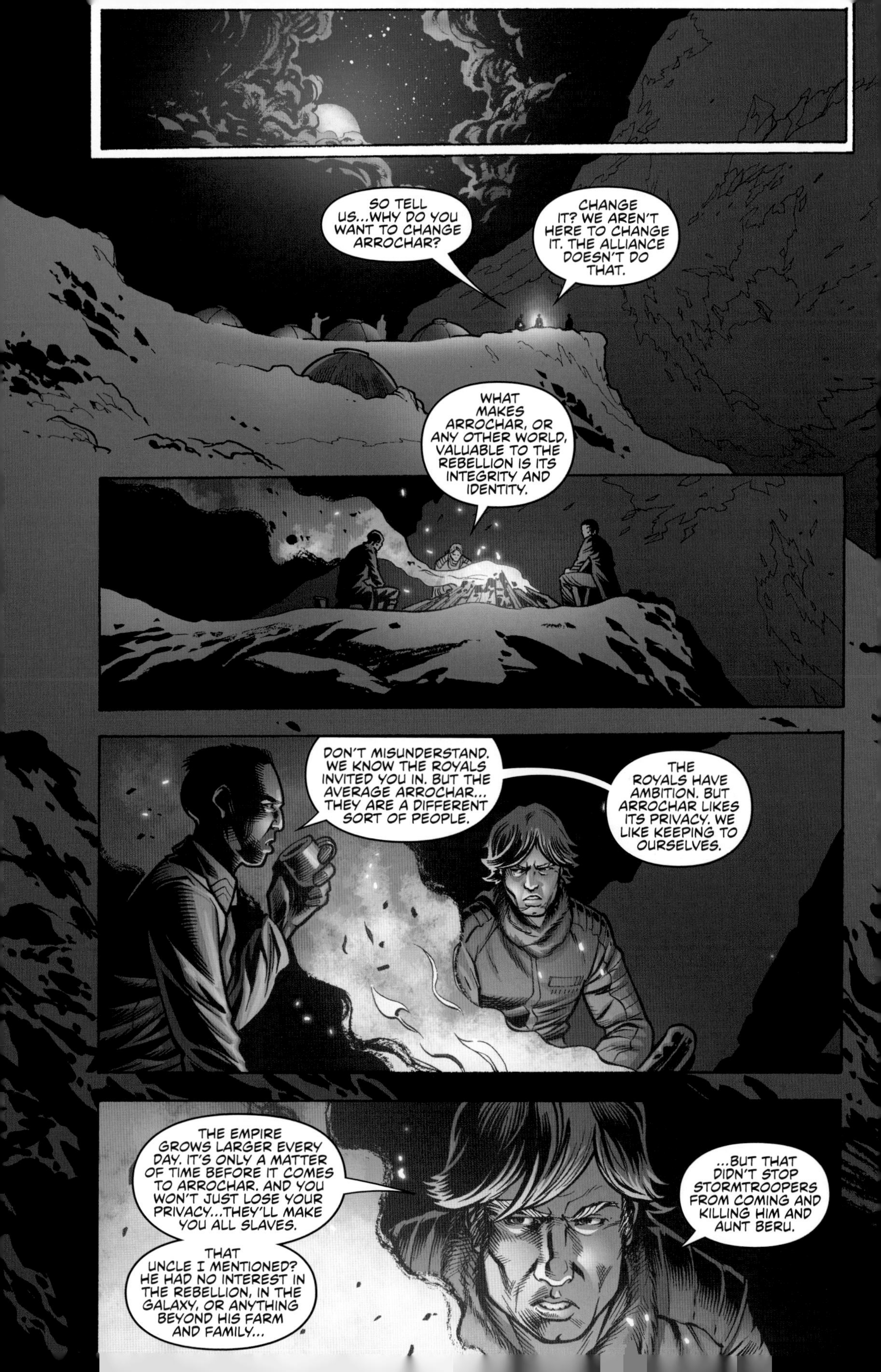
SO TELL US...WHY DO YOU WANT TO CHANGE ARROCHAR?
CHANGE IT? WE AREN'T HERE TO CHANGE IT. THE ALLIANCE DOESN'T DO THAT.
WHAT MAKES ARROCHAR, OR ANY OTHER WORLD, VALUABLE TO THE REBELLION IS ITS INTEGRITY AND IDENTITY.
DON'T MISUNDERSTAND. WE KNOW THE ROYALS INVITED YOU IN. BUT THE AVERAGE ARROCHAR... THEY ARE A DIFFERENT SORT OF PEOPLE.
THE ROYALS HAVE AMBITION. BUT ARROCHAR LIKES ITS PRIVACY. WE LIKE KEEPING TO OURSELVES.
THE EMPIRE GROWS LARGER EVERY DAY. IT'S ONLY A MATTER OF TIME BEFORE IT COMES TO ARROCHAR. AND YOU WON'T JUST LOSE YOUR PRIVACY...THEY'LL MAKE YOU ALL SLAVES.
THAT UNCLE I MENTIONED? HE HAD NO INTEREST IN THE REBELLION, IN THE GALAXY, OR ANYTHING BEYOND HIS FARM AND FAMILY...
...BUT THAT DIDN'T STOP STORMTROOPERS FROM COMING AND KILLING HIM AND AUNT BERU.

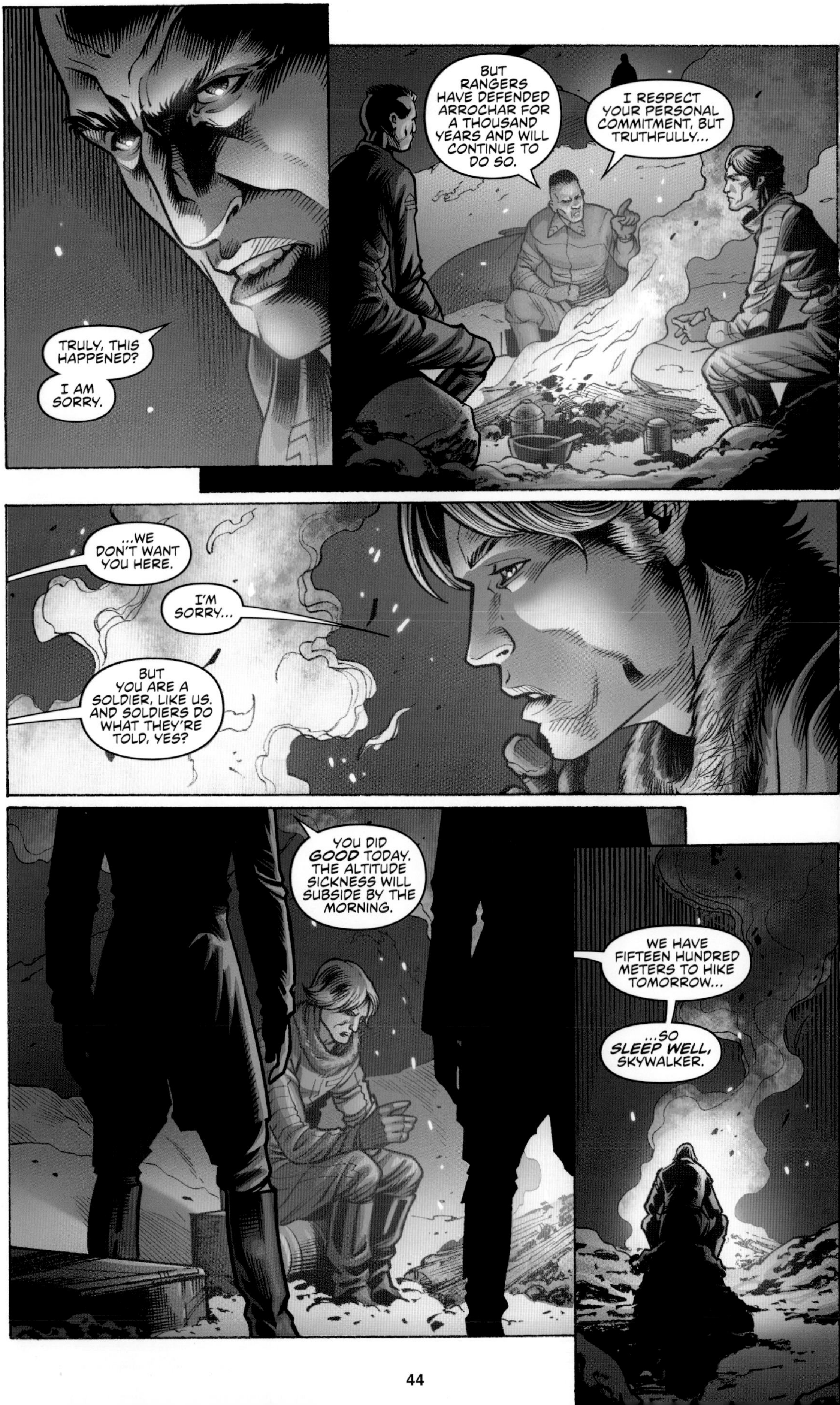
TRULY, THIS HAPPENED?
I AM SORRY.
BUT RANGERS HAVE DEFENDED ARROCHAR FOR A THOUSAND YEARS AND WILL CONTINUE TO DO SO.
I RESPECT YOUR PERSONAL COMMITMENT, BUT TRUTHFULLY...
...WE DON'T WANT YOU HERE.
I'M SORRY...
BUT YOU ARE A SOLDIER, LIKE US. AND SOLDIERS DO WHAT THEY'RE TOLD, YES?
YOU DID GOOD TODAY. THE ALTITUDE SICKNESS WILL SUBSIDE BY THE MORNING.
WE HAVE FIFTEEN HUNDRED METERS TO HIKE TOMORROW...
...SO SLEEP WELL, SKYWALKER.

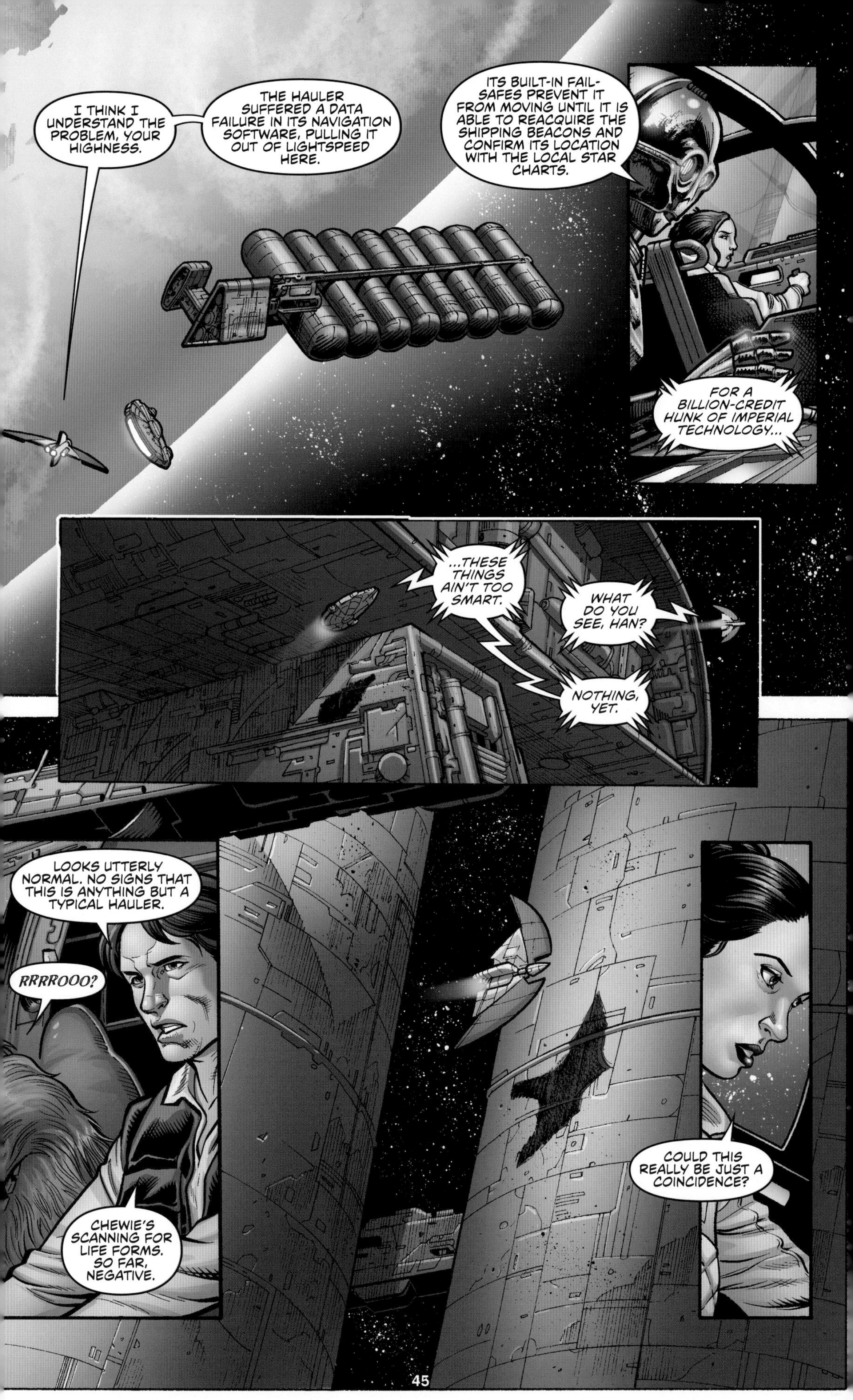
I THINK I UNDERSTAND THE PROBLEM, YOUR HIGHNESS.
THE HAULER SUFFERED A DATA FAILURE IN ITS NAVIGATION SOFTWARE, PULLING IT OUT OF LIGHTSPEED HERE.
ITS BUILT-IN FAIL-SAFES PREVENT IT FROM MOVING UNTIL IT IS ABLE TO REACQUIRE THE SHIPPING BEACONS AND CONFIRM ITS LOCATION WITH THE LOCAL STAR CHARTS.
FOR A BILLION-CREDIT HUNK OF IMPERIAL TECHNOLOGY...
...THESE THINGS AIN'T TOO SMART.
WHAT DO YOU SEE, HAN?
NOTHING, YET.
LOOKS UTTERLY NORMAL. NO SIGNS THAT THIS IS ANYTHING BUT A TYPICAL HAULER.
RRRROOO?
CHEWIE'S SCANNING FOR LIFE FORMS. SO FAR, NEGATIVE.
COULD THIS REALLY BE JUST A COINCIDENCE?

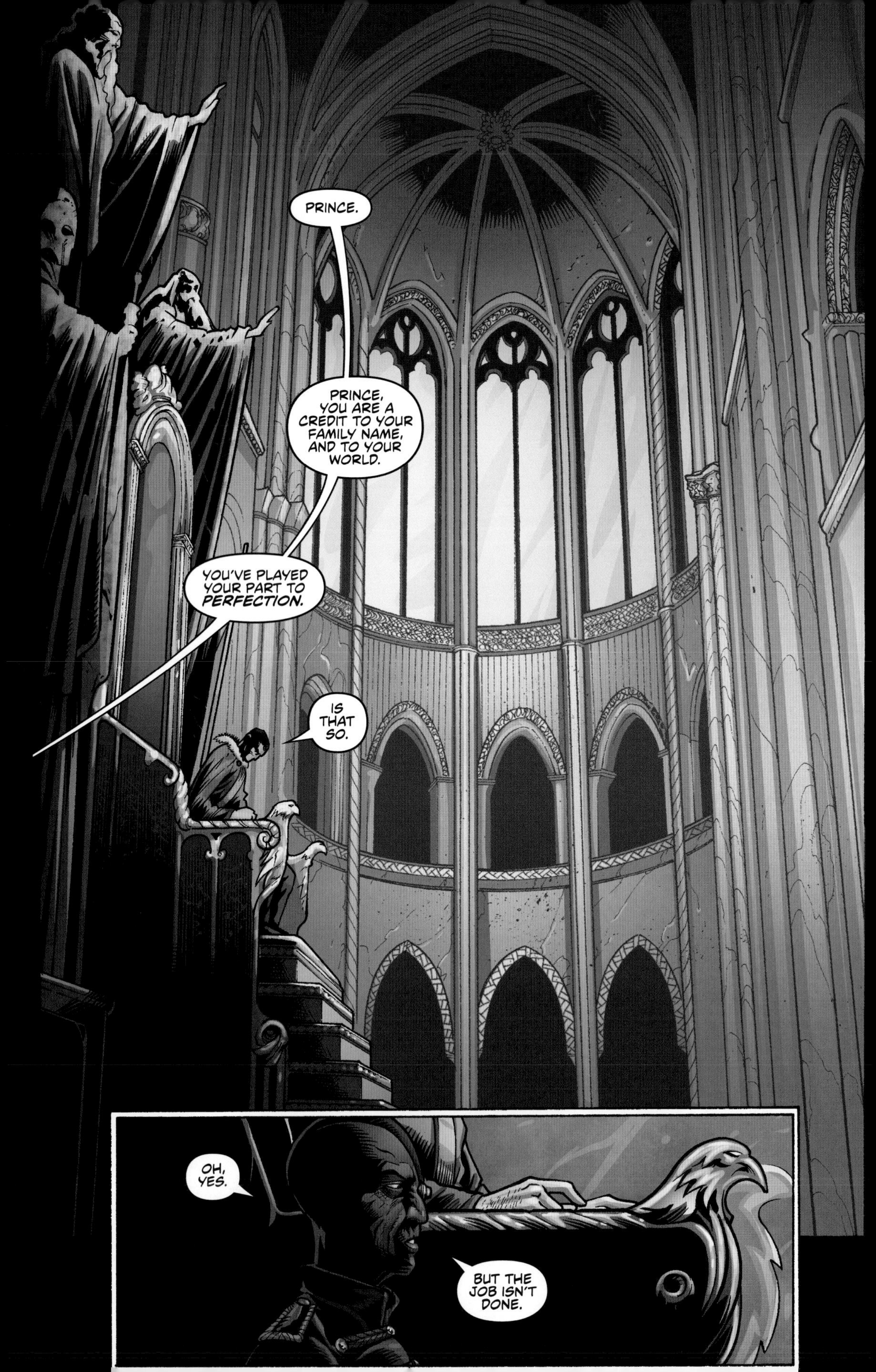
PRINCE.
PRINCE, YOU ARE A CREDIT TO YOUR FAMILY NAME, AND TO YOUR WORLD.
YOU'VE PLAYED YOUR PART TO PERFECTION.
IS THAT SO.
OH, YES.
BUT THE JOB ISN'T DONE.

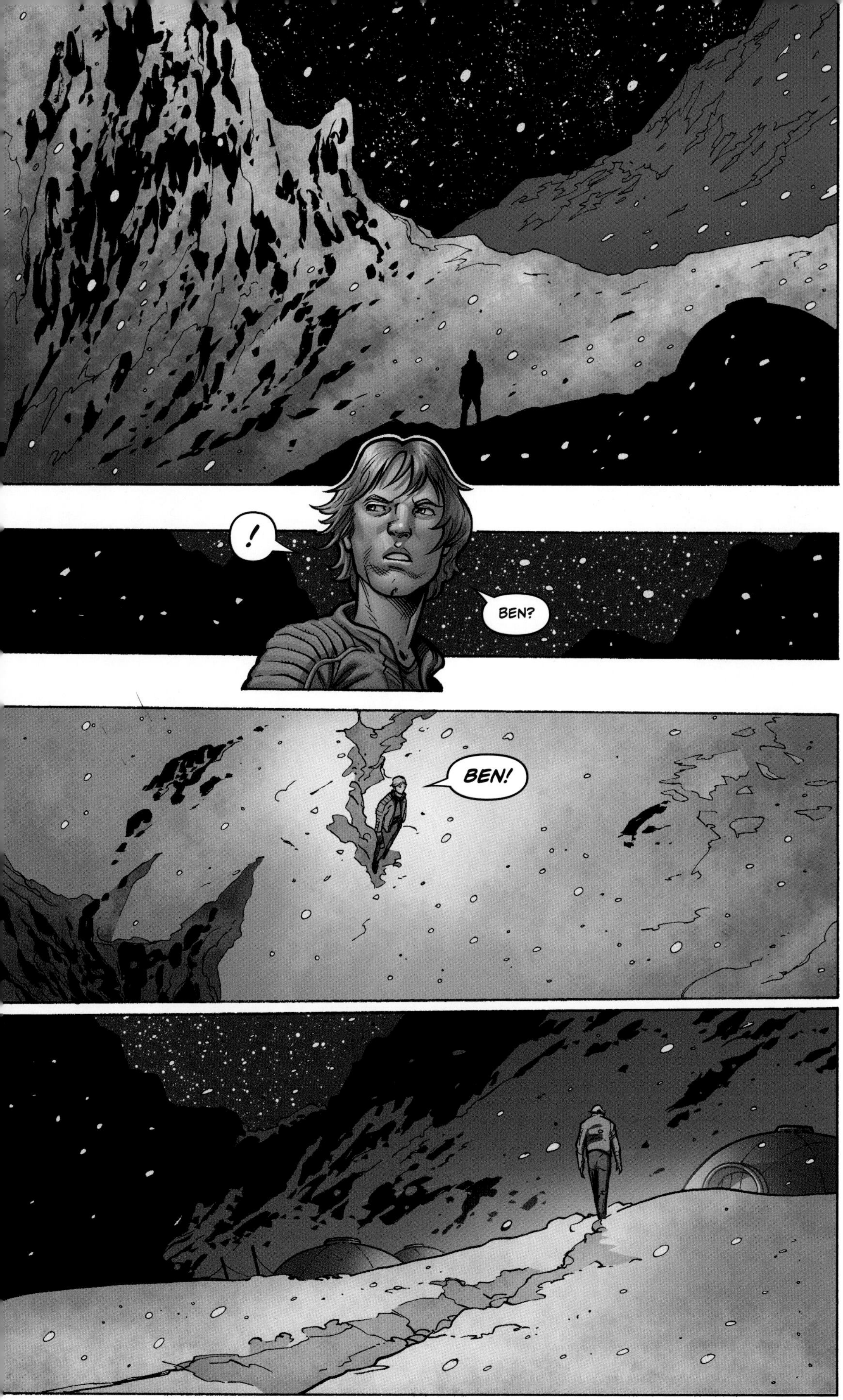

!
BEN?
BEN!

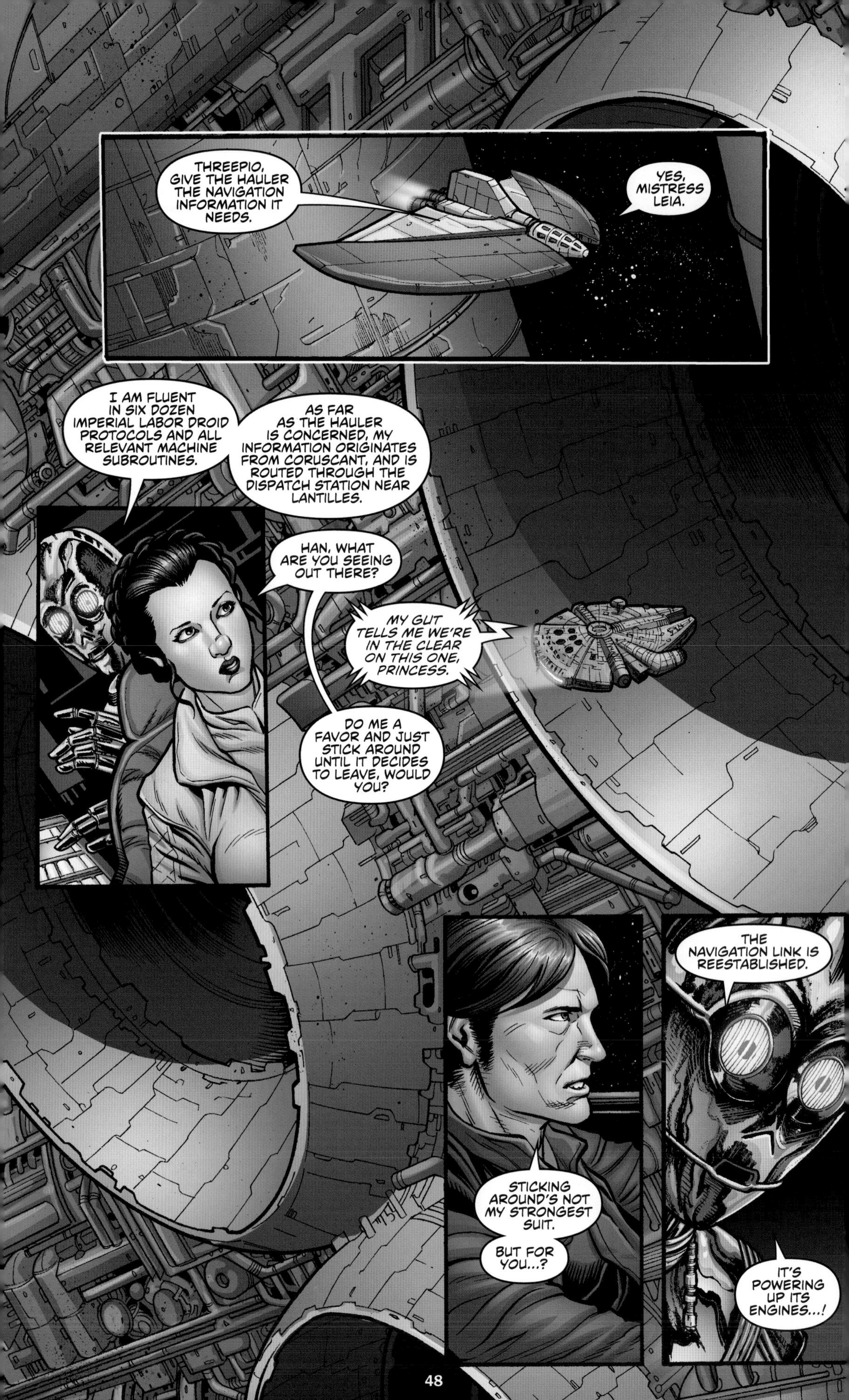

THREEPIO, GIVE THE HAULER THE NAVIGATION INFORMATION IT NEEDS.
YES, MISTRESS LEIA.
I AM FLUENT IN SIX DOZEN IMPERIAL LABOR DROID PROTOCOLS AND ALL RELEVANT MACHINE SUBROUTINES.
AS FAR AS THE HAULER IS CONCERNED, MY INFORMATION ORIGINATES FROM CORUSCANT, AND IS ROUTED THROUGH THE DISPATCH STATION NEAR LANTILLES.
HAN, WHAT ARE YOU SEEING OUT THERE?
MY GUT TELLS ME WE'RE IN THE CLEAR ON THIS ONE, PRINCESS.
DO ME A FAVOR AND JUST STICK AROUND UNTIL IT DECIDES TO LEAVE, WOULD YOU?
STICKING AROUND'S NOT MY STRONGEST SUIT.
BUT FOR YOU...?
THE NAVIGATION LINK IS REESTABLISHED.
IT'S POWERING UP ITS ENGINES...!

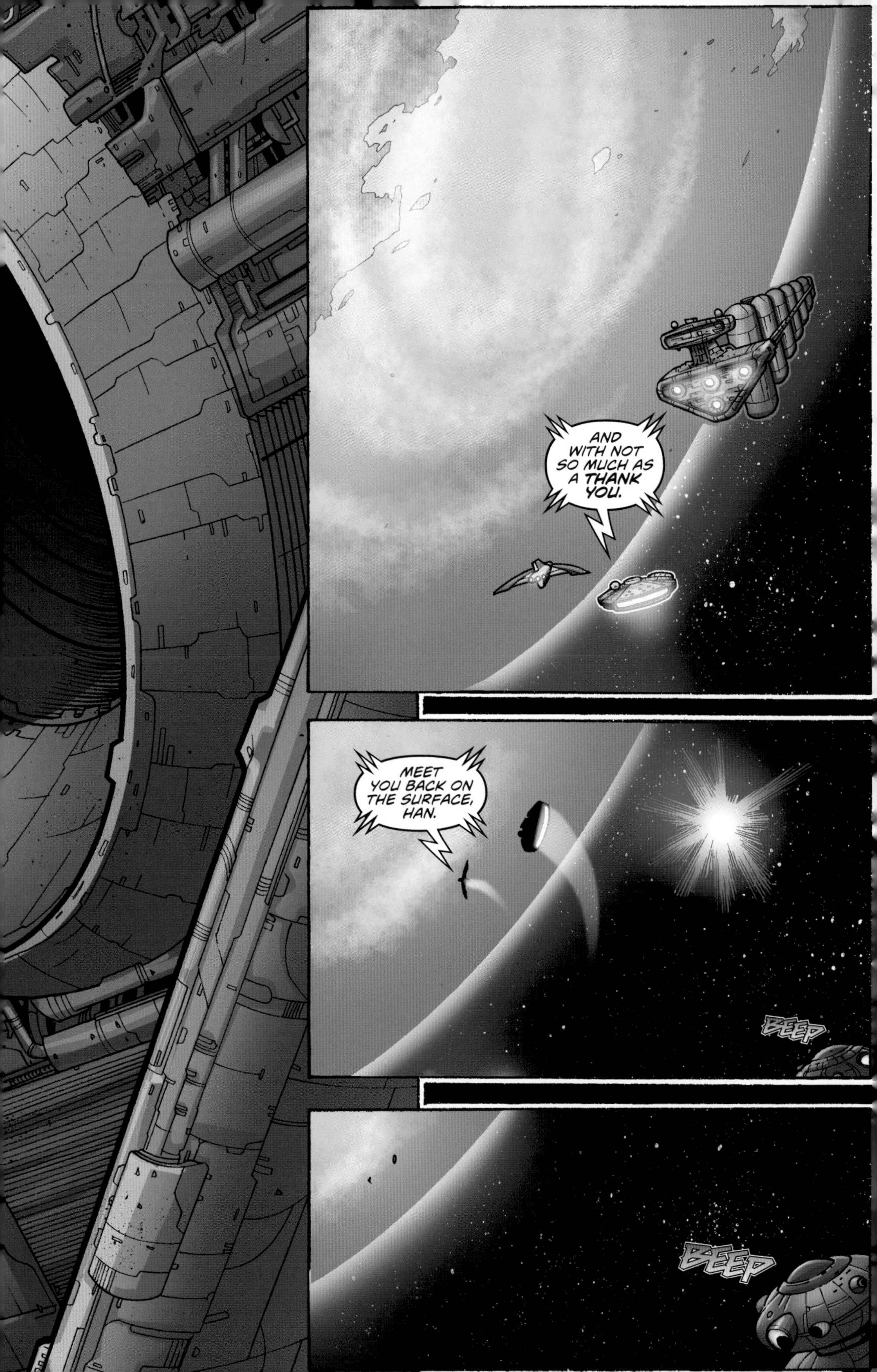
AND WITH NOT SO MUCH AS A THANK YOU.
MEET YOU BACK ON THE SURFACE, HAN.
BEEP
BEEP

BEEP

BEEP
BEEP
BEEP

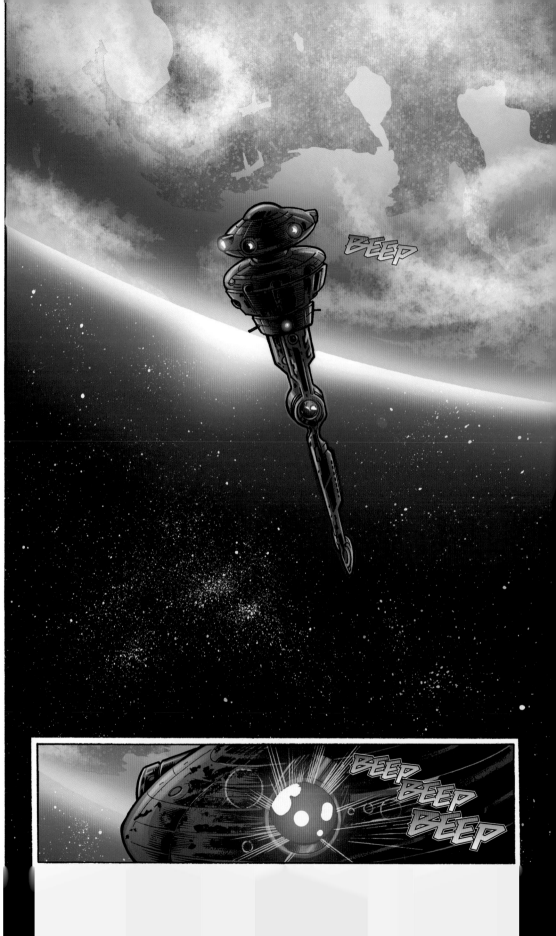

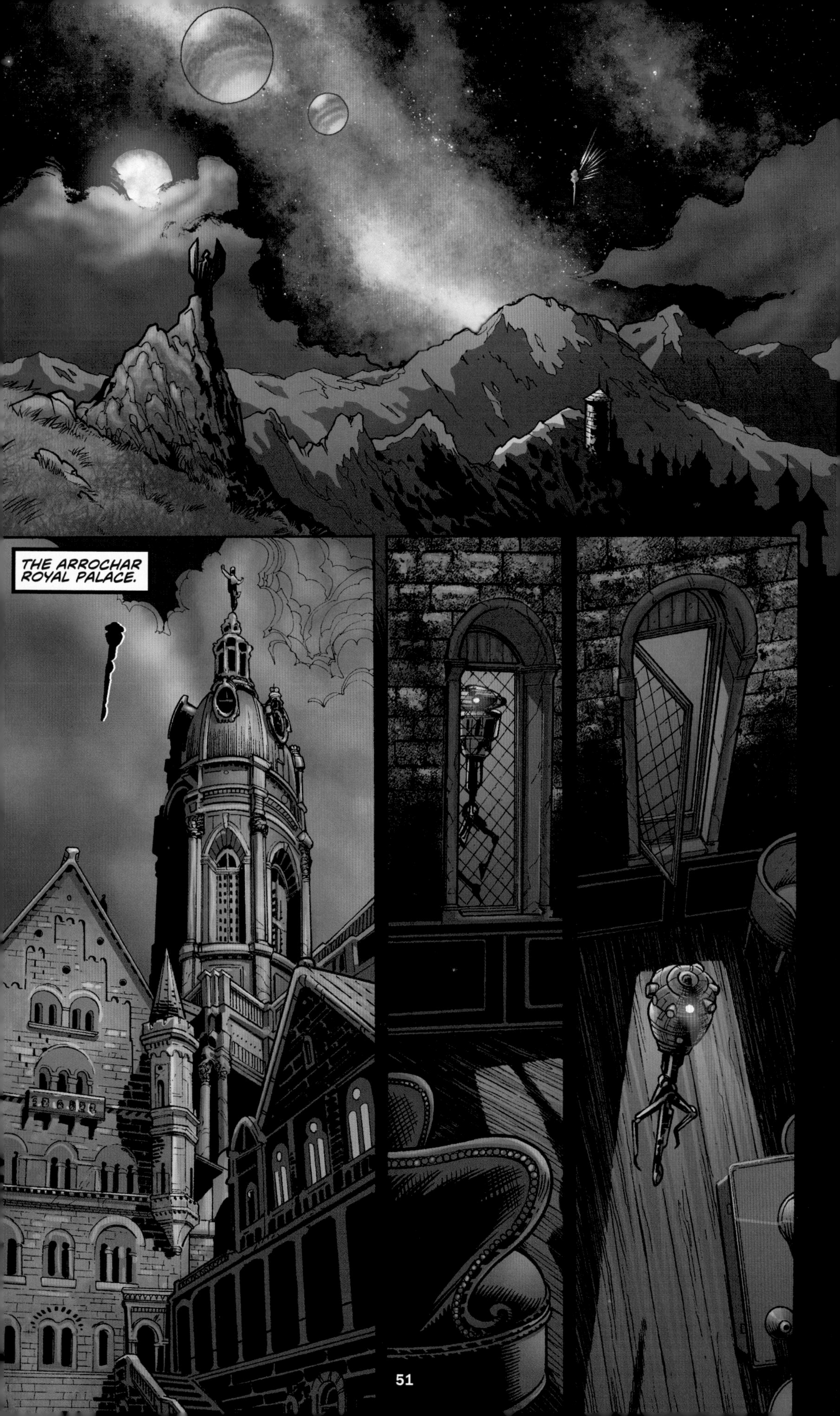
THE ARROCHAR ROYAL PALACE.

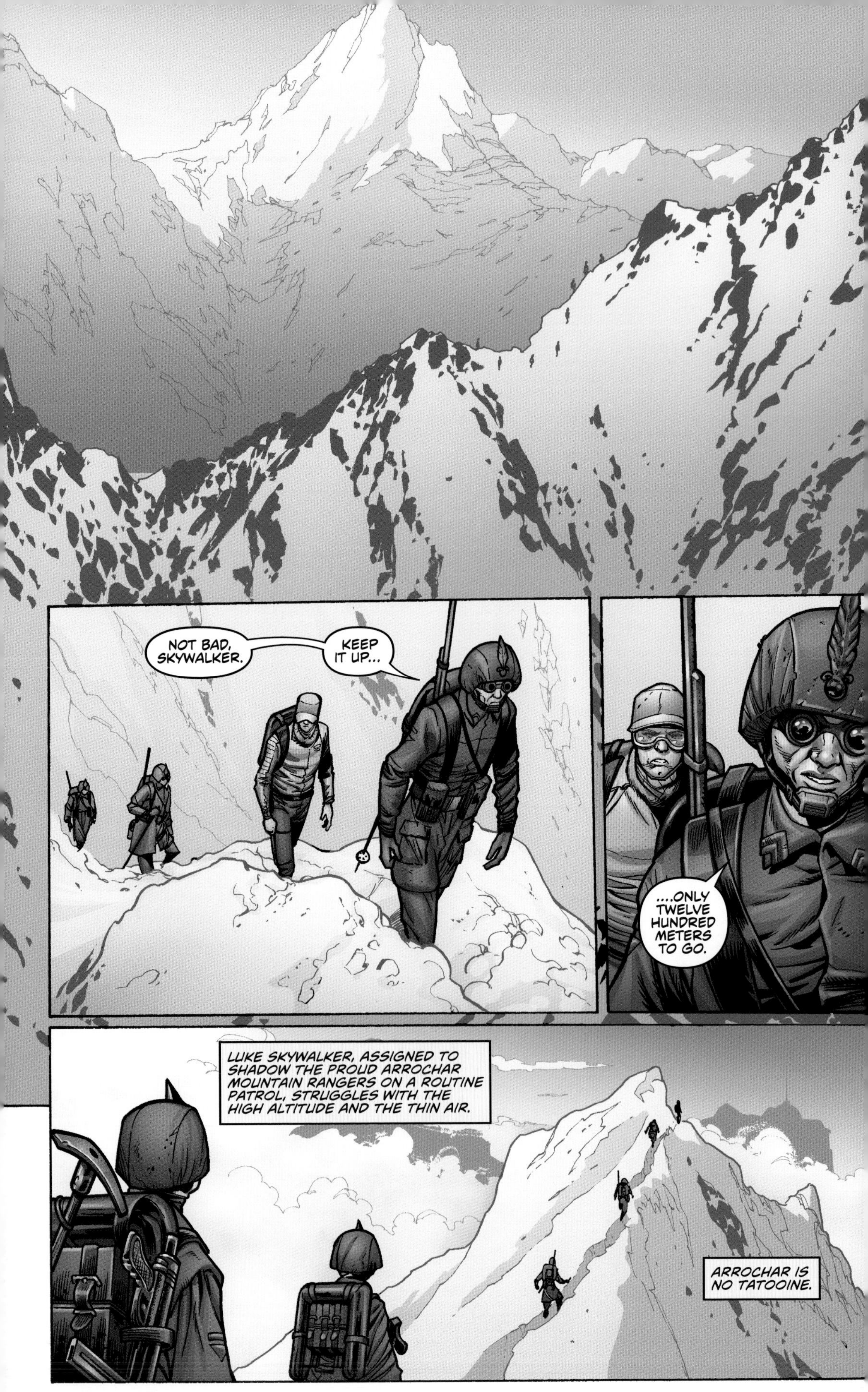
NOT BAD, SKYWALKER.
KEEP IT UP...
....ONLY TWELVE HUNDRED METERS TO GO.
LUKE SKYWALKER, ASSIGNED TO SHADOW THE PROUD ARROCHAR MOUNTAIN RANGERS ON A ROUTINE PATROL, STRUGGLES WITH THE HIGH ALTITUDE AND THE THIN AIR.
ARROCHAR IS NO TATOOINE.

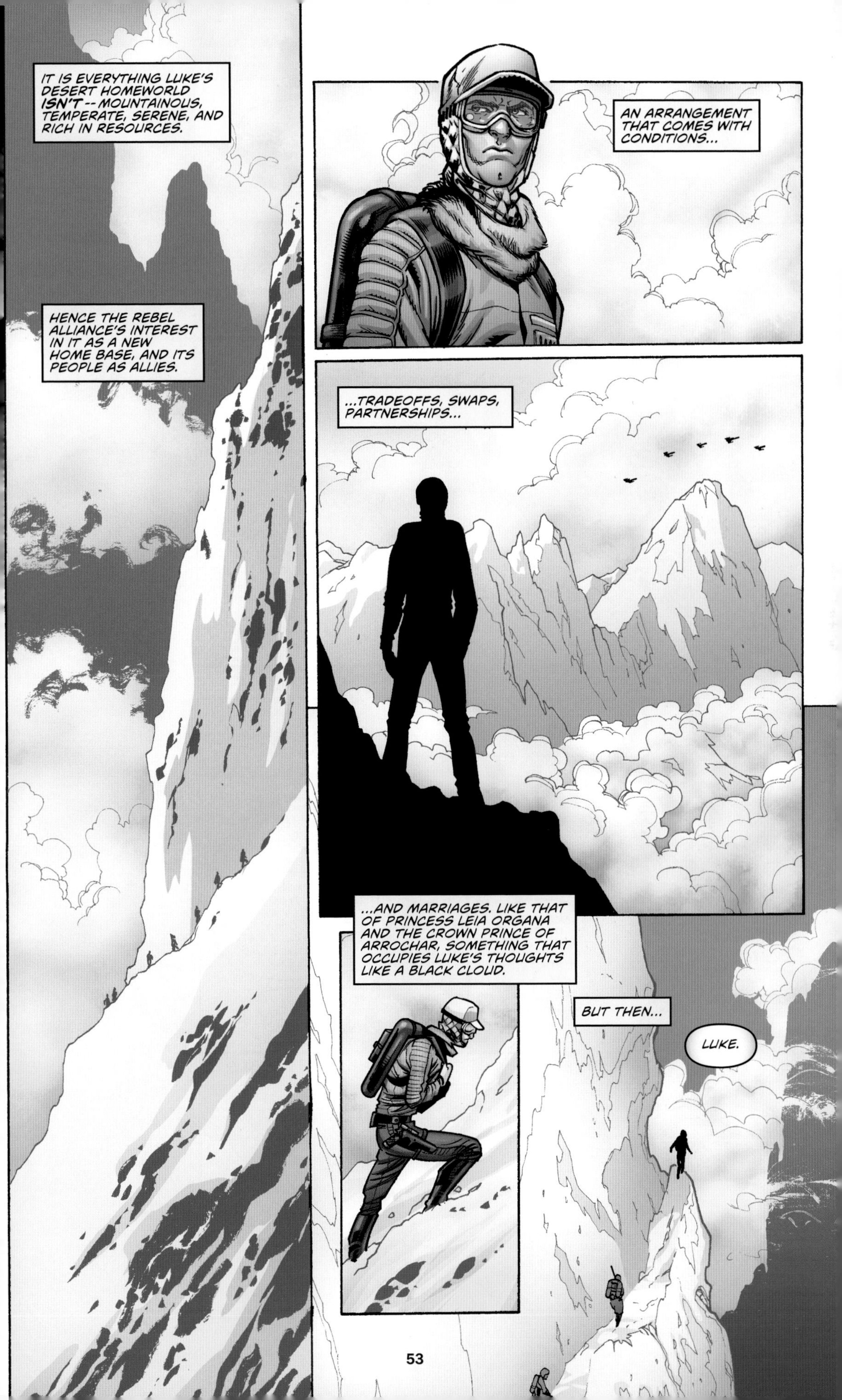
IT IS EVERYTHING LUKE'S DESERT HOMEWORLD ISN'T -- MOUNTAINOUS, TEMPERATE, SERENE, AND RICH IN RESOURCES.
HENCE THE REBEL ALLIANCE'S INTEREST IN IT AS A NEW HOME BASE, AND ITS PEOPLE AS ALLIES.
AN ARRANGEMENT THAT COMES WITH CONDITIONS...
...TRADEOFFS, SWAPS, PARTNERSHIPS...
...AND MARRIAGES. LIKE THAT OF PRINCESS LEIA ORGANA AND THE CROWN PRINCE OF ARROCHAR, SOMETHING THAT OCCUPIES LUKE'S THOUGHTS LIKE A BLACK CLOUD.
BUT THEN...
LUKE.

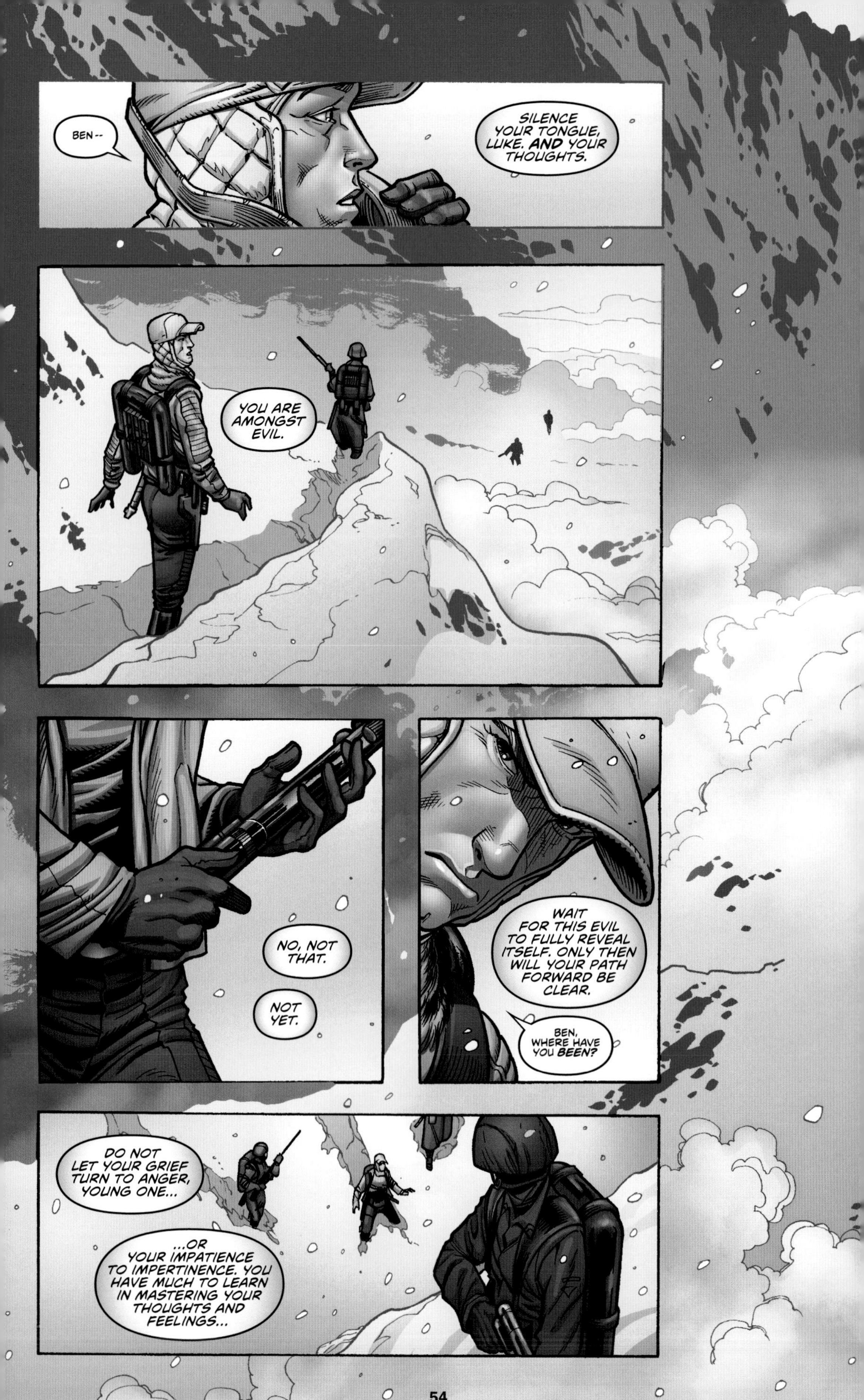
BEN--
SILENCE YOUR TONGUE, LUKE. AND YOUR THOUGHTS.
YOU ARE AMONGST EVIL.
NO, NOT THAT.
NOT YET.
WAIT FOR THIS EVIL TO FULLY REVEAL ITSELF. ONLY THEN WILL YOUR PATH FORWARD BE CLEAR.
BEN, WHERE HAVE YOU BEEN?
DO NOT LET YOUR GRIEF TURN TO ANGER, YOUNG ONE...
...OR YOUR IMPATIENCE TO IMPERTINENCE. YOU HAVE MUCH TO LEARN IN MASTERING YOUR THOUGHTS AND FEELINGS...

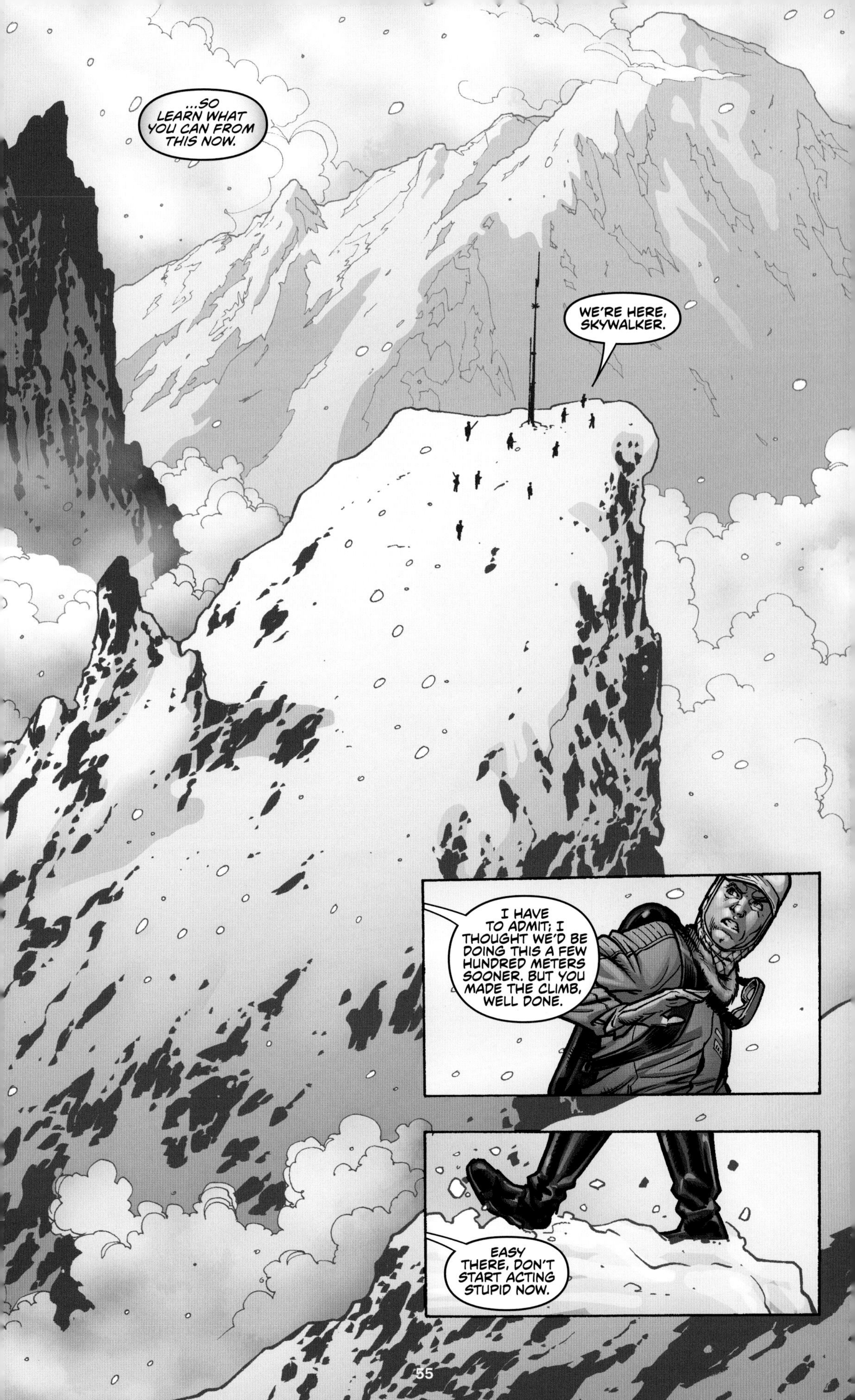
...SO LEARN WHAT YOU CAN FROM THIS NOW.
WE'RE HERE, SKYWALKER.
I HAVE TO ADMIT; I THOUGHT WE'D BE DOING THIS A FEW HUNDRED METERS SOONER. BUT YOU MADE THE CLIMB, WELL DONE.
EASY THERE, DON'T START ACTING STUPID NOW.

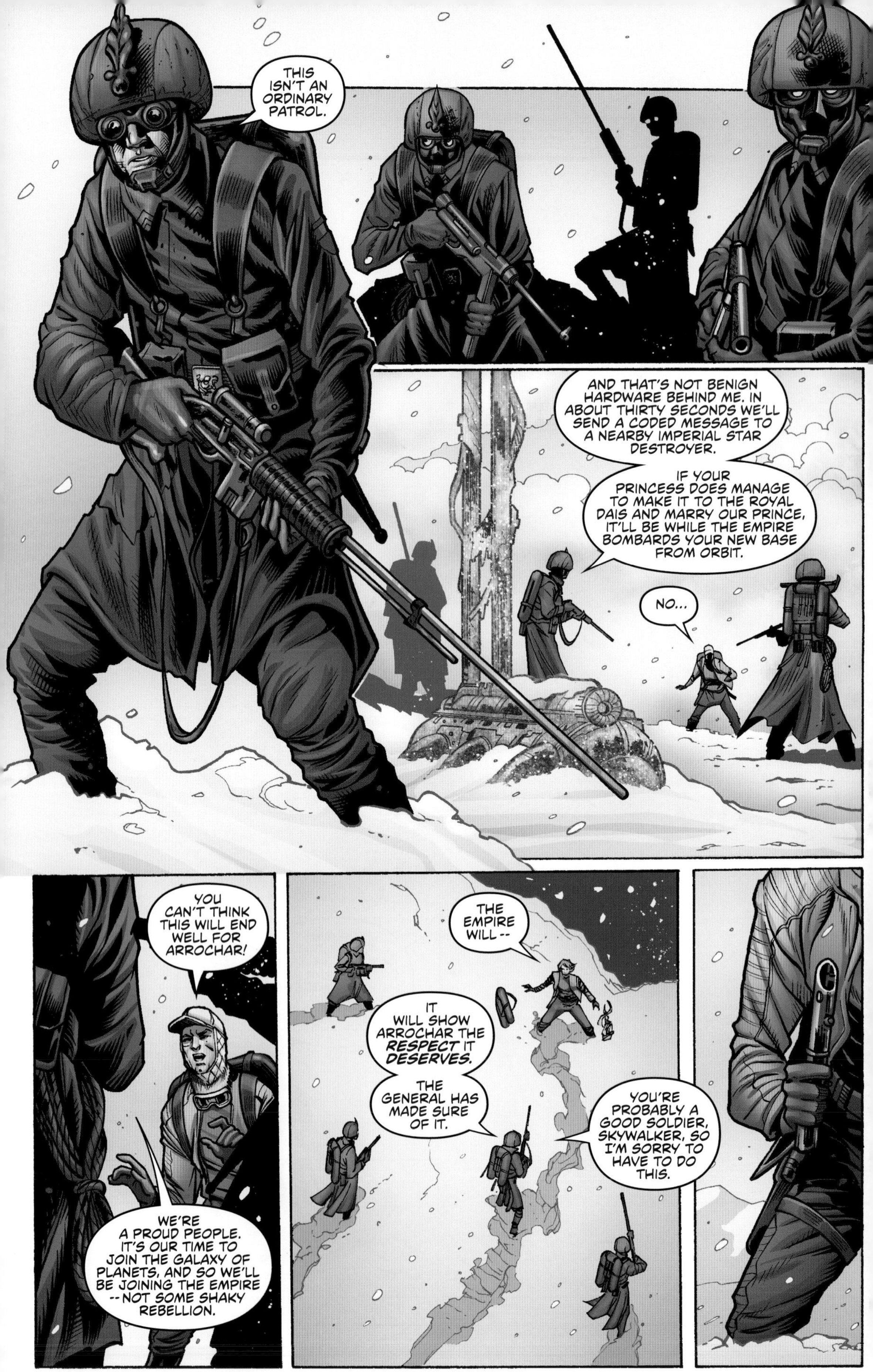
THIS ISN'T AN ORDINARY PATROL.
AND THAT'S NOT BENIGN HARDWARE BEHIND ME. IN ABOUT THIRTY SECONDS WE'LL SEND A CODED MESSAGE TO A NEARBY IMPERIAL STAR DESTROYER.
IF YOUR PRINCESS DOES MANAGE TO MAKE IT TO THE ROYAL DAIS AND MARRY OUR PRINCE, IT'LL BE WHILE THE EMPIRE BOMBARDS YOUR NEW BASE FROM ORBIT.
NO...
YOU CAN'T THINK THIS WILL END WELL FOR ARROCHAR!
WE'RE A PROUD PEOPLE. IT'S OUR TIME TO JOIN THE GALAXY OF PLANETS, AND SO WE'LL BE JOINING THE EMPIRE --NOT SOME SHAKY REBELLION.
THE EMPIRE WILL --
IT WILL SHOW ARROCHAR THE *RESPECT* IT *DESERVES.*
THE GENERAL HAS MADE SURE OF IT.
YOU'RE PROBABLY A GOOD SOLDIER, SKYWALKER, SO I'M SORRY TO HAVE TO DO THIS.

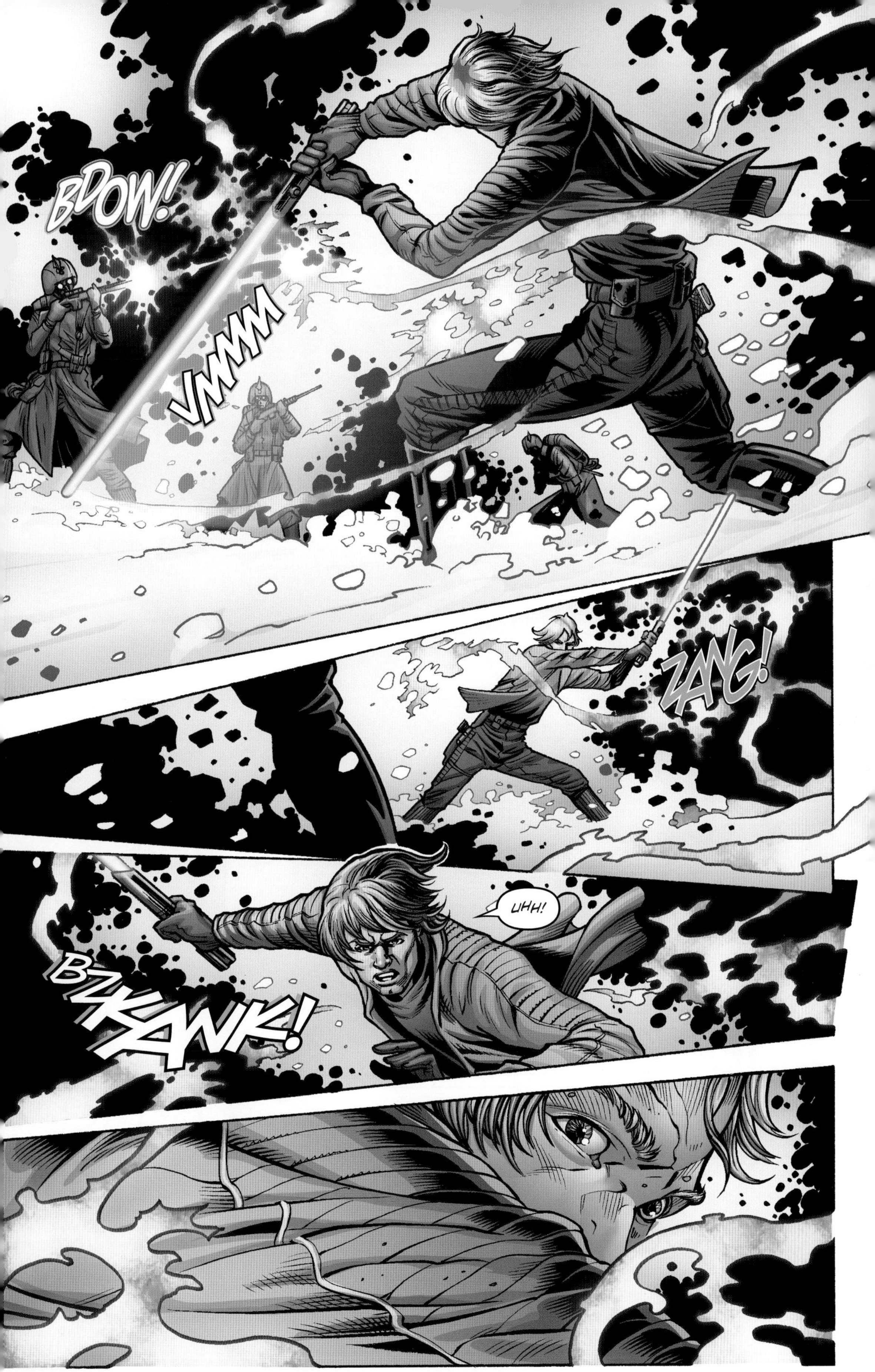
BDOW!
VMMM
ZANG!
UHH!
BZZKANK!

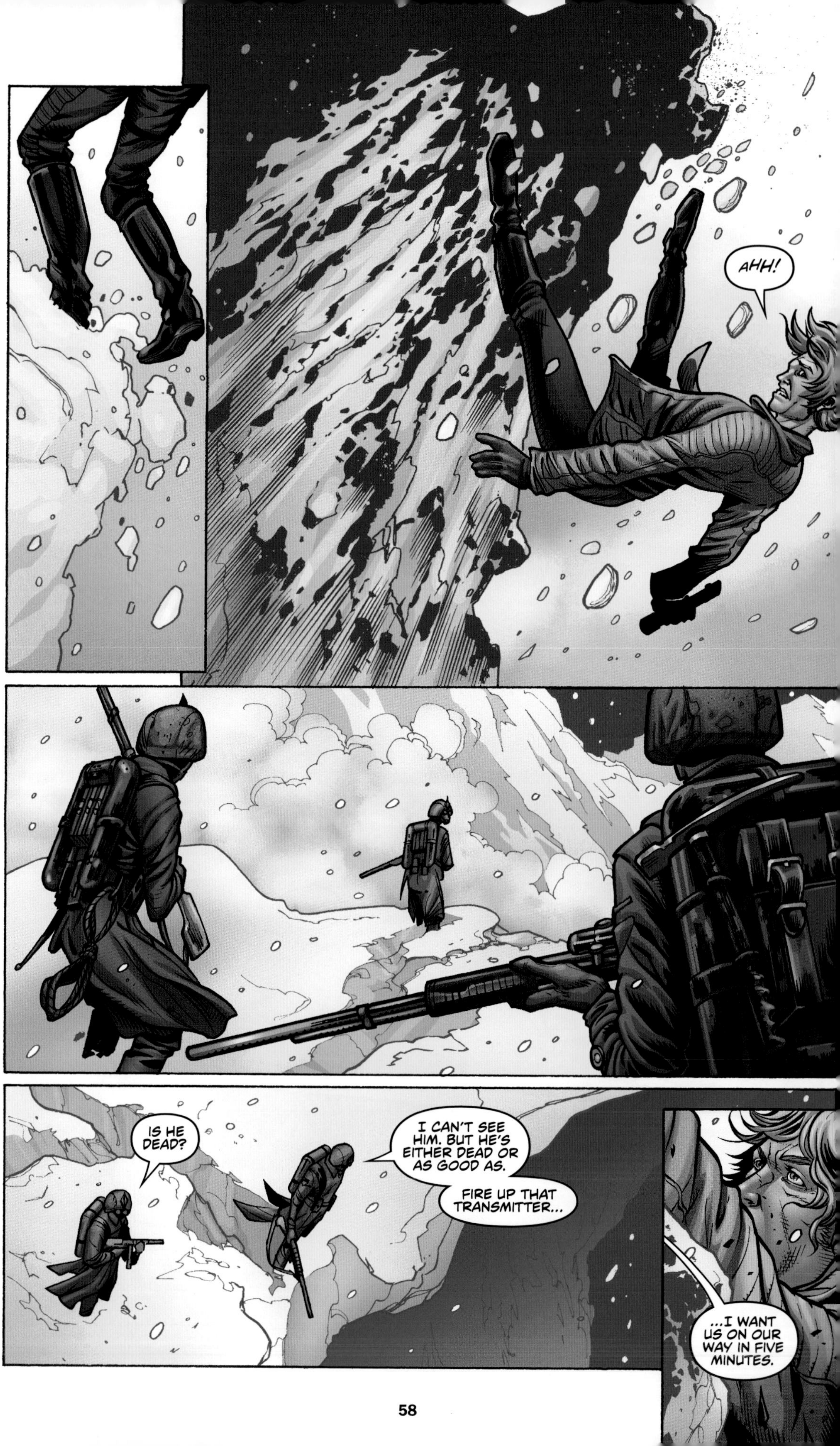
AHH!
IS HE DEAD?
I CAN'T SEE HIM. BUT HE'S EITHER DEAD OR AS GOOD AS.
FIRE UP THAT TRANSMITTER...
...I WANT US ON OUR WAY IN FIVE MINUTES.

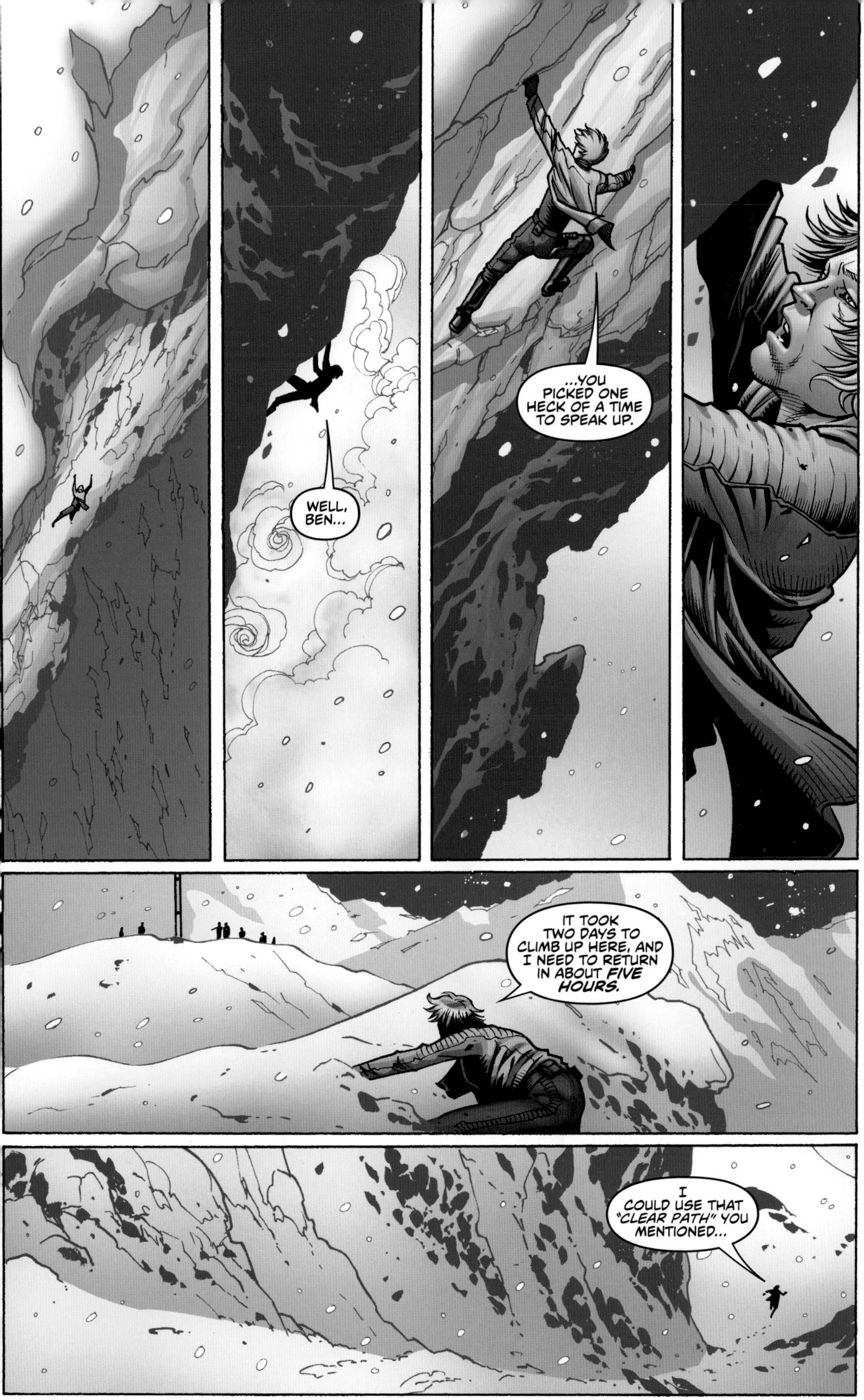
WELL, BEN...
...YOU PICKED ONE HECK OF A TIME TO SPEAK UP.
IT TOOK TWO DAYS TO CLIMB UP HERE, AND I NEED TO RETURN IN ABOUT *FIVE HOURS.*
I COULD USE THAT "CLEAR PATH" YOU MENTIONED...

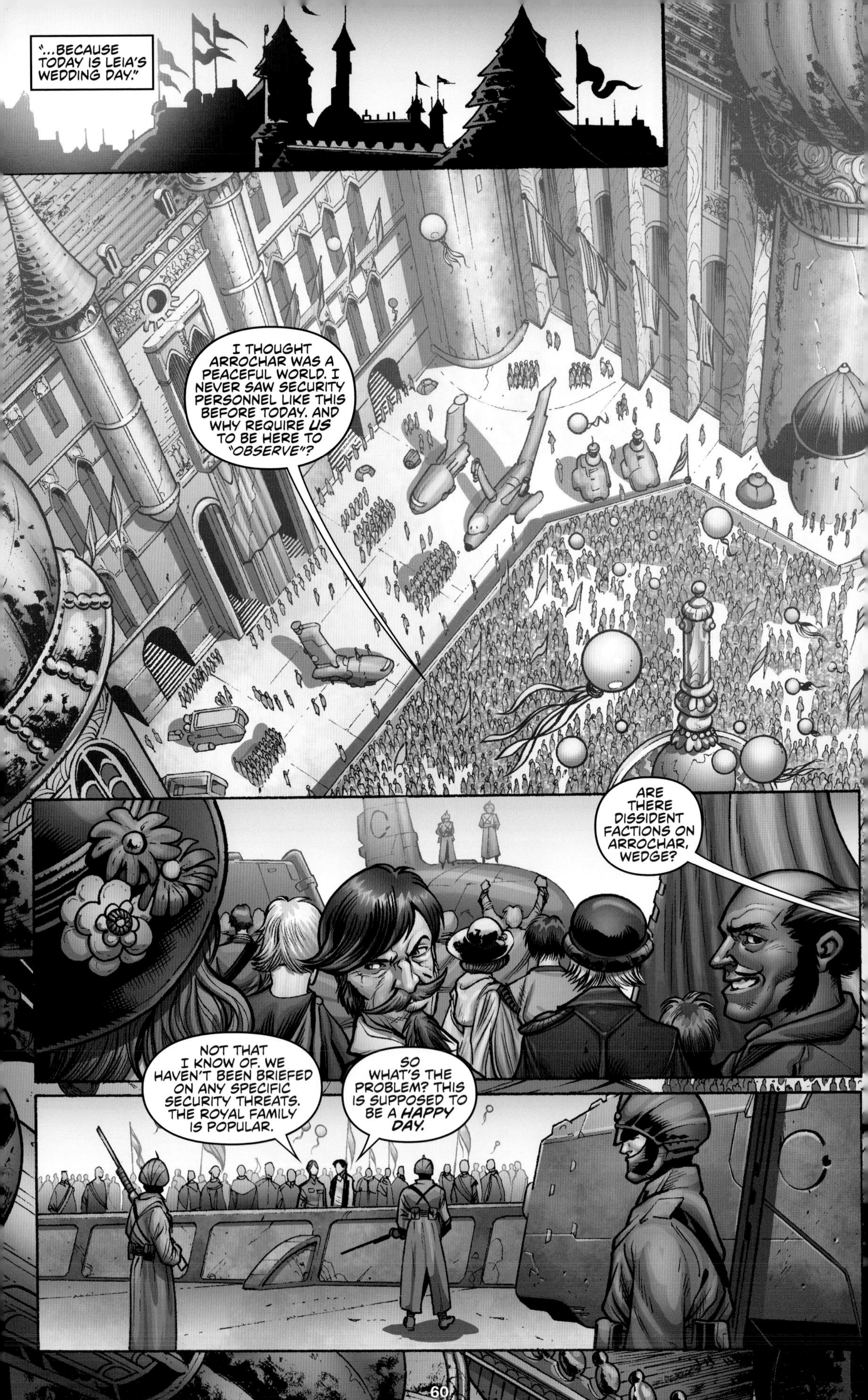
"...BECAUSE TODAY IS LEIA'S WEDDING DAY."
I THOUGHT ARROCHAR WAS A PEACEFUL WORLD. I NEVER SAW SECURITY PERSONNEL LIKE THIS BEFORE TODAY. AND WHY REQUIRE *US* TO BE HERE TO *"OBSERVE"*?
ARE THERE DISSIDENT FACTIONS ON ARROCHAR, WEDGE?
NOT THAT I KNOW OF. WE HAVEN'T BEEN BRIEFED ON ANY SPECIFIC SECURITY THREATS. THE ROYAL FAMILY IS POPULAR.
SO WHAT'S THE PROBLEM? THIS IS SUPPOSED TO BE A *HAPPY DAY*.

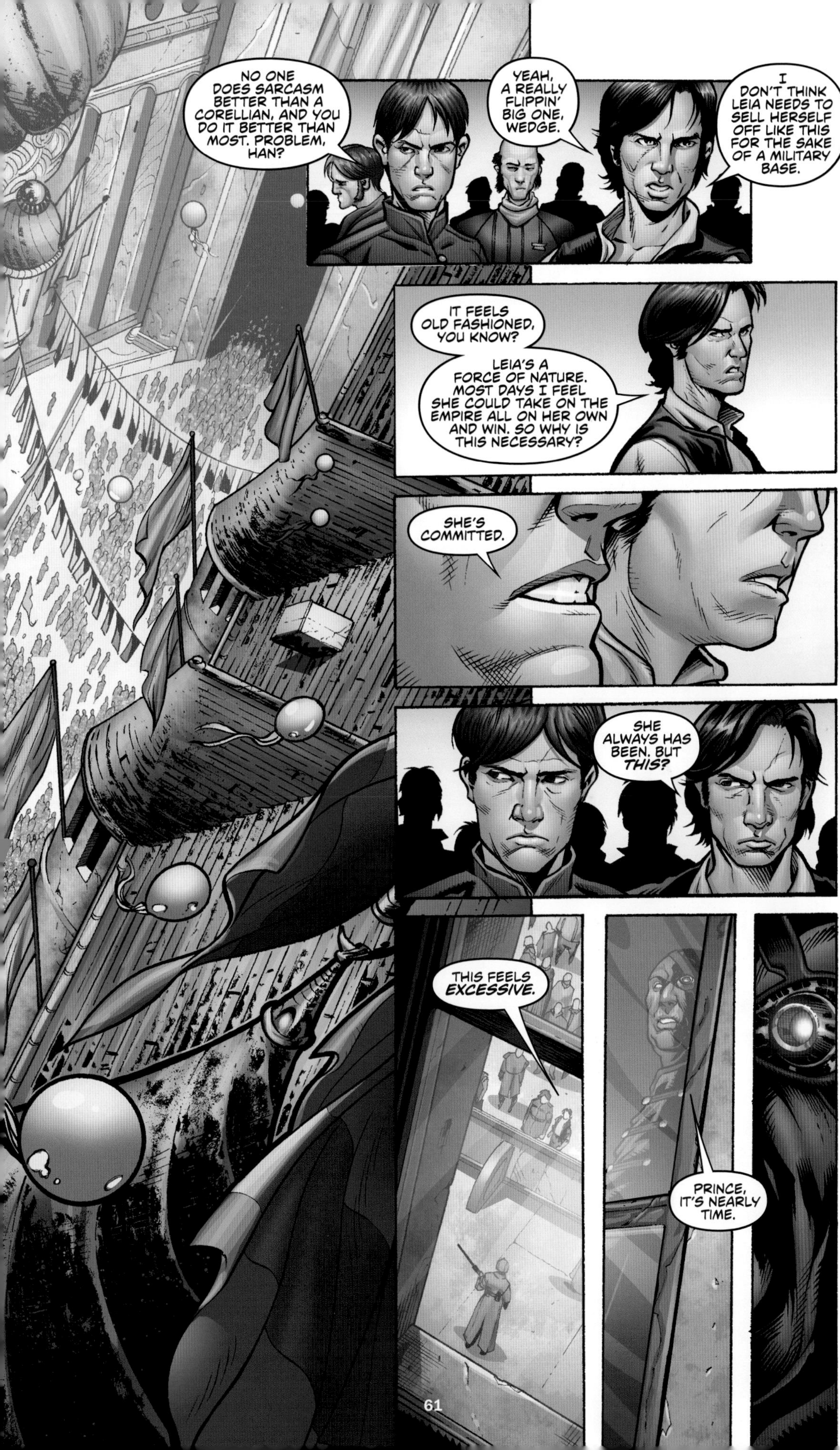
NO ONE DOES SARCASM BETTER THAN A CORELLIAN, AND YOU DO IT BETTER THAN MOST. PROBLEM, HAN?
YEAH, A REALLY FLIPPIN' BIG ONE, WEDGE.
I DON'T THINK LEIA NEEDS TO SELL HERSELF OFF LIKE THIS FOR THE SAKE OF A MILITARY BASE.
IT FEELS OLD FASHIONED, YOU KNOW?
LEIA'S A FORCE OF NATURE. MOST DAYS I FEEL SHE COULD TAKE ON THE EMPIRE ALL ON HER OWN AND WIN. SO WHY IS THIS NECESSARY?
SHE'S COMMITTED.
SHE ALWAYS HAS BEEN. BUT *THIS?*
THIS FEELS *EXCESSIVE.*
PRINCE, IT'S NEARLY TIME.

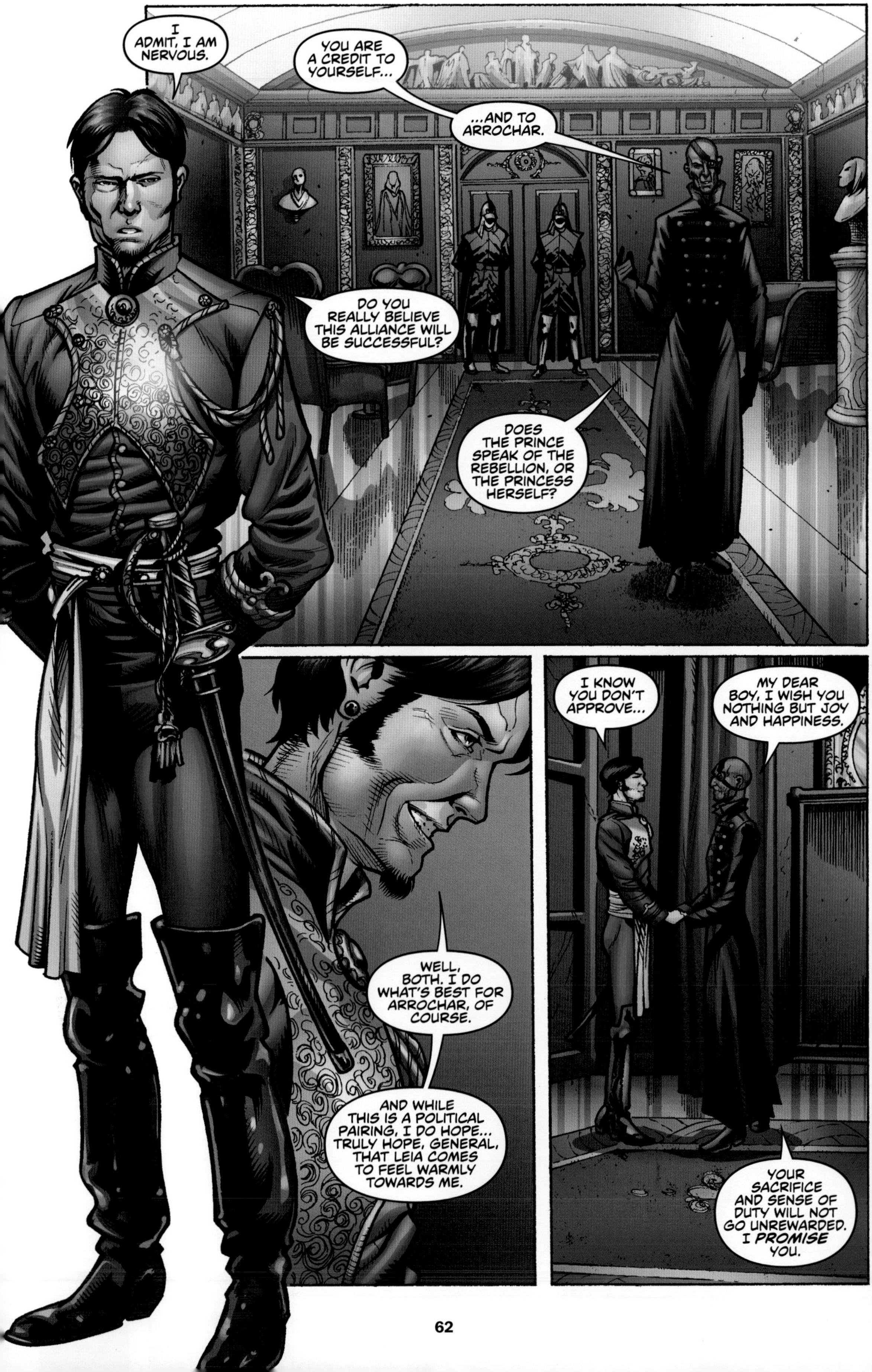
I ADMIT, I AM NERVOUS.
YOU ARE A CREDIT TO YOURSELF...
...AND TO ARROCHAR.
DO YOU REALLY BELIEVE THIS ALLIANCE WILL BE SUCCESSFUL?
DOES THE PRINCE SPEAK OF THE REBELLION, OR THE PRINCESS HERSELF?
WELL, BOTH. I DO WHAT'S BEST FOR ARROCHAR, OF COURSE.
AND WHILE THIS IS A POLITICAL PAIRING, I DO HOPE... TRULY HOPE, GENERAL, THAT LEIA COMES TO FEEL WARMLY TOWARDS ME.
I KNOW YOU DON'T APPROVE...
MY DEAR BOY, I WISH YOU NOTHING BUT JOY AND HAPPINESS.
YOUR SACRIFICE AND SENSE OF DUTY WILL NOT GO UNREWARDED. I *PROMISE* YOU.

THIS WILL BE A DAY WELL REMEMBERED IN ARROCHAR HISTORY. CHILDREN WILL SING THE STORY OF THIS DAY FOR GENERATIONS TO COME.

I LONGED FOR MILITARY SERVICE, GENERAL, TO BE A PILOT, OR ONE OF THE RANGERS, PERHAPS.

YOUR FATHER, THE KING, CHOSE A DIFFERENT PATH FOR YOU.

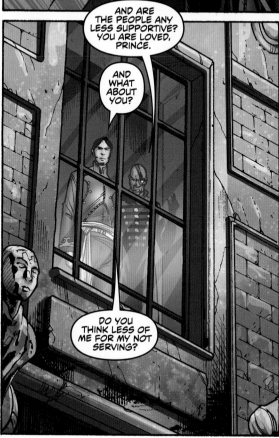

AND ARE THE PEOPLE ANY LESS SUPPORTIVE? YOU ARE LOVED, PRINCE.

AND WHAT ABOUT YOU?

DO YOU THINK LESS OF ME FOR MY NOT SERVING?

DO NOT WORRY...

THERE MAY BE TIME FOR THAT YET.

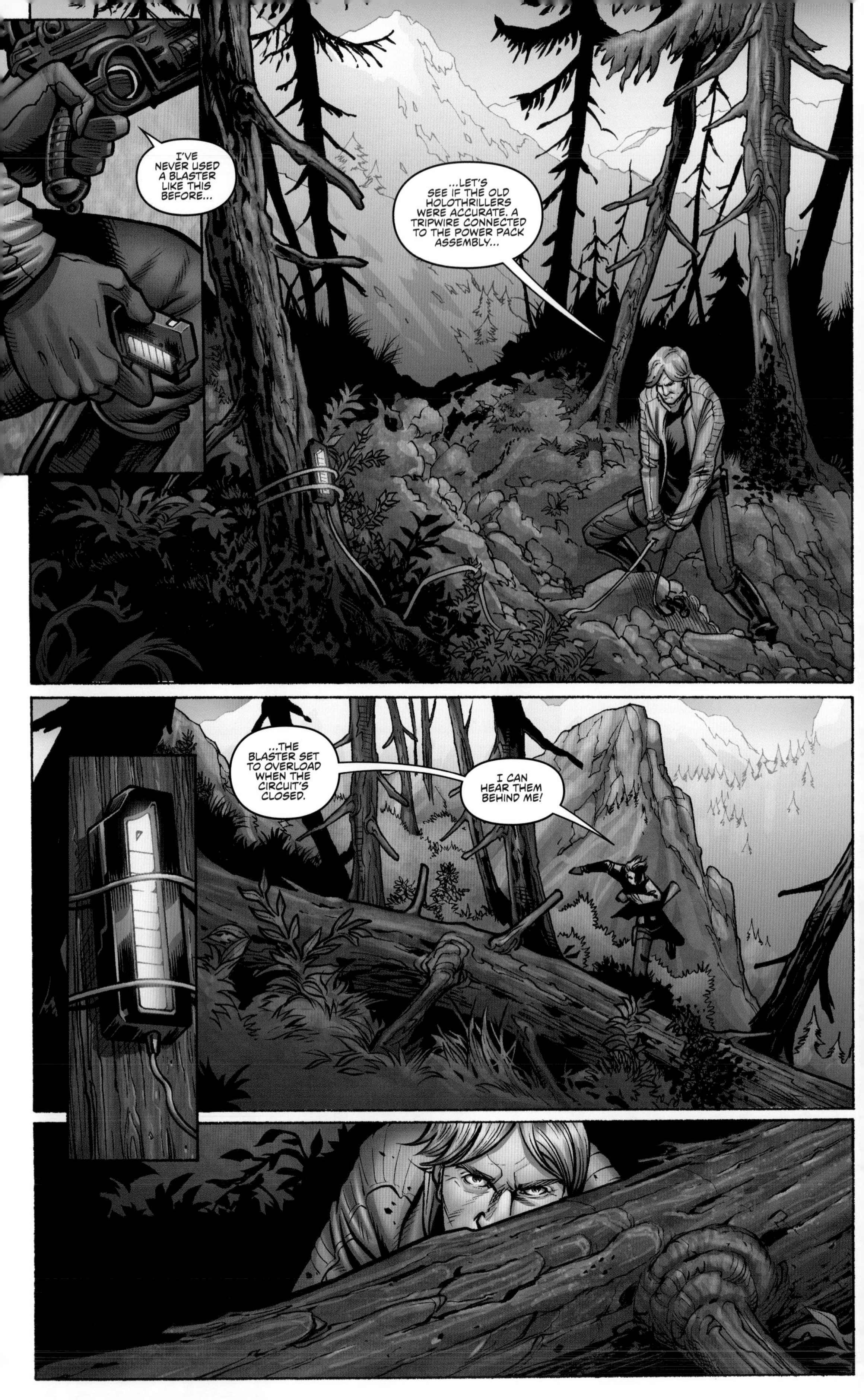

I'VE NEVER USED A BLASTER LIKE THIS BEFORE...
...LET'S SEE IF THE OLD HOLOTHRILLERS WERE ACCURATE. A TRIPWIRE CONNECTED TO THE POWER PACK ASSEMBLY...
...THE BLASTER SET TO OVERLOAD WHEN THE CIRCUIT'S CLOSED.
I CAN HEAR THEM BEHIND ME!

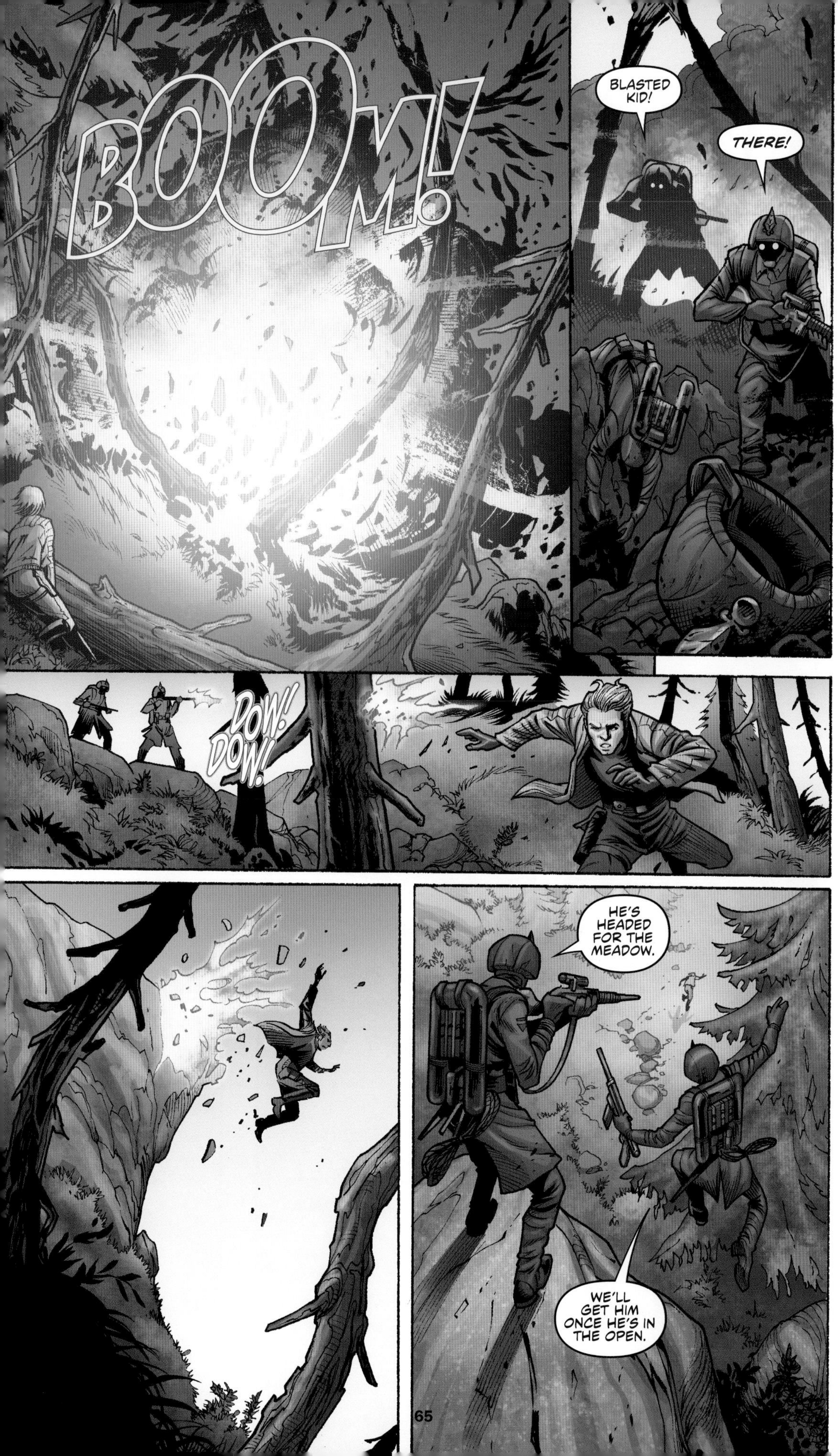
BOOM!
BLASTED KID!
THERE!
DOW! DOW!
HE'S HEADED FOR THE MEADOW.
WE'LL GET HIM ONCE HE'S IN THE OPEN.

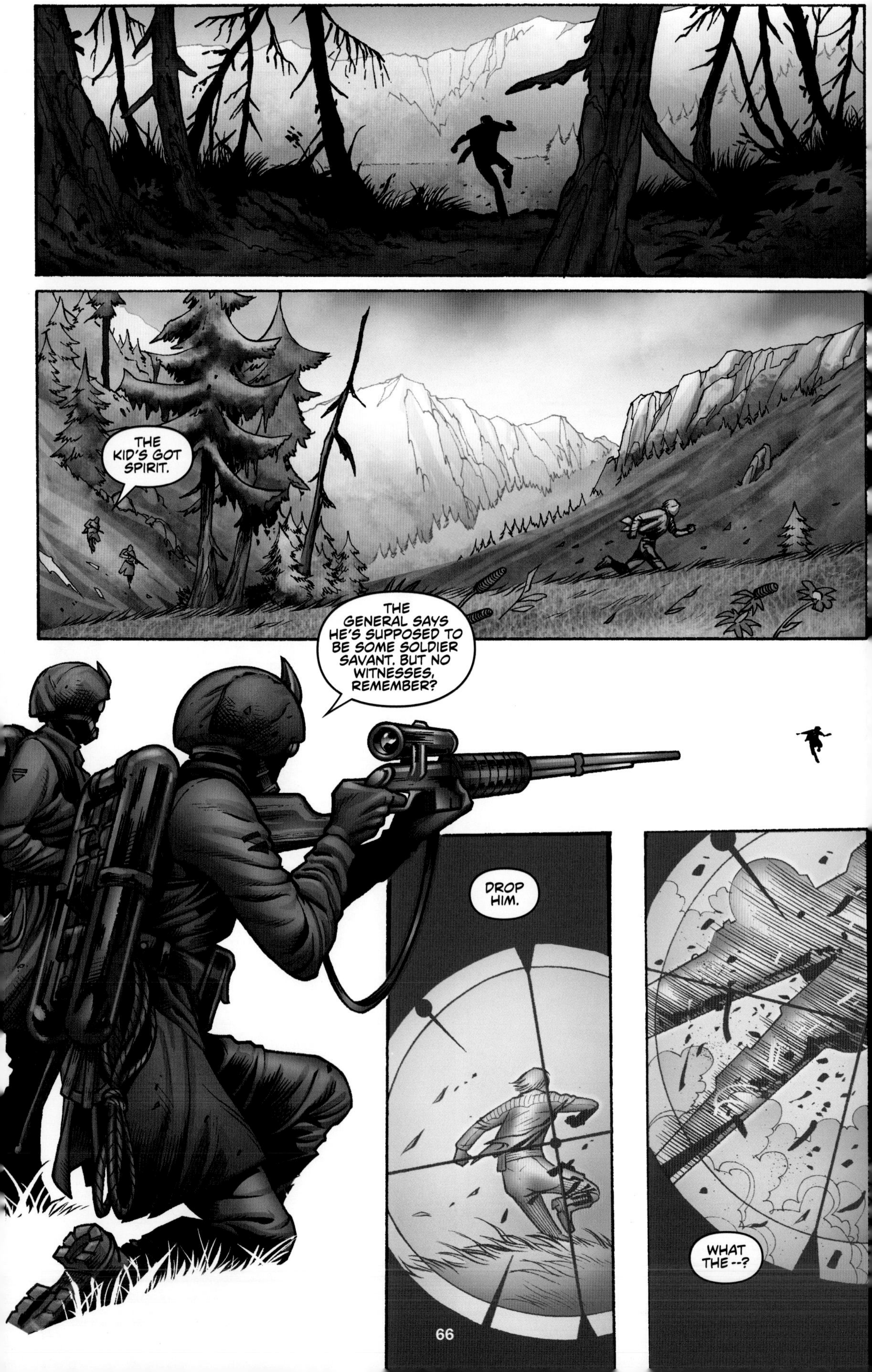
THE KID'S GOT SPIRIT.
THE GENERAL SAYS HE'S SUPPOSED TO BE SOME SOLDIER SAVANT. BUT NO WITNESSES, REMEMBER?
DROP HIM.
WHAT THE--?

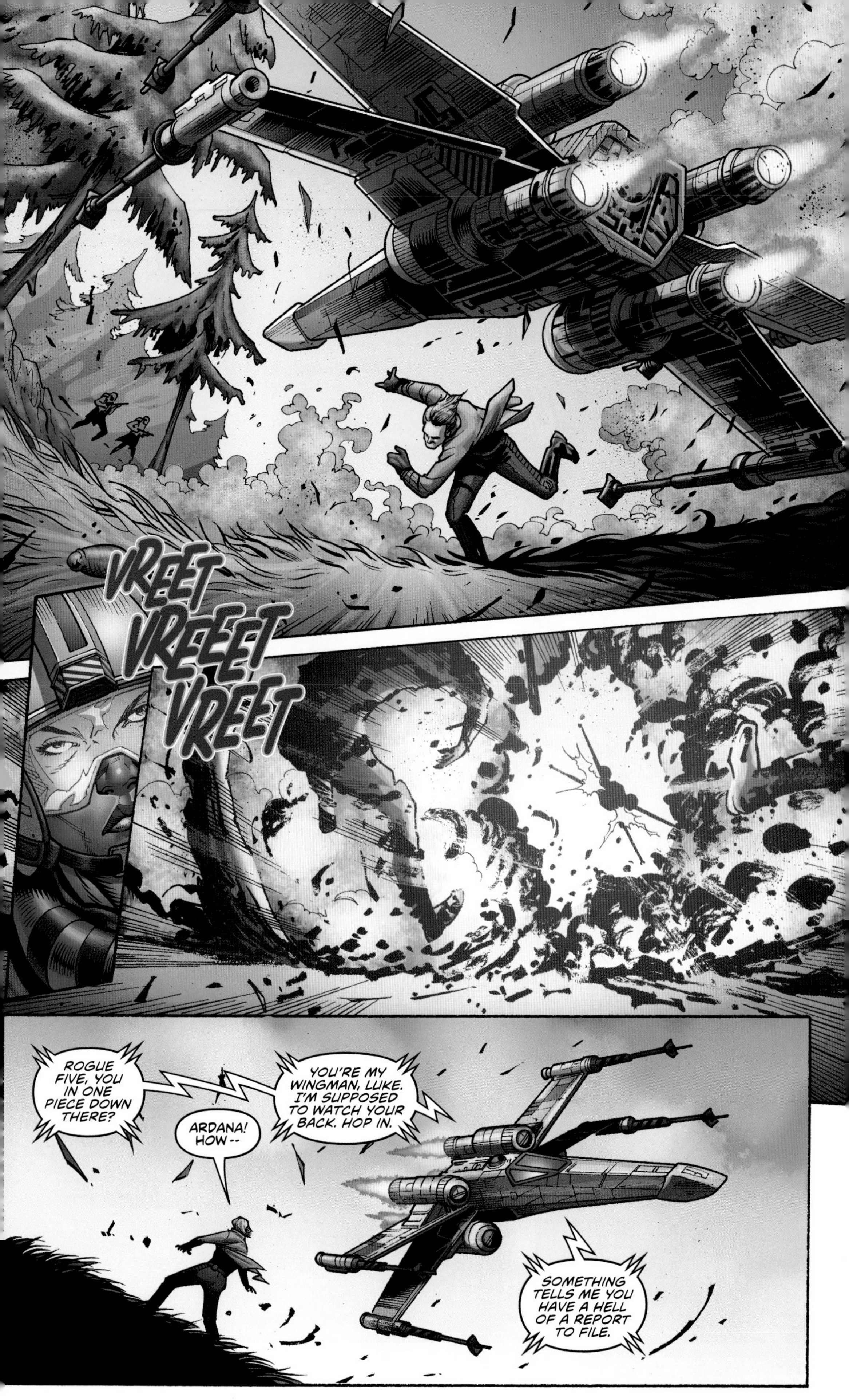
VREET
VREEET
VREET
ROGUE FIVE, YOU IN ONE PIECE DOWN THERE?
ARDANA! HOW --
YOU'RE MY WINGMAN, LUKE. I'M SUPPOSED TO WATCH YOUR BACK. HOP IN.
SOMETHING TELLS ME YOU HAVE A HELL OF A REPORT TO FILE.

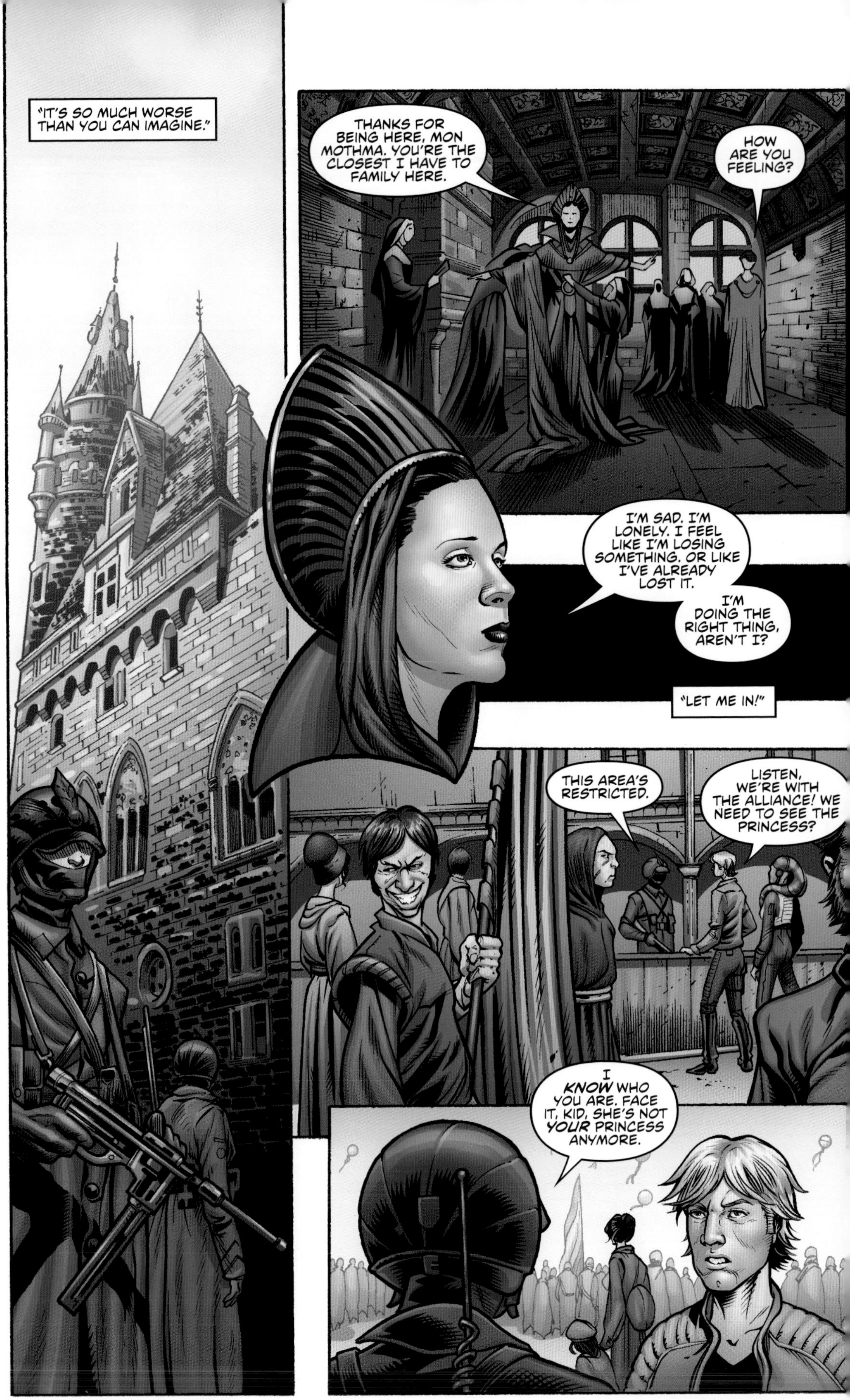
"IT'S SO MUCH WORSE THAN YOU CAN IMAGINE."
THANKS FOR BEING HERE, MON MOTHMA. YOU'RE THE CLOSEST I HAVE TO FAMILY HERE.
HOW ARE YOU FEELING?
I'M SAD. I'M LONELY. I FEEL LIKE I'M LOSING SOMETHING. OR LIKE I'VE ALREADY LOST IT.
I'M DOING THE RIGHT THING, AREN'T I?
"LET ME IN!"
THIS AREA'S RESTRICTED.
LISTEN, WE'RE WITH THE ALLIANCE! WE NEED TO SEE THE PRINCESS?
I KNOW WHO YOU ARE. FACE IT, KID, SHE'S NOT YOUR PRINCESS ANYMORE.

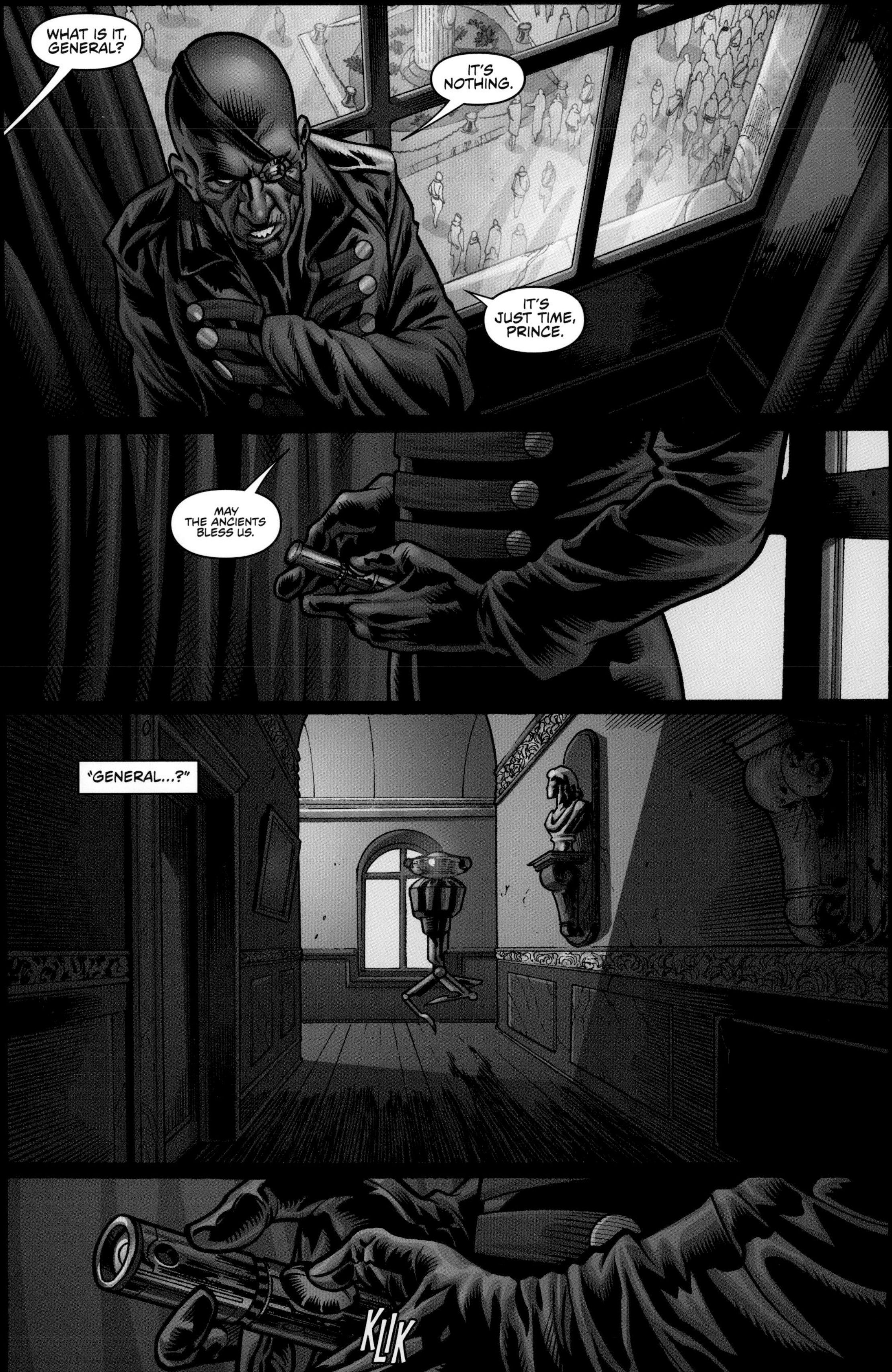

WHAT IS IT, GENERAL?
IT'S NOTHING.
IT'S JUST TIME, PRINCE.
MAY THE ANCIENTS BLESS US.
"GENERAL...?"
KLIK

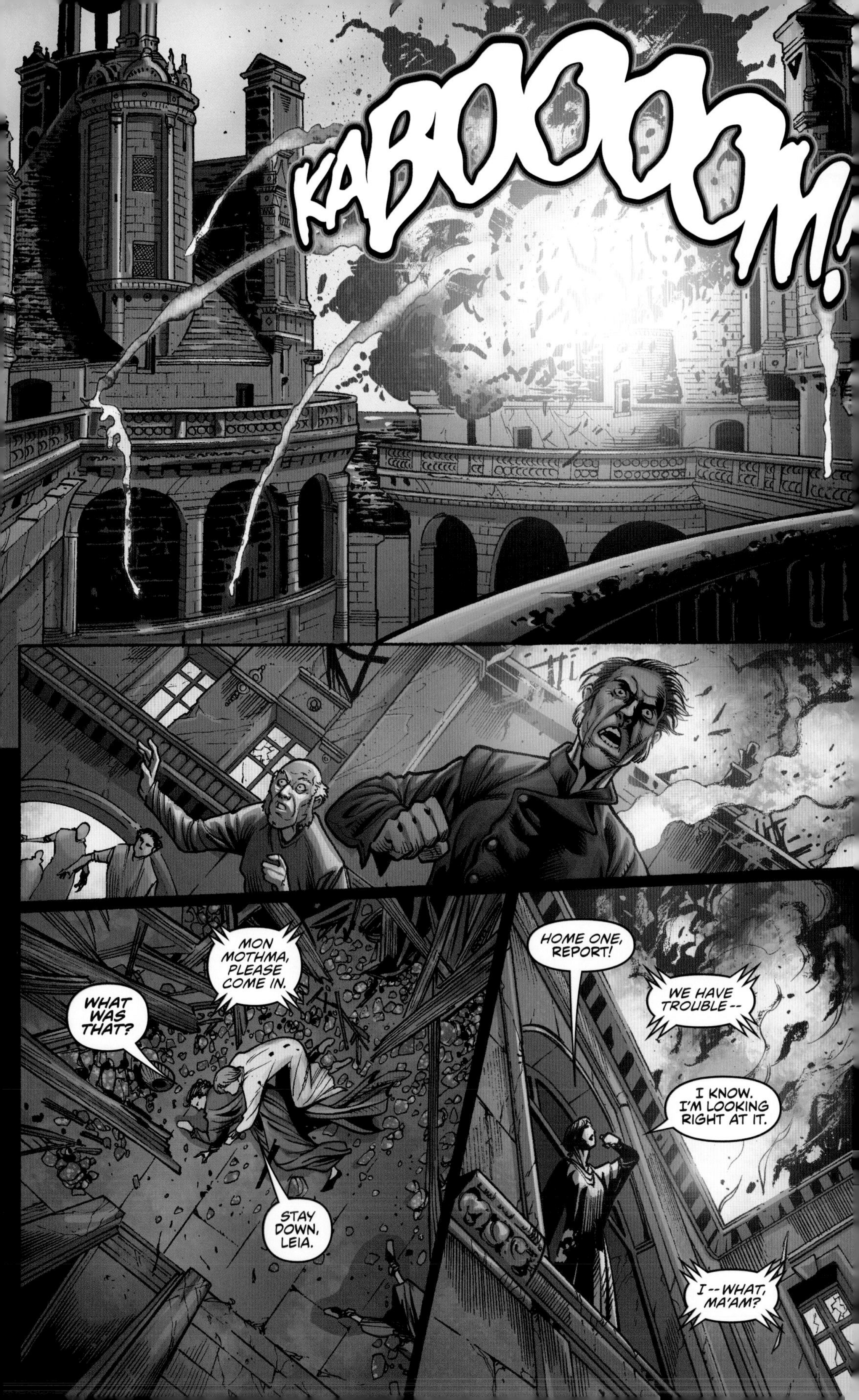
KABOOOOM!
WHAT WAS THAT?
MON MOTHMA, PLEASE COME IN.
STAY DOWN, LEIA.
HOME ONE, REPORT!
WE HAVE TROUBLE --
I KNOW. I'M LOOKING RIGHT AT IT.
I -- WHAT, MA'AM?

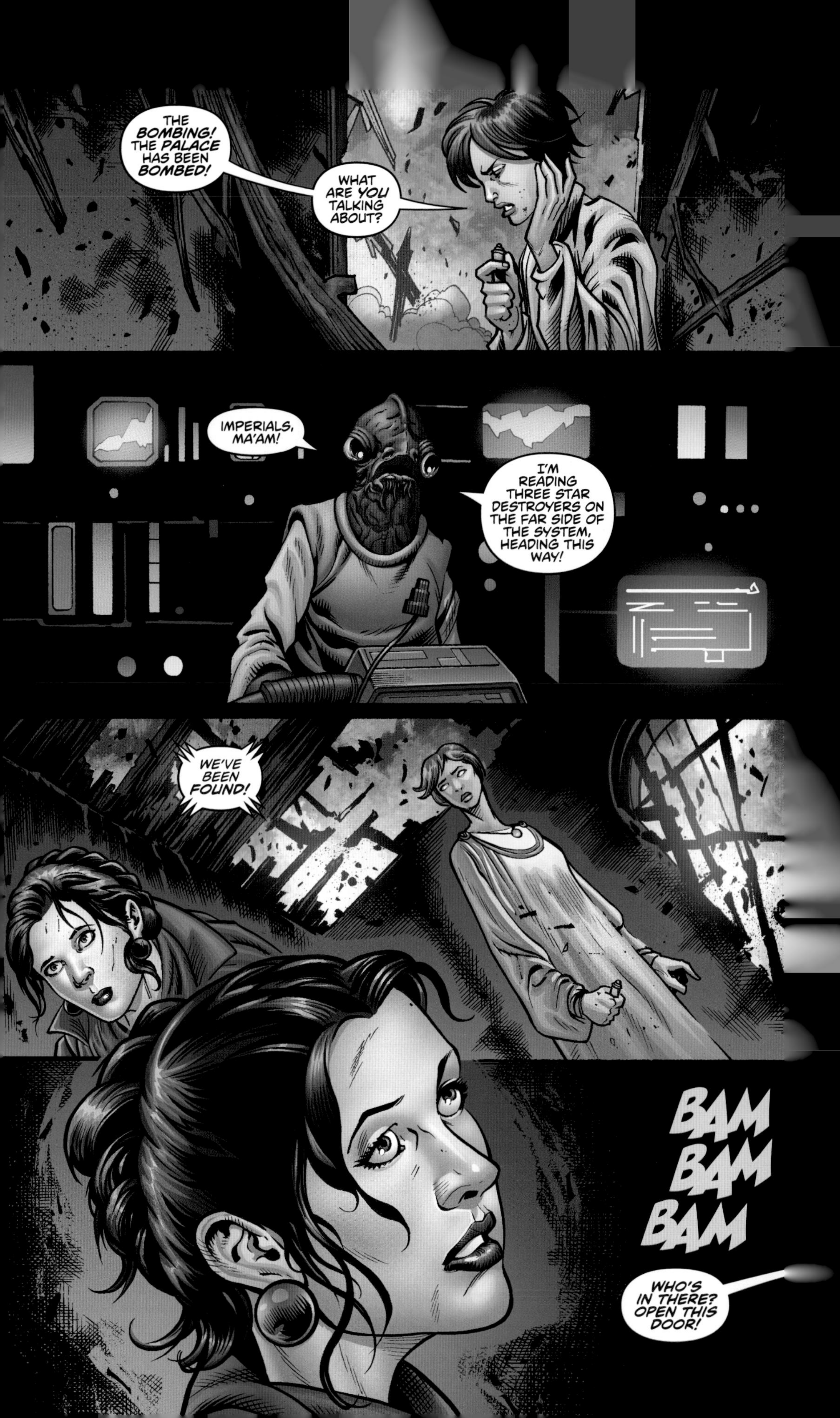
THE BOMBING! THE PALACE HAS BEEN BOMBED!
WHAT ARE YOU TALKING ABOUT?
IMPERIALS, MA'AM!
I'M READING THREE STAR DESTROYERS ON THE FAR SIDE OF THE SYSTEM, HEADING THIS WAY!
WE'VE BEEN FOUND!
BAM BAM BAM
WHO'S IN THERE? OPEN THIS DOOR!

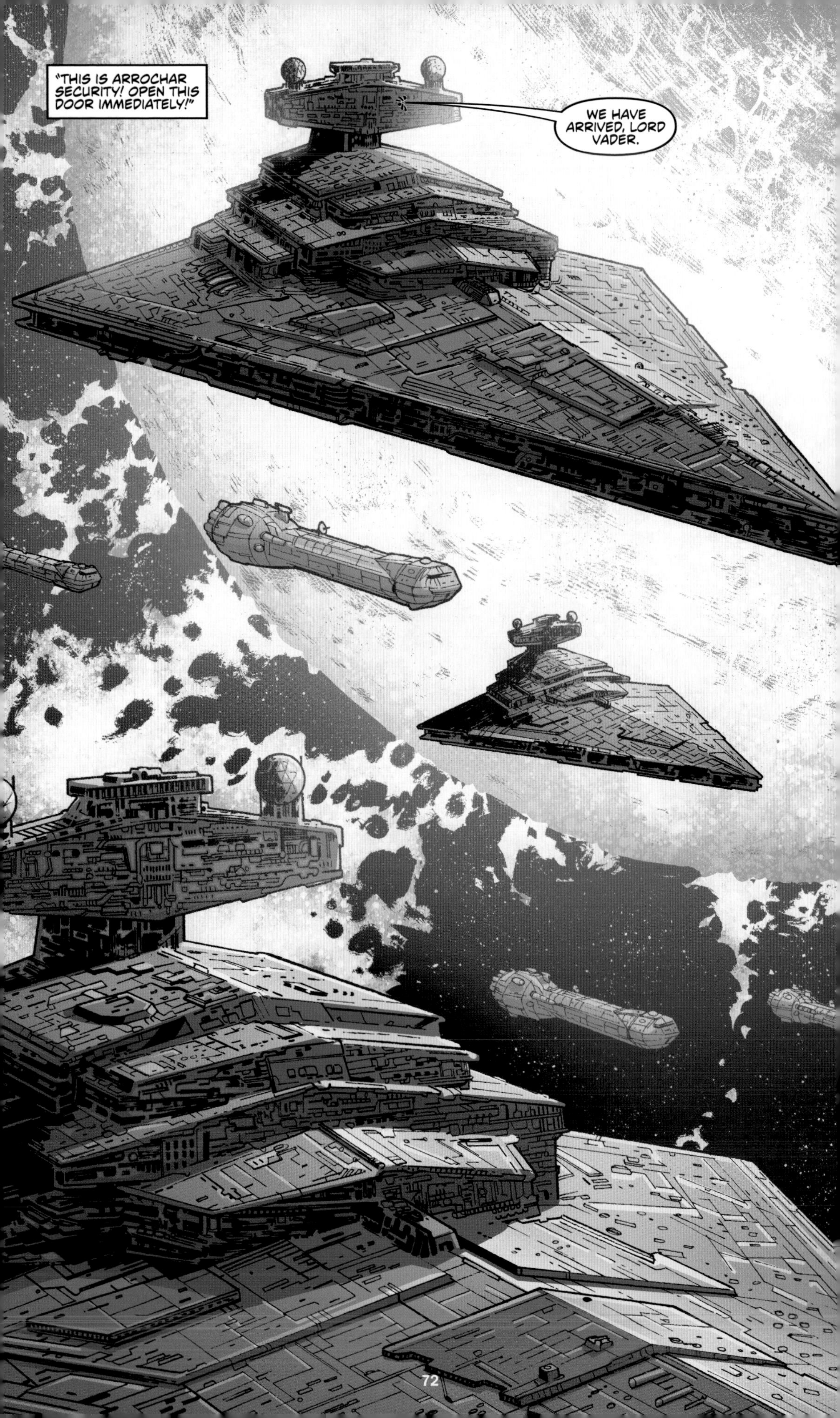
"THIS IS ARROCHAR SECURITY! OPEN THIS DOOR IMMEDIATELY!"
WE HAVE ARRIVED, LORD VADER.

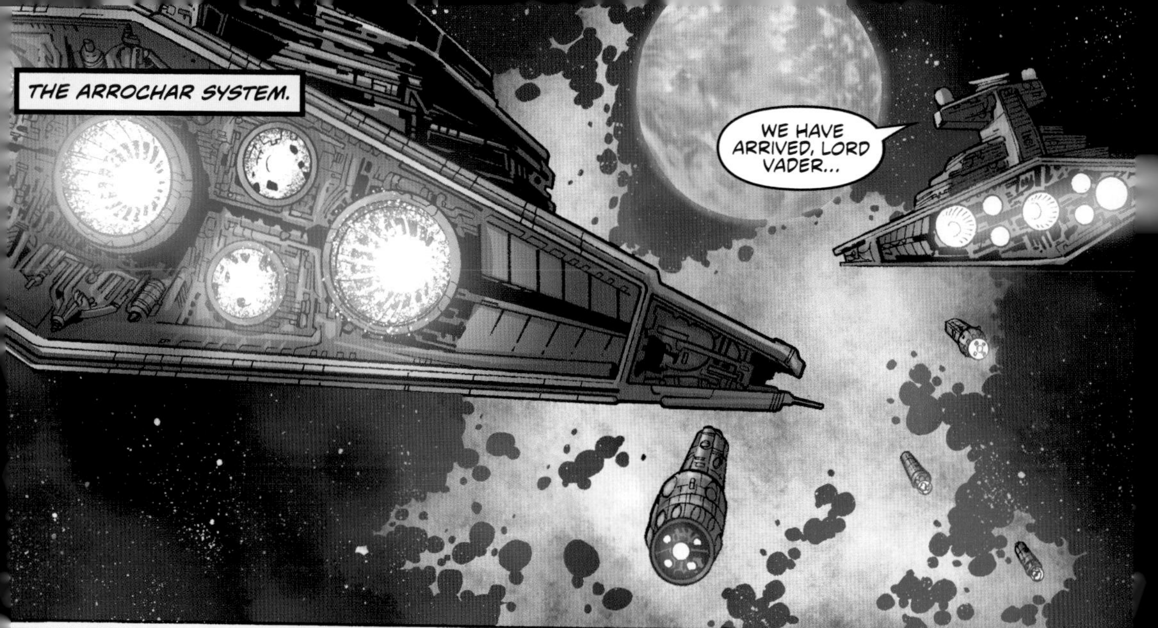
THE ARROCHAR SYSTEM.
WE HAVE ARRIVED, LORD VADER...

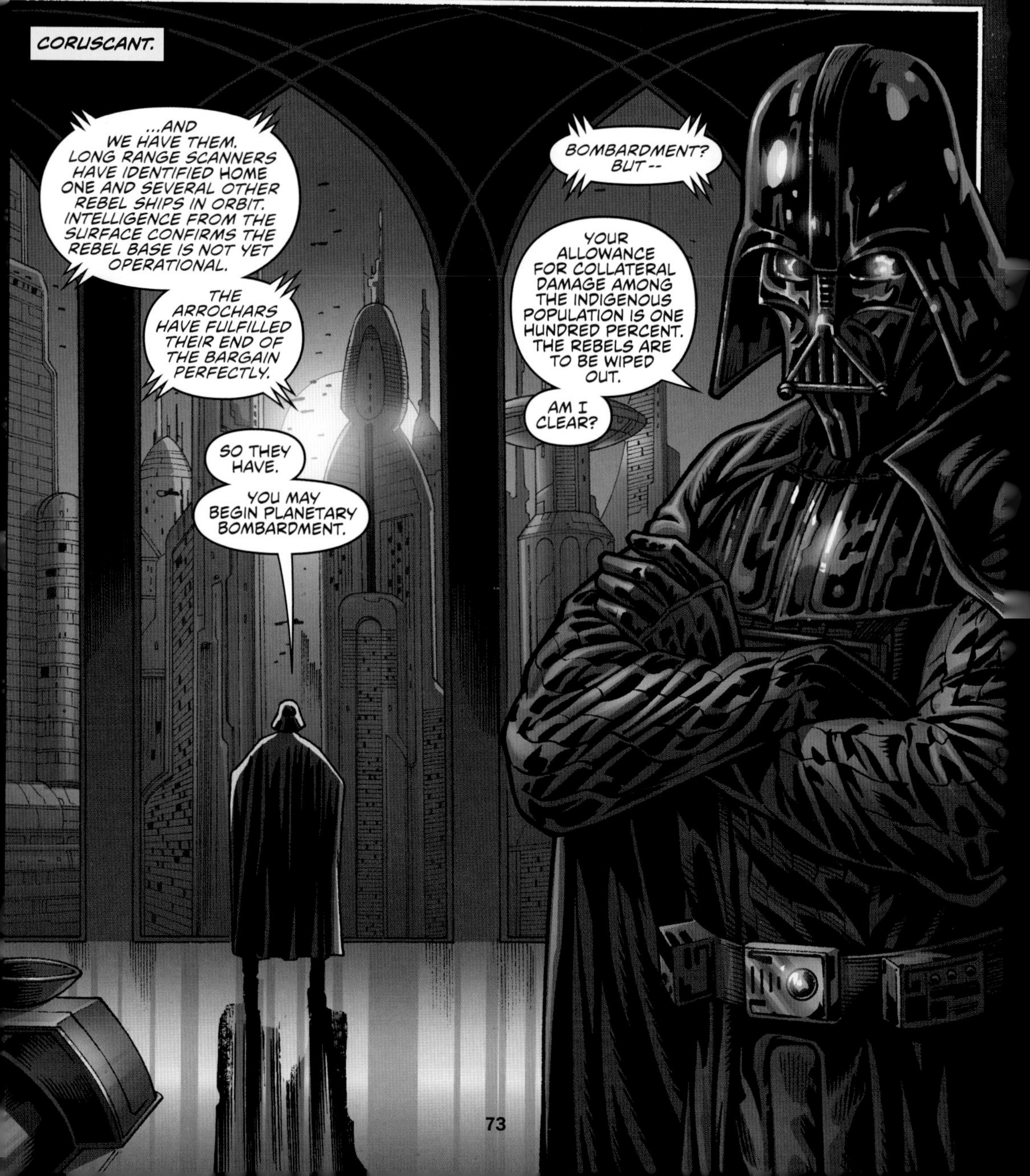
CORUSCANT.
...AND WE HAVE THEM. LONG RANGE SCANNERS HAVE IDENTIFIED HOME ONE AND SEVERAL OTHER REBEL SHIPS IN ORBIT. INTELLIGENCE FROM THE SURFACE CONFIRMS THE REBEL BASE IS NOT YET OPERATIONAL.
THE ARROCHARS HAVE FULFILLED THEIR END OF THE BARGAIN PERFECTLY.
SO THEY HAVE.
YOU MAY BEGIN PLANETARY BOMBARDMENT.
BOMBARDMENT? BUT --
YOUR ALLOWANCE FOR COLLATERAL DAMAGE AMONG THE INDIGENOUS POPULATION IS ONE HUNDRED PERCENT. THE REBELS ARE TO BE WIPED OUT.
AM I CLEAR?

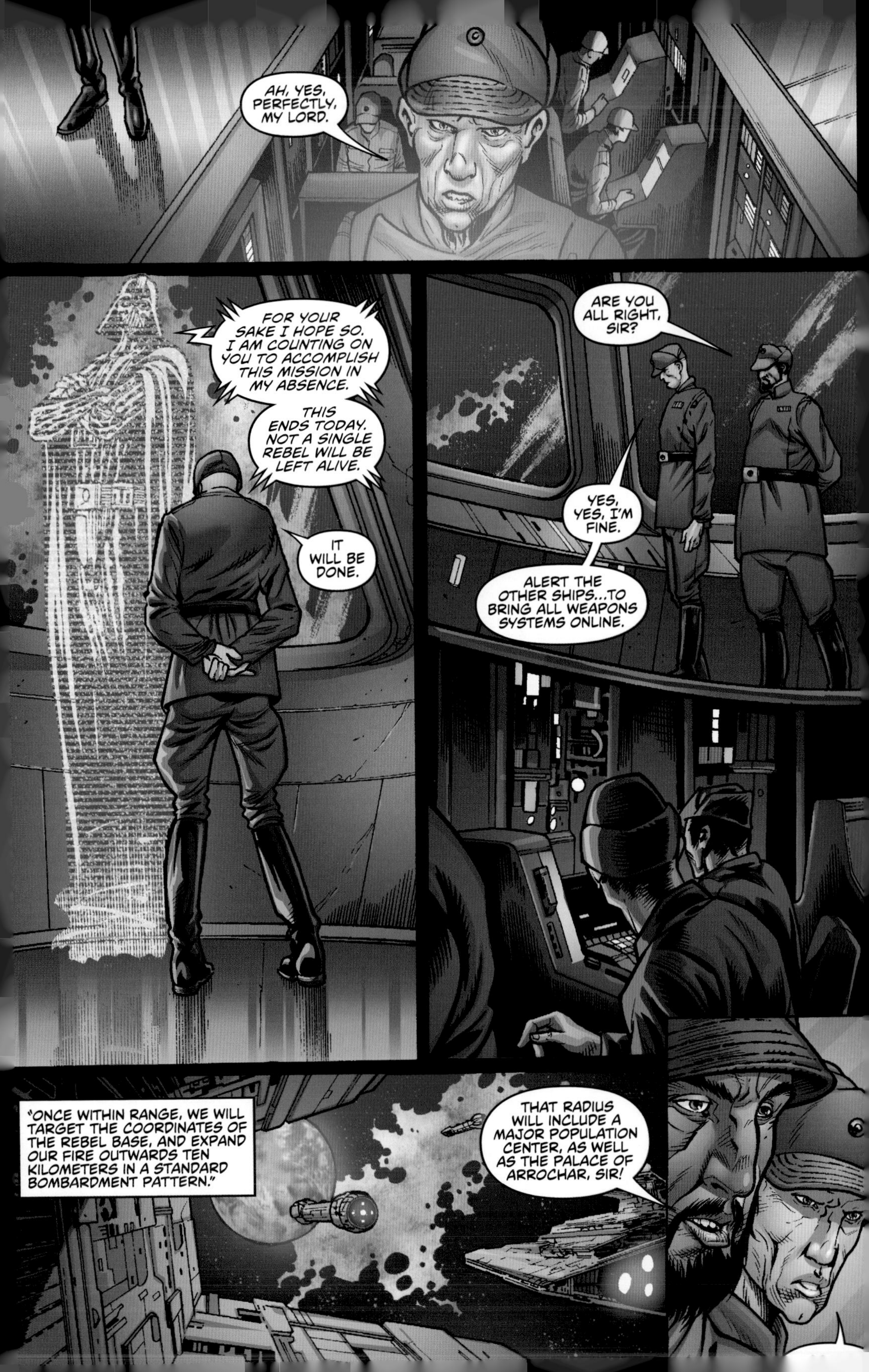
AH, YES, PERFECTLY, MY LORD.
FOR YOUR SAKE I HOPE SO. I AM COUNTING ON YOU TO ACCOMPLISH THIS MISSION IN MY ABSENCE.
THIS ENDS TODAY. NOT A SINGLE REBEL WILL BE LEFT ALIVE.
IT WILL BE DONE.
ARE YOU ALL RIGHT, SIR?
YES, YES, I'M FINE.
ALERT THE OTHER SHIPS...TO BRING ALL WEAPONS SYSTEMS ONLINE.
"ONCE WITHIN RANGE, WE WILL TARGET THE COORDINATES OF THE REBEL BASE, AND EXPAND OUR FIRE OUTWARDS TEN KILOMETERS IN A STANDARD BOMBARDMENT PATTERN."
THAT RADIUS WILL INCLUDE A MAJOR POPULATION CENTER, AS WELL AS THE PALACE OF ARROCHAR, SIR!

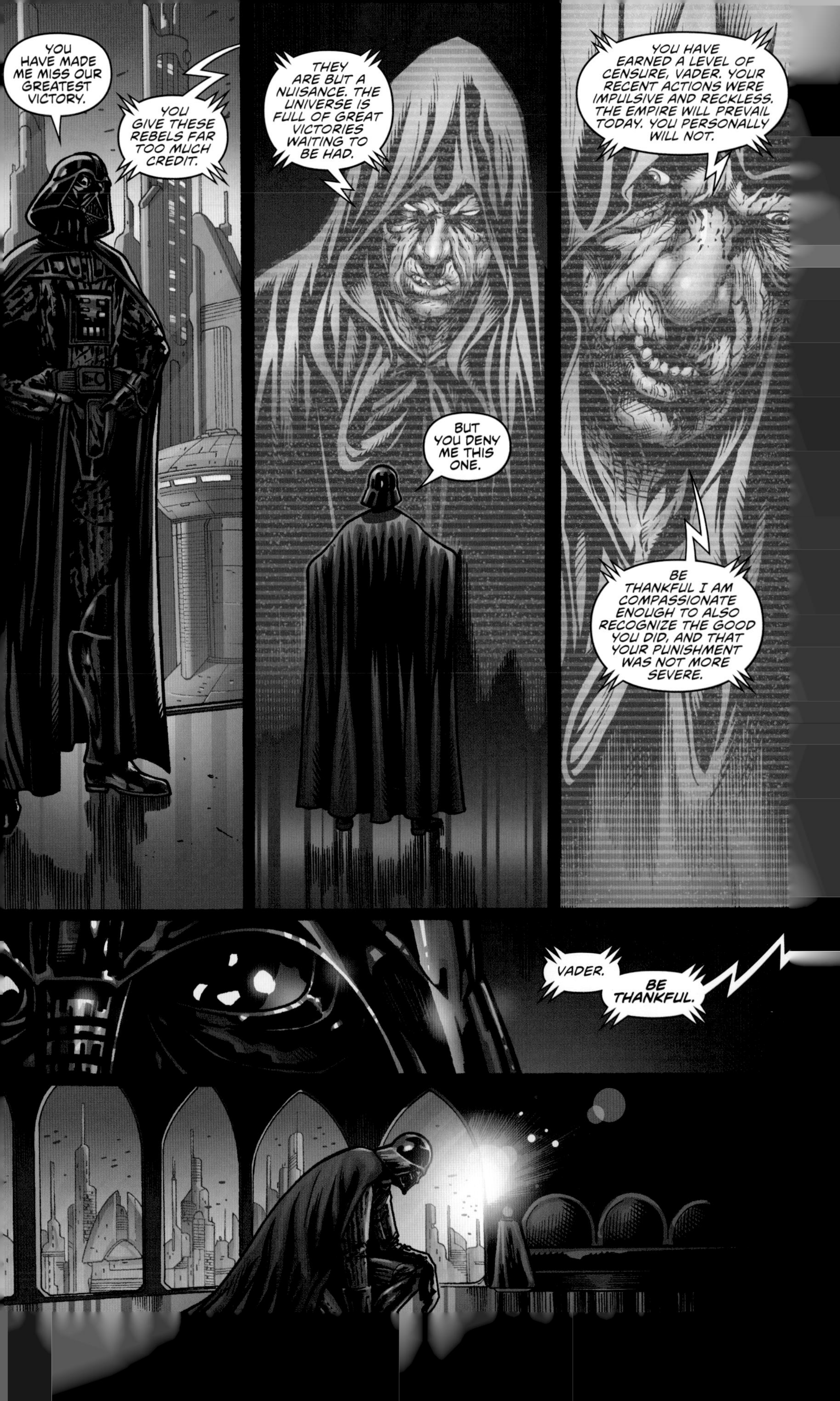
YOU HAVE MADE ME MISS OUR GREATEST VICTORY.
YOU GIVE THESE REBELS FAR TOO MUCH CREDIT.
THEY ARE BUT A NUISANCE. THE UNIVERSE IS FULL OF GREAT VICTORIES WAITING TO BE HAD.
BUT YOU DENY ME THIS ONE.
YOU HAVE EARNED A LEVEL OF CENSURE, VADER. YOUR RECENT ACTIONS WERE IMPULSIVE AND RECKLESS. THE EMPIRE WILL PREVAIL TODAY. YOU PERSONALLY WILL NOT.
BE THANKFUL I AM COMPASSIONATE ENOUGH TO ALSO RECOGNIZE THE GOOD YOU DID, AND THAT YOUR PUNISHMENT WAS NOT MORE SEVERE.
VADER.
BE THANKFUL.

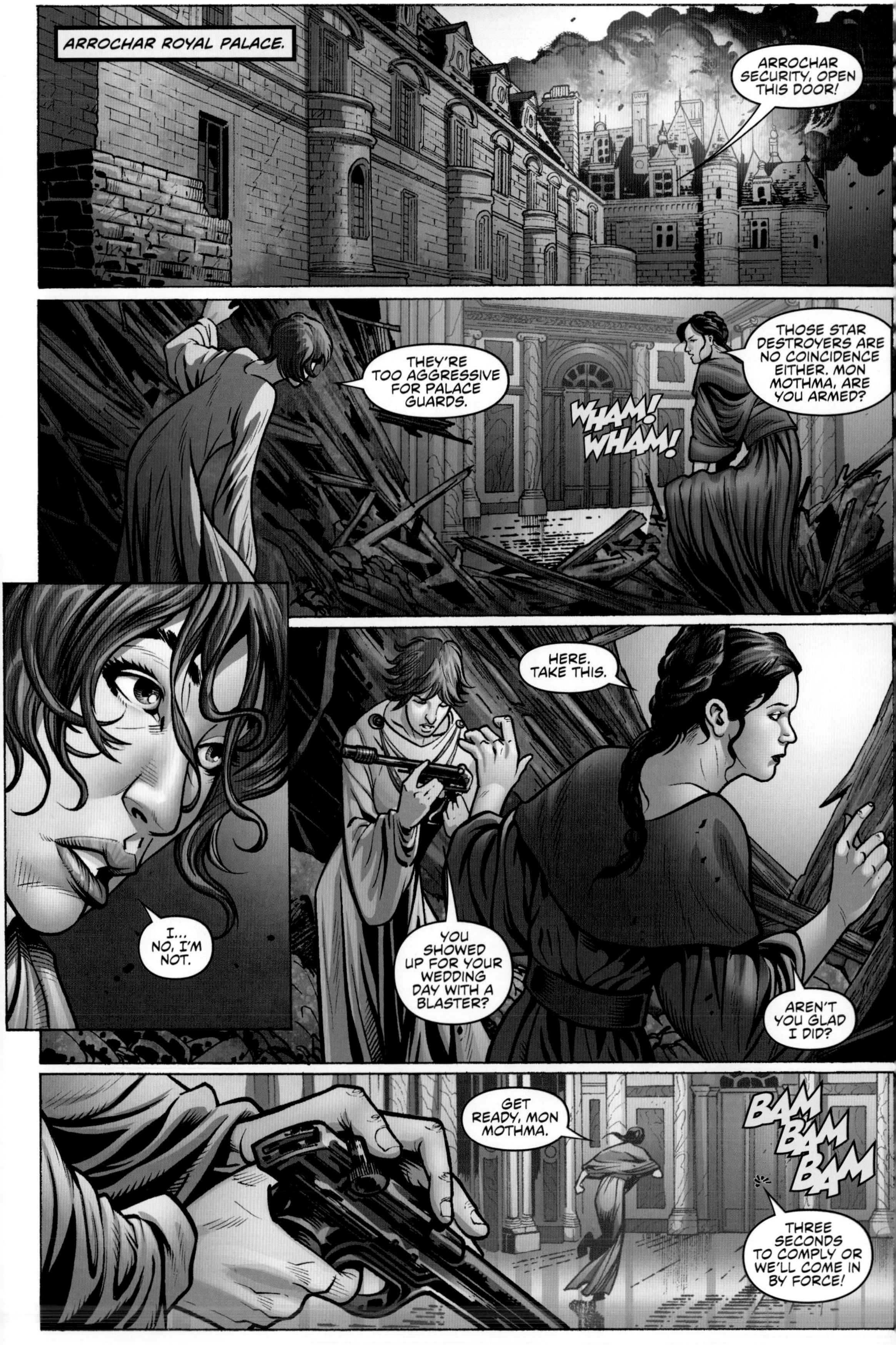
ARROCHAR ROYAL PALACE.
ARROCHAR SECURITY, OPEN THIS DOOR!
THEY'RE TOO AGGRESSIVE FOR PALACE GUARDS.
WHAM! WHAM!
THOSE STAR DESTROYERS ARE NO COINCIDENCE EITHER. MON MOTHMA, ARE YOU ARMED?
I... NO, I'M NOT.
HERE. TAKE THIS.
YOU SHOWED UP FOR YOUR WEDDING DAY WITH A BLASTER?
AREN'T YOU GLAD I DID?
GET READY, MON MOTHMA.
BAM BAM BAM
THREE SECONDS TO COMPLY OR WE'LL COME IN BY FORCE!

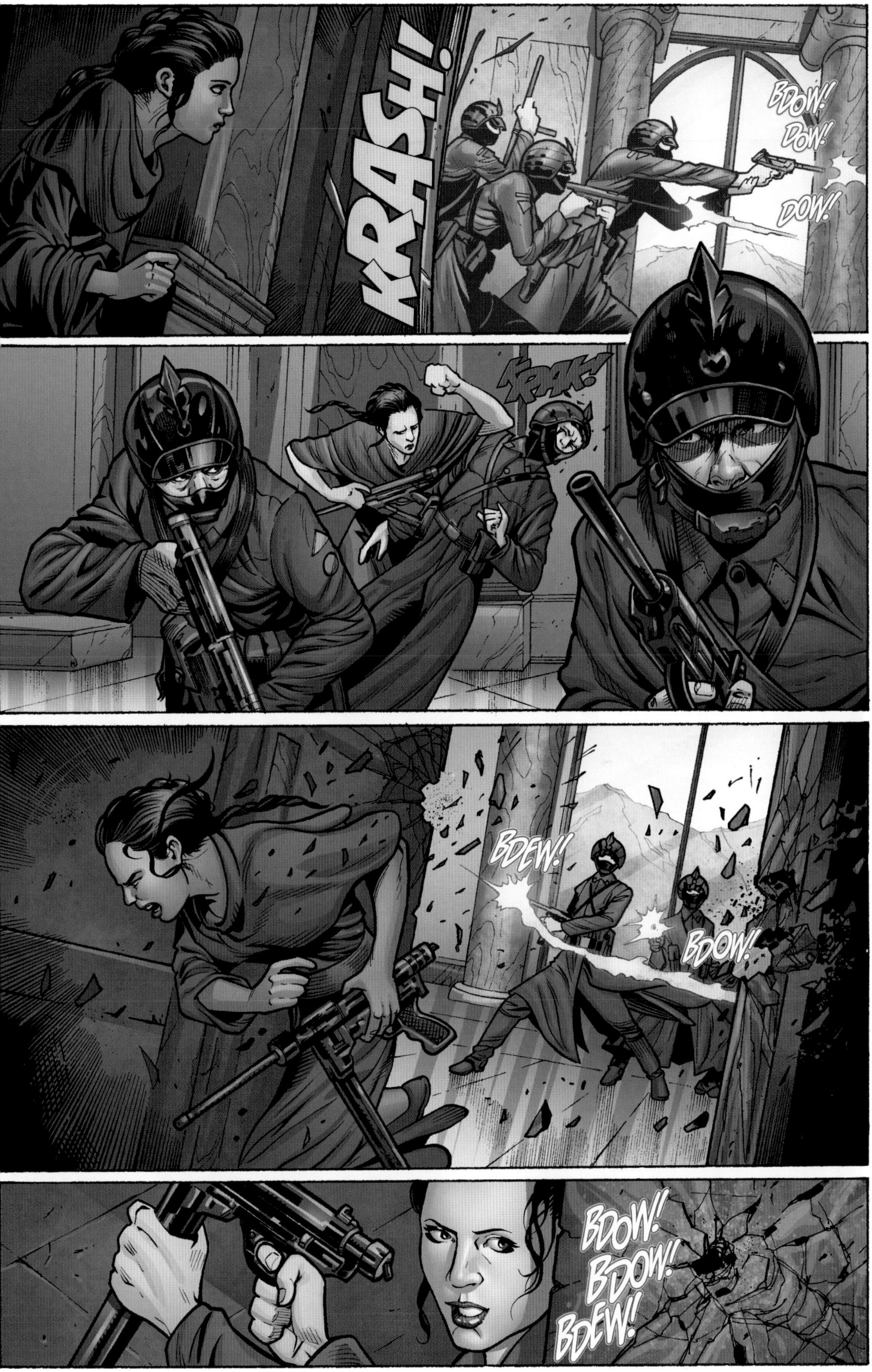
KRASH!
BDOW! DOW!
DOW!
KRAK!
BDEW!
BDOW!
BDOW!
BDOW!
BDEW!

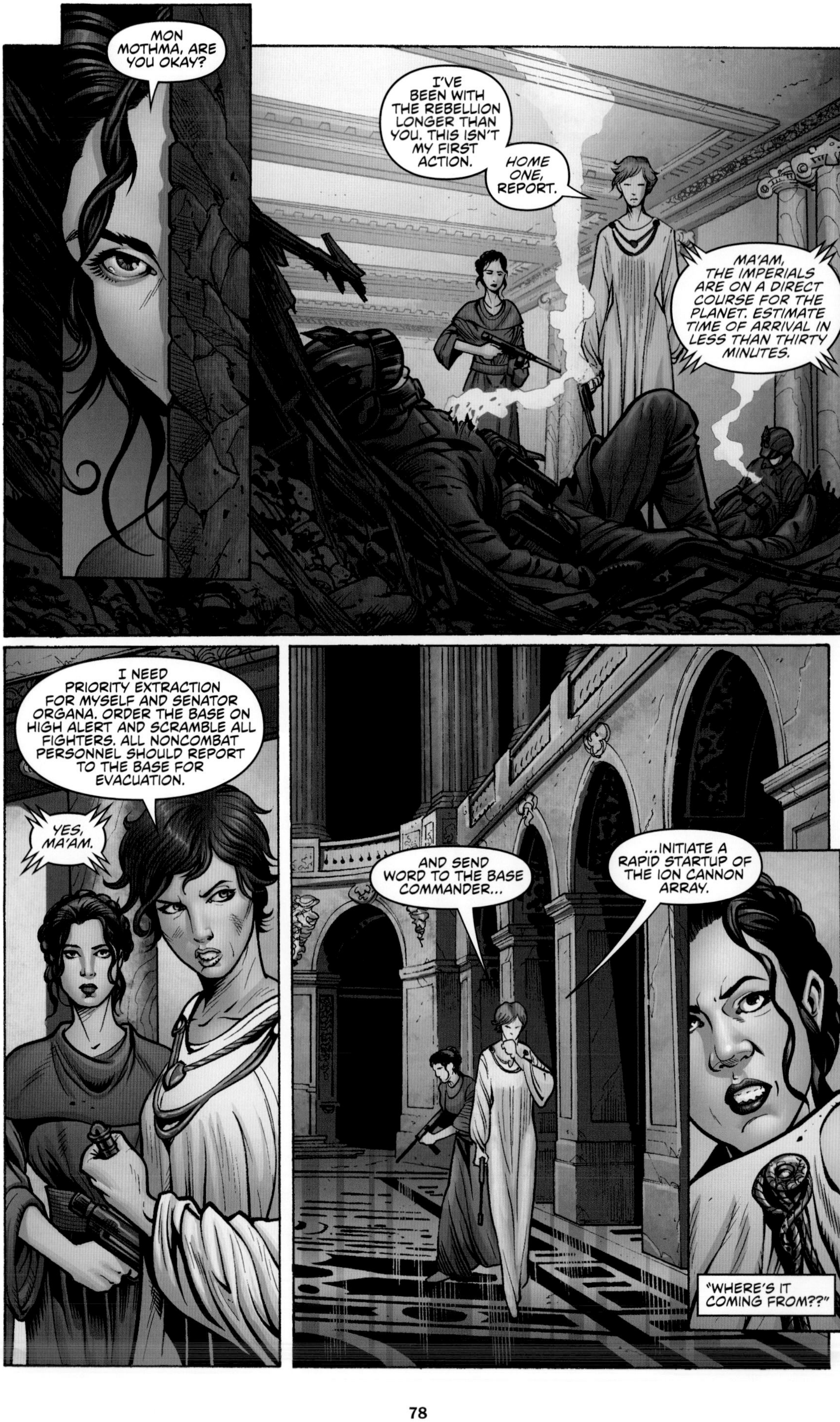
MON MOTHMA, ARE YOU OKAY?
I'VE BEEN WITH THE REBELLION LONGER THAN YOU. THIS ISN'T MY FIRST ACTION.
HOME ONE, REPORT.
MA'AM, THE IMPERIALS ARE ON A DIRECT COURSE FOR THE PLANET. ESTIMATE TIME OF ARRIVAL IN LESS THAN THIRTY MINUTES.
I NEED PRIORITY EXTRACTION FOR MYSELF AND SENATOR ORGANA. ORDER THE BASE ON HIGH ALERT AND SCRAMBLE ALL FIGHTERS. ALL NONCOMBAT PERSONNEL SHOULD REPORT TO THE BASE FOR EVACUATION.
YES, MA'AM.
AND SEND WORD TO THE BASE COMMANDER...
...INITIATE A RAPID STARTUP OF THE ION CANNON ARRAY.
"WHERE'S IT COMING FROM??"

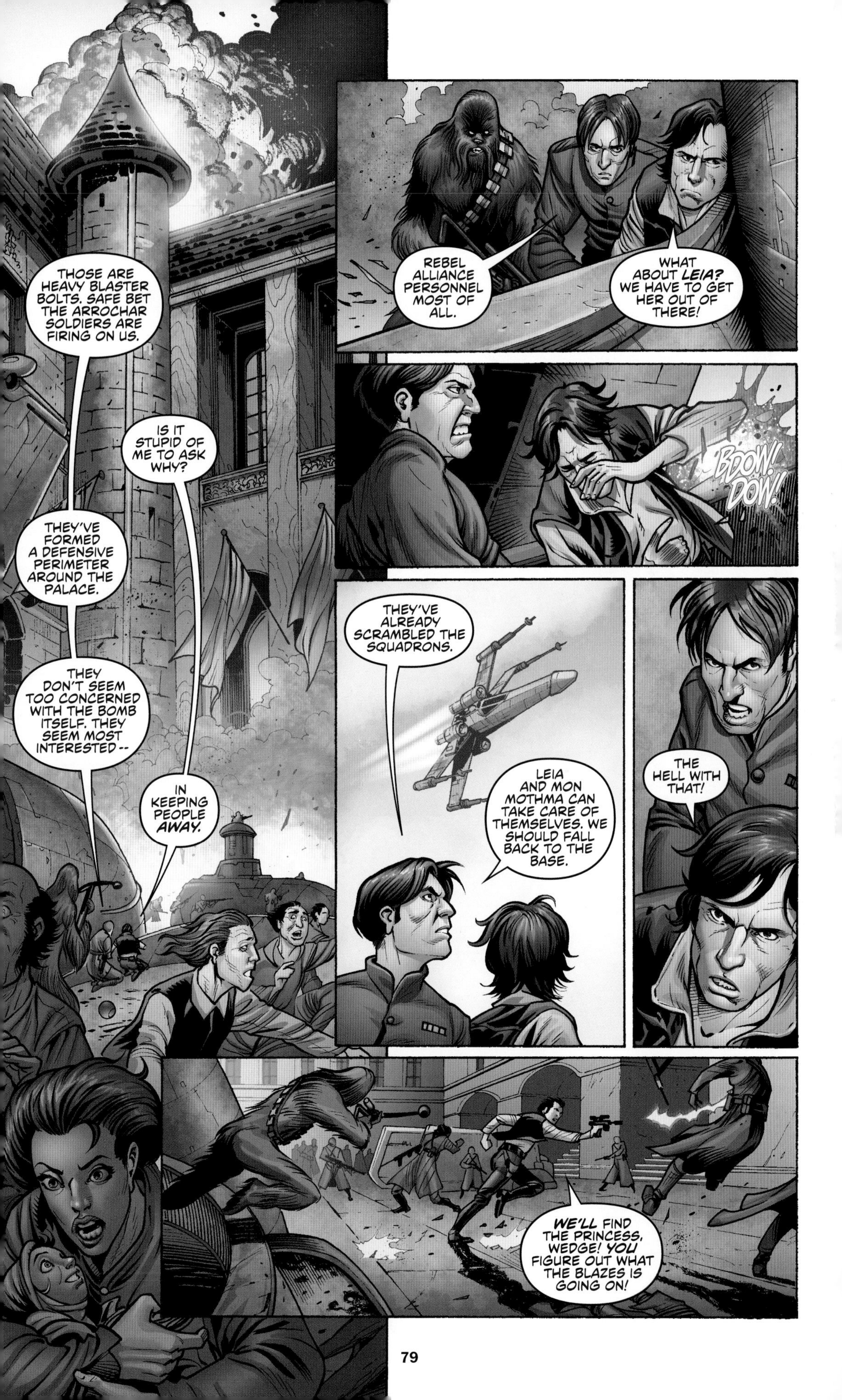
THOSE ARE HEAVY BLASTER BOLTS. SAFE BET THE ARROCHAR SOLDIERS ARE FIRING ON US.
IS IT STUPID OF ME TO ASK WHY?
THEY'VE FORMED A DEFENSIVE PERIMETER AROUND THE PALACE.
THEY DON'T SEEM TOO CONCERNED WITH THE BOMB ITSELF. THEY SEEM MOST INTERESTED --
IN KEEPING PEOPLE AWAY.
REBEL ALLIANCE PERSONNEL MOST OF ALL.
WHAT ABOUT LEIA? WE HAVE TO GET HER OUT OF THERE!
BDOW! DOW!
THEY'VE ALREADY SCRAMBLED THE SQUADRONS.
LEIA AND MON MOTHMA CAN TAKE CARE OF THEMSELVES. WE SHOULD FALL BACK TO THE BASE.
THE HELL WITH THAT!
WE'LL FIND THE PRINCESS, WEDGE! YOU FIGURE OUT WHAT THE BLAZES IS GOING ON!

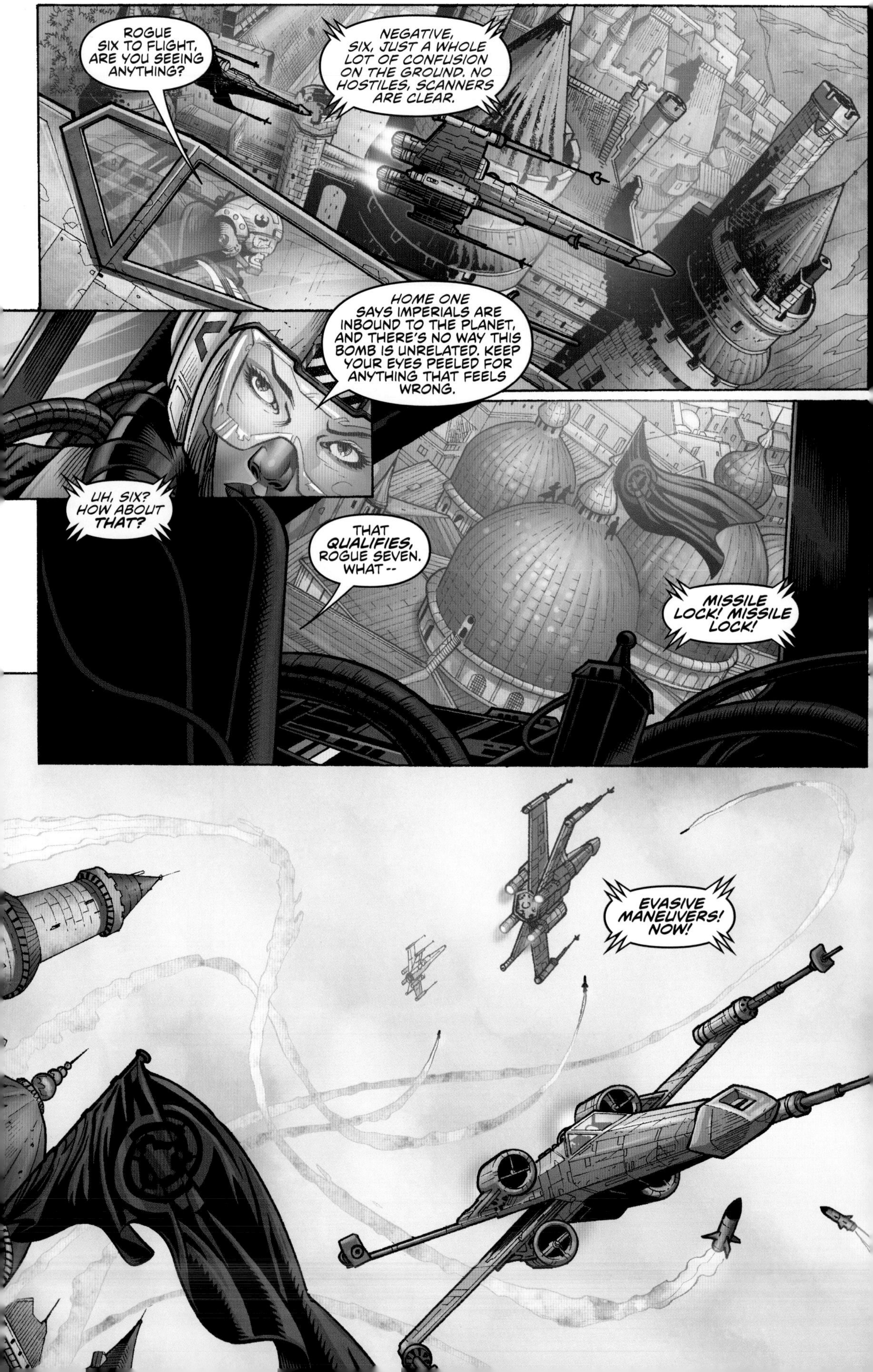
ROGUE SIX TO FLIGHT, ARE YOU SEEING ANYTHING?
NEGATIVE, SIX, JUST A WHOLE LOT OF CONFUSION ON THE GROUND. NO HOSTILES, SCANNERS ARE CLEAR.
HOME ONE SAYS IMPERIALS ARE INBOUND TO THE PLANET, AND THERE'S NO WAY THIS BOMB IS UNRELATED. KEEP YOUR EYES PEELED FOR ANYTHING THAT FEELS WRONG.
UH, SIX? HOW ABOUT THAT?
THAT QUALIFIES, ROGUE SEVEN. WHAT --
MISSILE LOCK! MISSILE LOCK!
EVASIVE MANEUVERS! NOW!

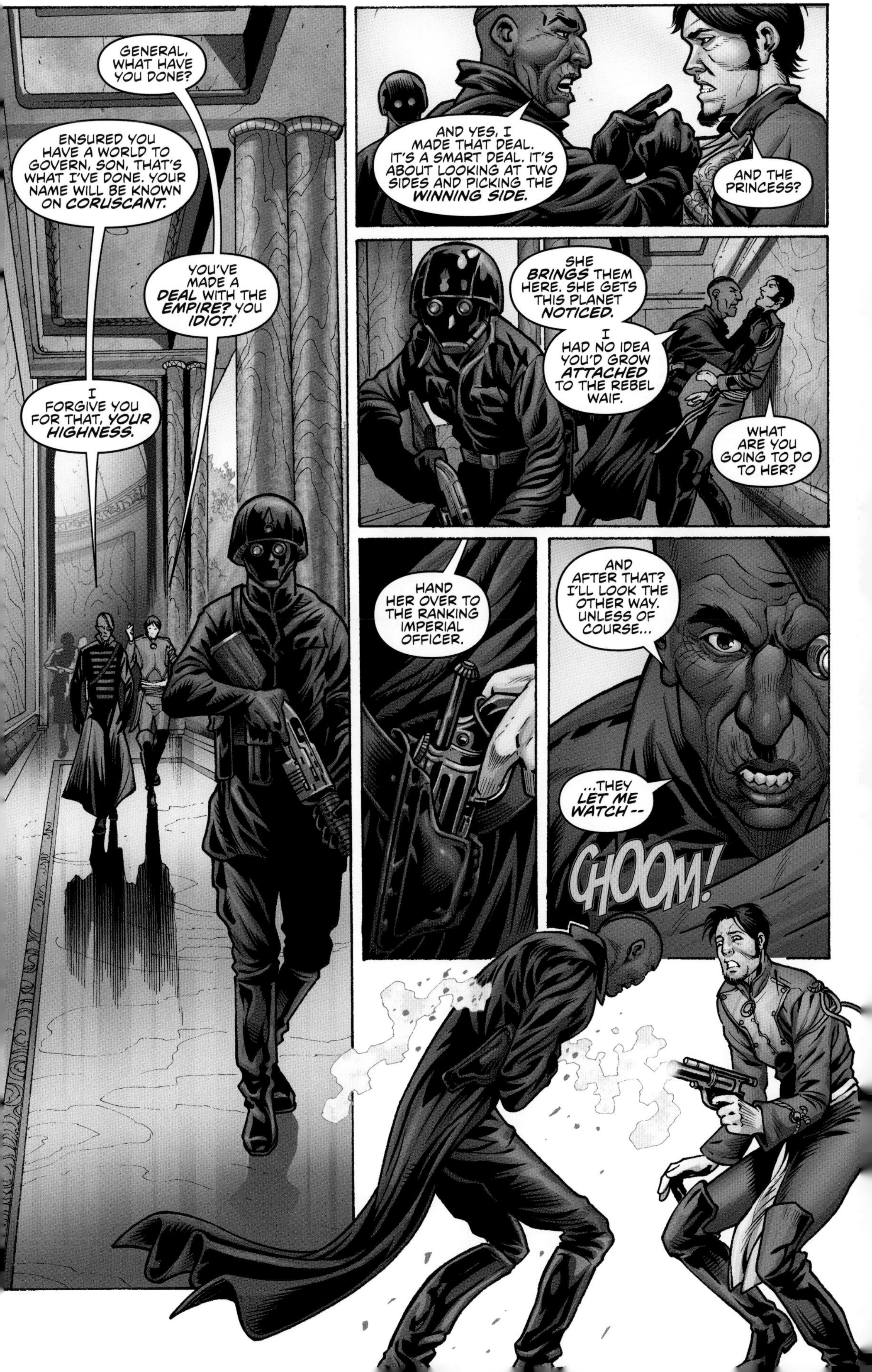
GENERAL, WHAT HAVE YOU DONE?
ENSURED YOU HAVE A WORLD TO GOVERN, SON, THAT'S WHAT I'VE DONE. YOUR NAME WILL BE KNOWN ON CORUSCANT.
YOU'VE MADE A DEAL WITH THE EMPIRE? YOU IDIOT!
I FORGIVE YOU FOR THAT, YOUR HIGHNESS.
AND YES, I MADE THAT DEAL. IT'S A SMART DEAL. IT'S ABOUT LOOKING AT TWO SIDES AND PICKING THE WINNING SIDE.
AND THE PRINCESS?
SHE BRINGS THEM HERE. SHE GETS THIS PLANET NOTICED.
I HAD NO IDEA YOU'D GROW ATTACHED TO THE REBEL WAIF.
WHAT ARE YOU GOING TO DO TO HER?
HAND HER OVER TO THE RANKING IMPERIAL OFFICER.
AND AFTER THAT? I'LL LOOK THE OTHER WAY. UNLESS OF COURSE...
...THEY LET ME WATCH --
CHOOM!

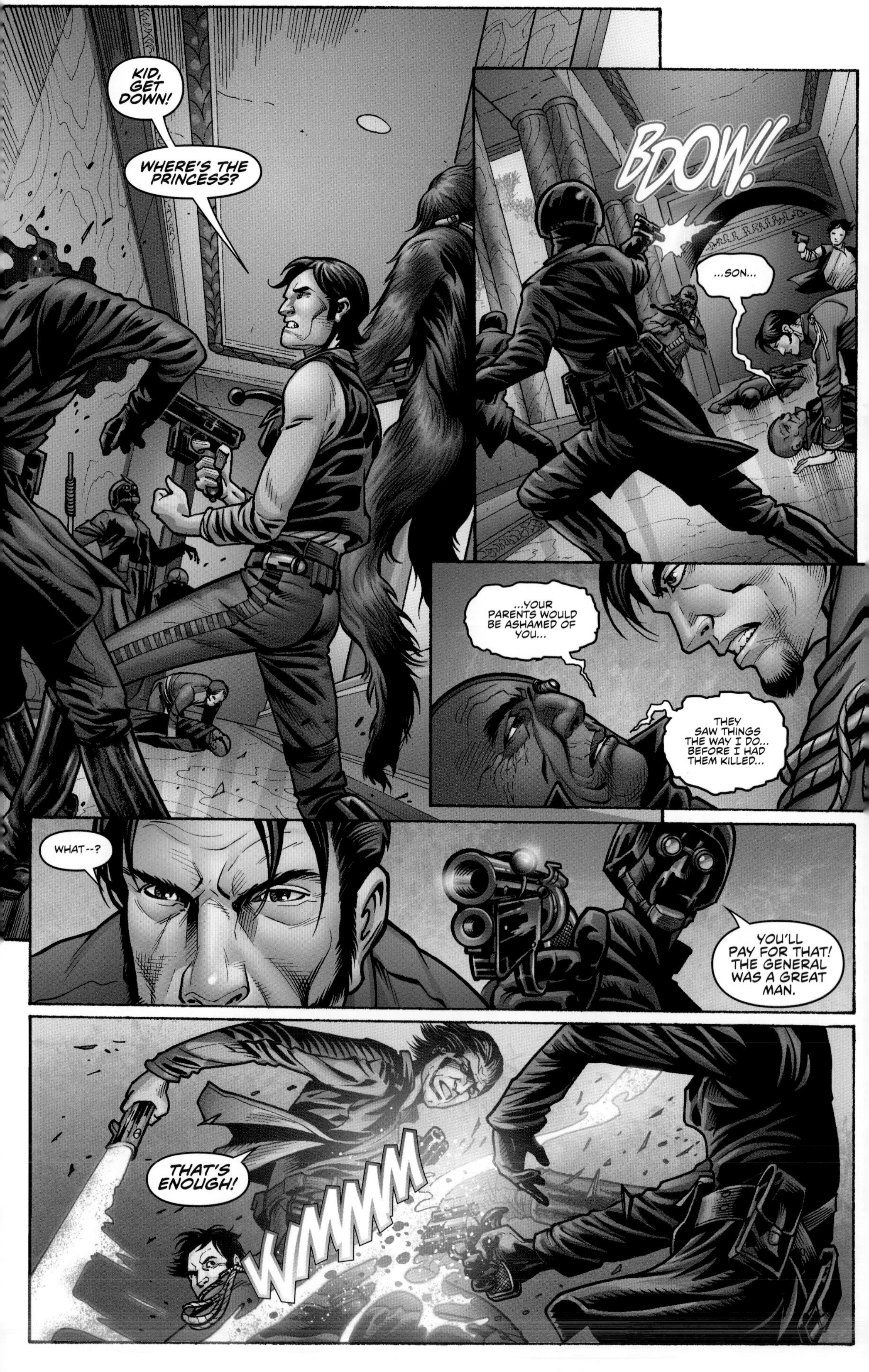

KID, GET DOWN!
WHERE'S THE PRINCESS?
BDOW!
...SON...
...YOUR PARENTS WOULD BE ASHAMED OF YOU...
THEY SAW THINGS THE WAY I DO... BEFORE I HAD THEM KILLED...
WHAT--?
YOU'LL PAY FOR THAT! THE GENERAL WAS A GREAT MAN.
THAT'S ENOUGH!
WMMMM

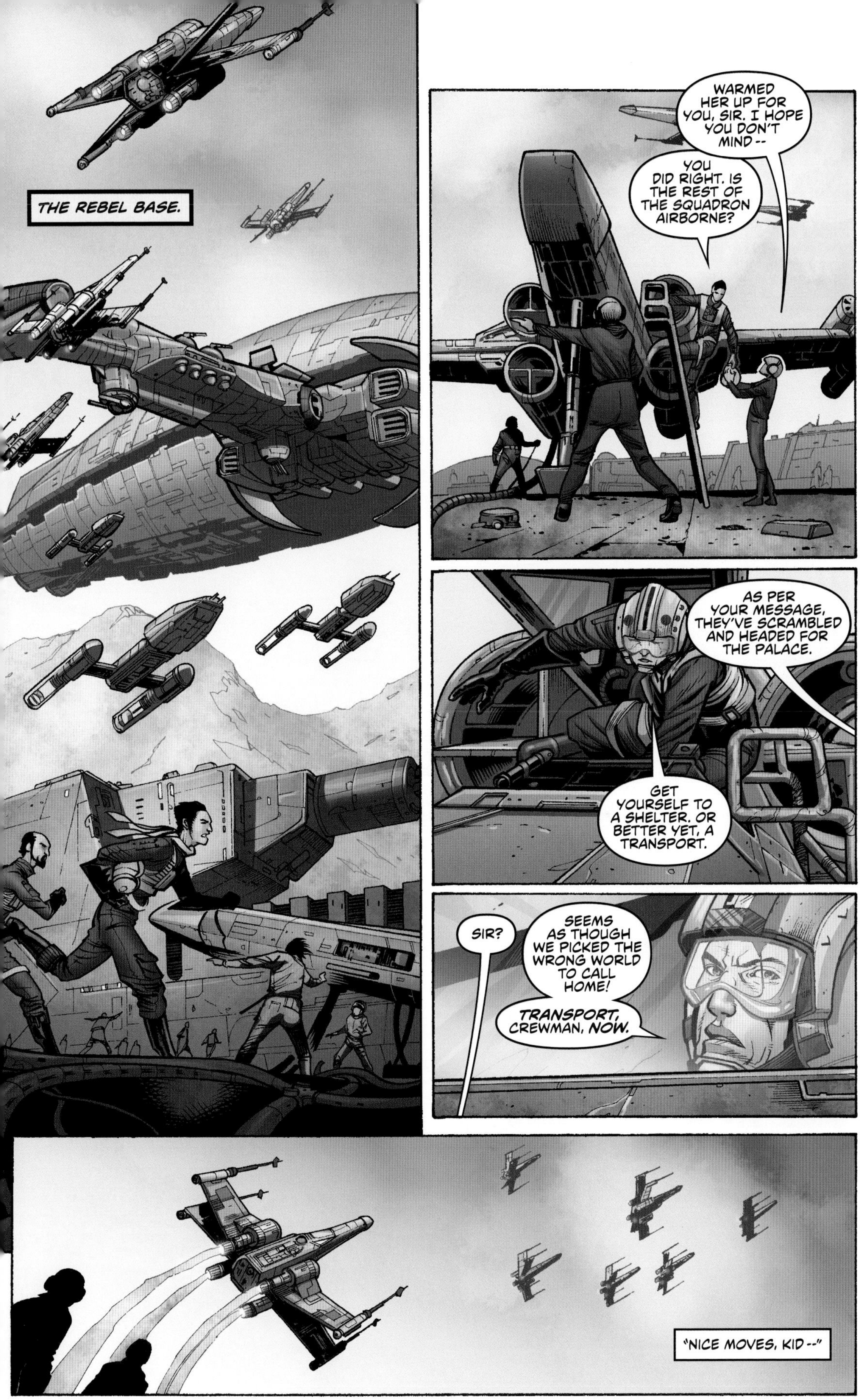
THE REBEL BASE.
WARMED HER UP FOR YOU, SIR. I HOPE YOU DON'T MIND --
YOU DID RIGHT. IS THE REST OF THE SQUADRON AIRBORNE?
AS PER YOUR MESSAGE, THEY'VE SCRAMBLED AND HEADED FOR THE PALACE.
GET YOURSELF TO A SHELTER. OR BETTER YET, A TRANSPORT.
SIR?
SEEMS AS THOUGH WE PICKED THE WRONG WORLD TO CALL HOME!
TRANSPORT, CREWMAN, NOW.
"NICE MOVES, KID --"

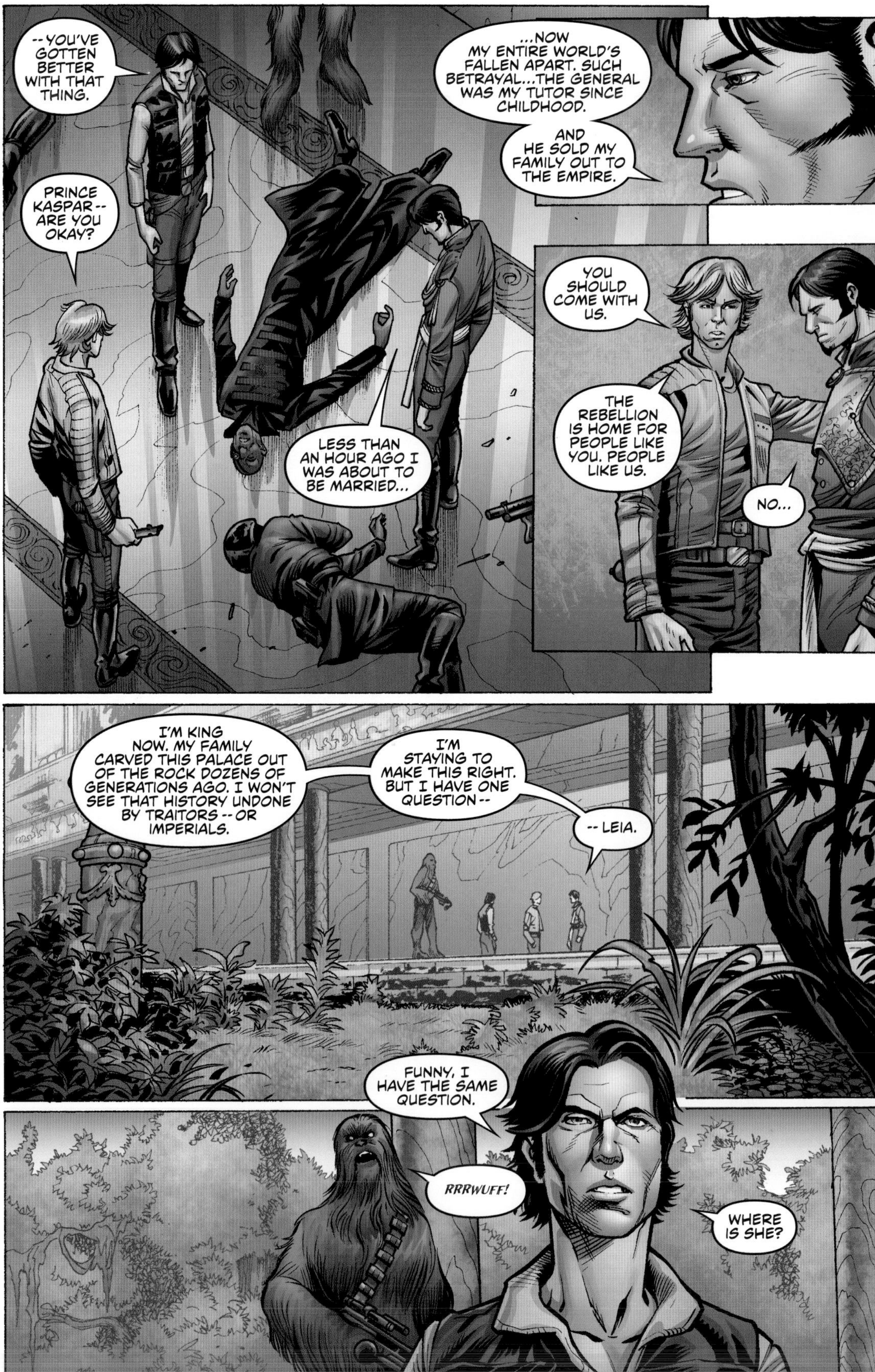
--YOU'VE GOTTEN BETTER WITH THAT THING.
PRINCE KASPAR--ARE YOU OKAY?
LESS THAN AN HOUR AGO I WAS ABOUT TO BE MARRIED...
...NOW MY ENTIRE WORLD'S FALLEN APART. SUCH BETRAYAL...THE GENERAL WAS MY TUTOR SINCE CHILDHOOD.
AND HE SOLD MY FAMILY OUT TO THE EMPIRE.
YOU SHOULD COME WITH US.
THE REBELLION IS HOME FOR PEOPLE LIKE YOU. PEOPLE LIKE US.
NO...
I'M KING NOW. MY FAMILY CARVED THIS PALACE OUT OF THE ROCK DOZENS OF GENERATIONS AGO. I WON'T SEE THAT HISTORY UNDONE BY TRAITORS--OR IMPERIALS.
I'M STAYING TO MAKE THIS RIGHT. BUT I HAVE ONE QUESTION--
--LEIA.
FUNNY, I HAVE THE SAME QUESTION.
RRRWUFF!
WHERE IS SHE?

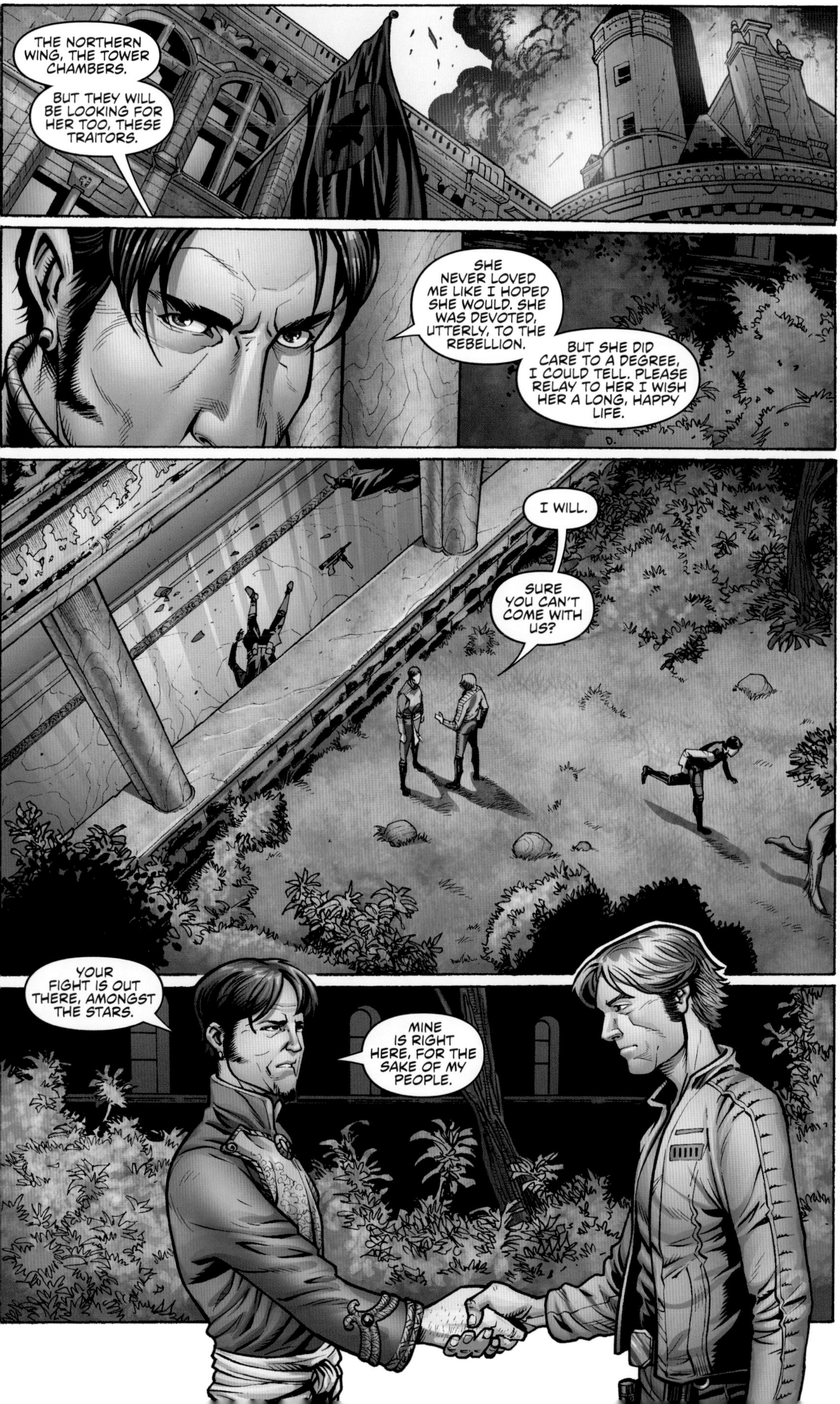
THE NORTHERN WING, THE TOWER CHAMBERS.
BUT THEY WILL BE LOOKING FOR HER TOO, THESE TRAITORS.
SHE NEVER LOVED ME LIKE I HOPED SHE WOULD. SHE WAS DEVOTED, UTTERLY, TO THE REBELLION.
BUT SHE DID CARE TO A DEGREE, I COULD TELL. PLEASE RELAY TO HER I WISH HER A LONG, HAPPY LIFE.
I WILL.
SURE YOU CAN'T COME WITH US?
YOUR FIGHT IS OUT THERE, AMONGST THE STARS.
MINE IS RIGHT HERE, FOR THE SAKE OF MY PEOPLE.

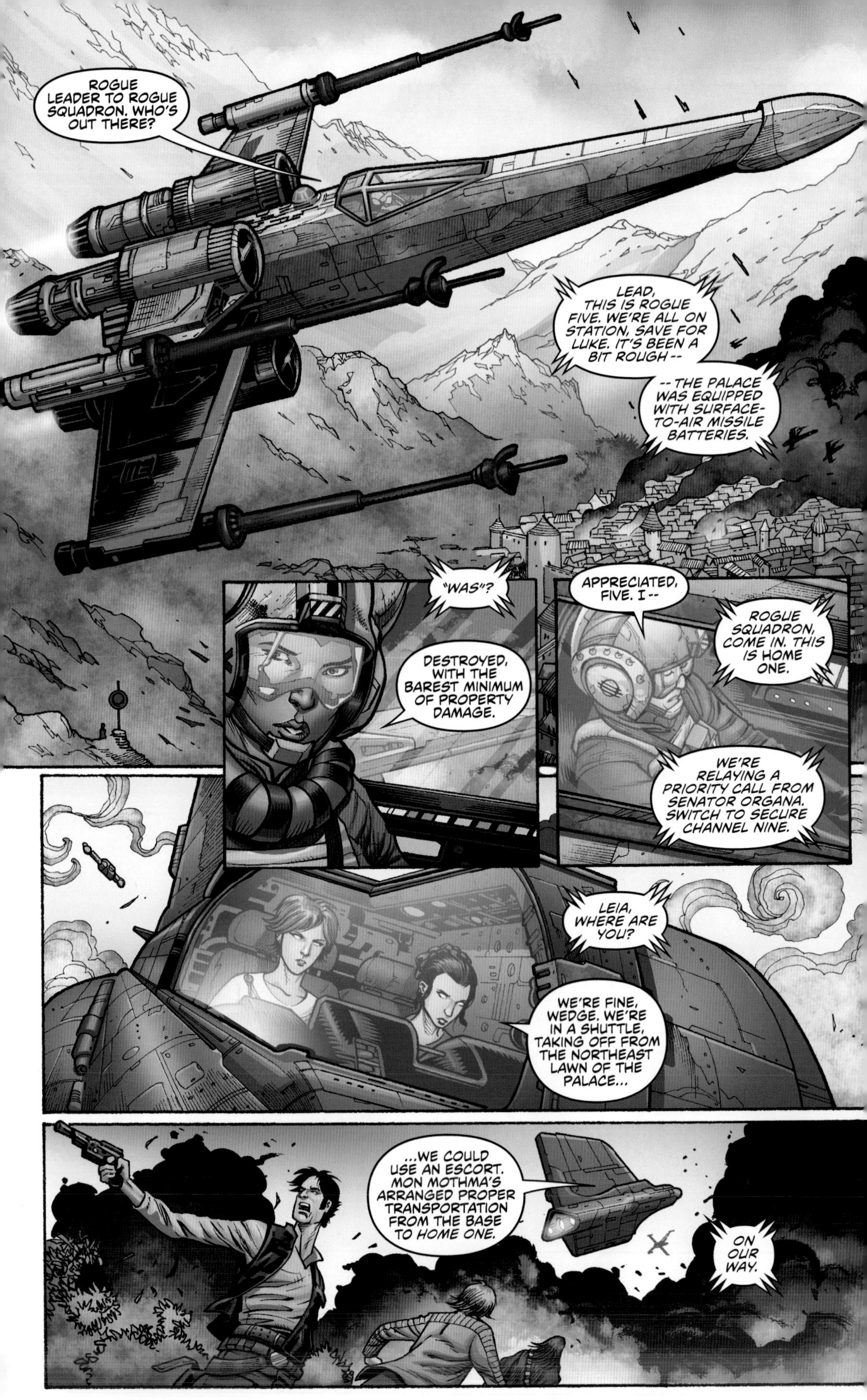
ROGUE LEADER TO ROGUE SQUADRON. WHO'S OUT THERE?
LEAD, THIS IS ROGUE FIVE. WE'RE ALL ON STATION, SAVE FOR LUKE. IT'S BEEN A BIT ROUGH --
-- THE PALACE WAS EQUIPPED WITH SURFACE-TO-AIR MISSILE BATTERIES.
"WAS"?
DESTROYED, WITH THE BAREST MINIMUM OF PROPERTY DAMAGE.
APPRECIATED, FIVE. I --
ROGUE SQUADRON, COME IN. THIS IS HOME ONE.
WE'RE RELAYING A PRIORITY CALL FROM SENATOR ORGANA. SWITCH TO SECURE CHANNEL NINE.
LEIA, WHERE ARE YOU?
WE'RE FINE, WEDGE. WE'RE IN A SHUTTLE, TAKING OFF FROM THE NORTHEAST LAWN OF THE PALACE...
...WE COULD USE AN ESCORT. MON MOTHMA'S ARRANGED PROPER TRANSPORTATION FROM THE BASE TO HOME ONE.
ON OUR WAY.

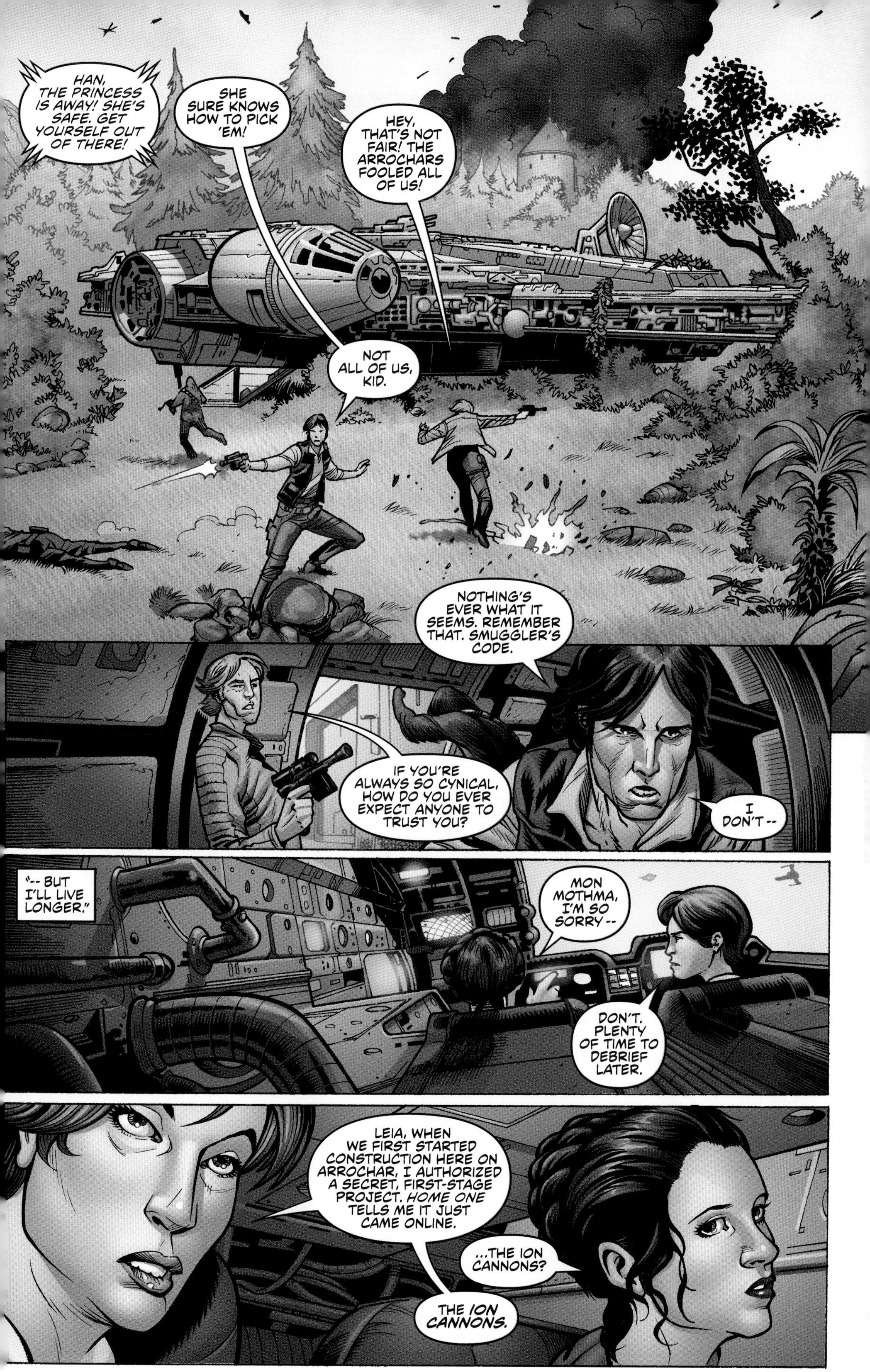
HAN, THE PRINCESS IS AWAY! SHE'S SAFE. GET YOURSELF OUT OF THERE!
SHE SURE KNOWS HOW TO PICK 'EM!
HEY, THAT'S NOT FAIR! THE ARROCHARS FOOLED ALL OF US!
NOT ALL OF US, KID.
NOTHING'S EVER WHAT IT SEEMS. REMEMBER THAT. SMUGGLER'S CODE.
IF YOU'RE ALWAYS SO CYNICAL, HOW DO YOU EVER EXPECT ANYONE TO TRUST YOU?
I DON'T --
"-- BUT I'LL LIVE LONGER."
MON MOTHMA, I'M SO SORRY --
DON'T. PLENTY OF TIME TO DEBRIEF LATER.
LEIA, WHEN WE FIRST STARTED CONSTRUCTION HERE ON ARROCHAR, I AUTHORIZED A SECRET, FIRST-STAGE PROJECT. *HOME ONE* TELLS ME IT JUST CAME ONLINE.
...THE ION CANNONS?
THE *ION CANNONS.*

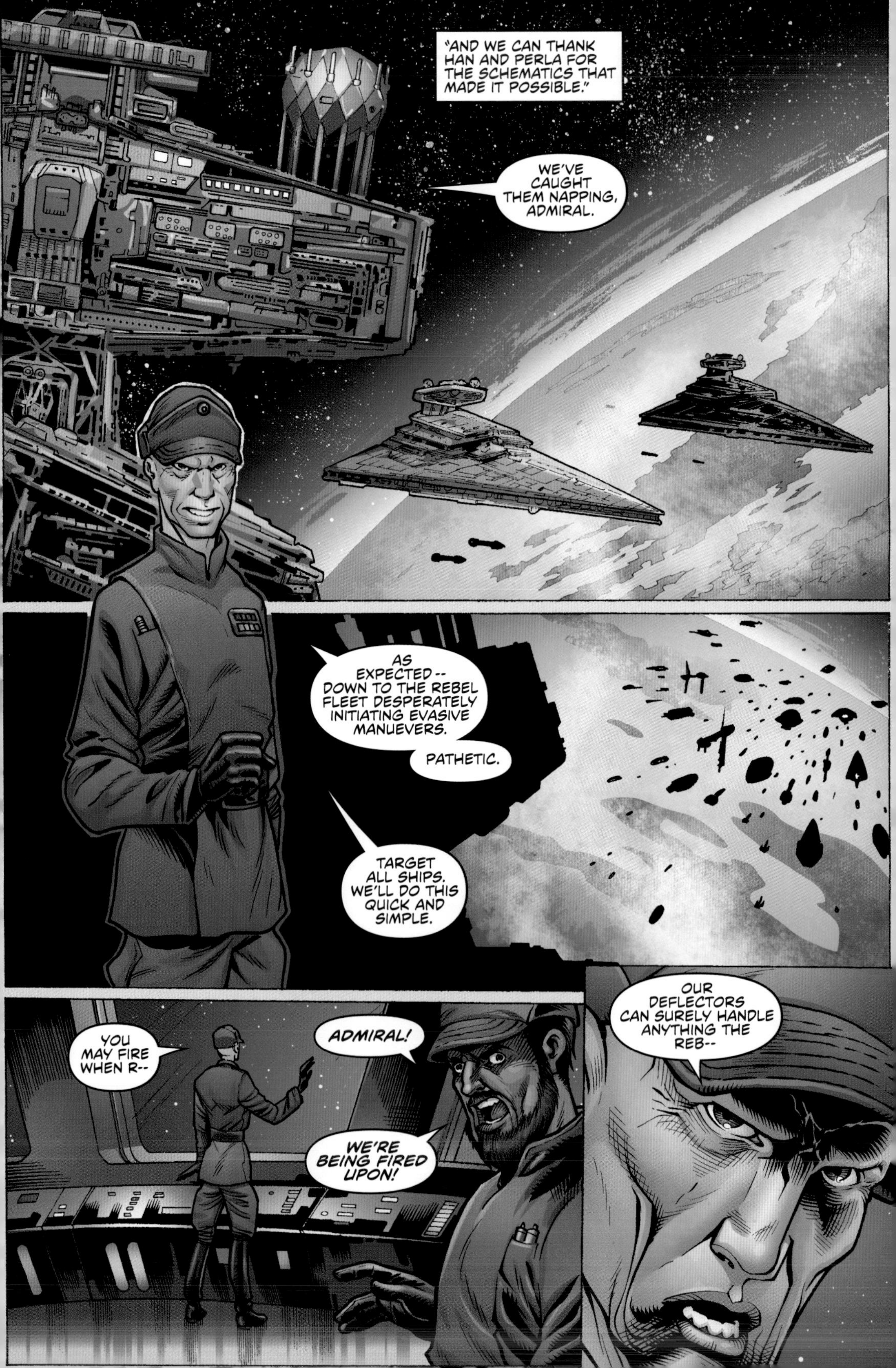
"AND WE CAN THANK HAN AND PERLA FOR THE SCHEMATICS THAT MADE IT POSSIBLE."
WE'VE CAUGHT THEM NAPPING, ADMIRAL.
AS EXPECTED -- DOWN TO THE REBEL FLEET DESPERATELY INITIATING EVASIVE MANUEVERS.
PATHETIC.
TARGET ALL SHIPS. WE'LL DO THIS QUICK AND SIMPLE.
YOU MAY FIRE WHEN R--
ADMIRAL!
WE'RE BEING FIRED UPON!
OUR DEFLECTORS CAN SURELY HANDLE ANYTHING THE REB--

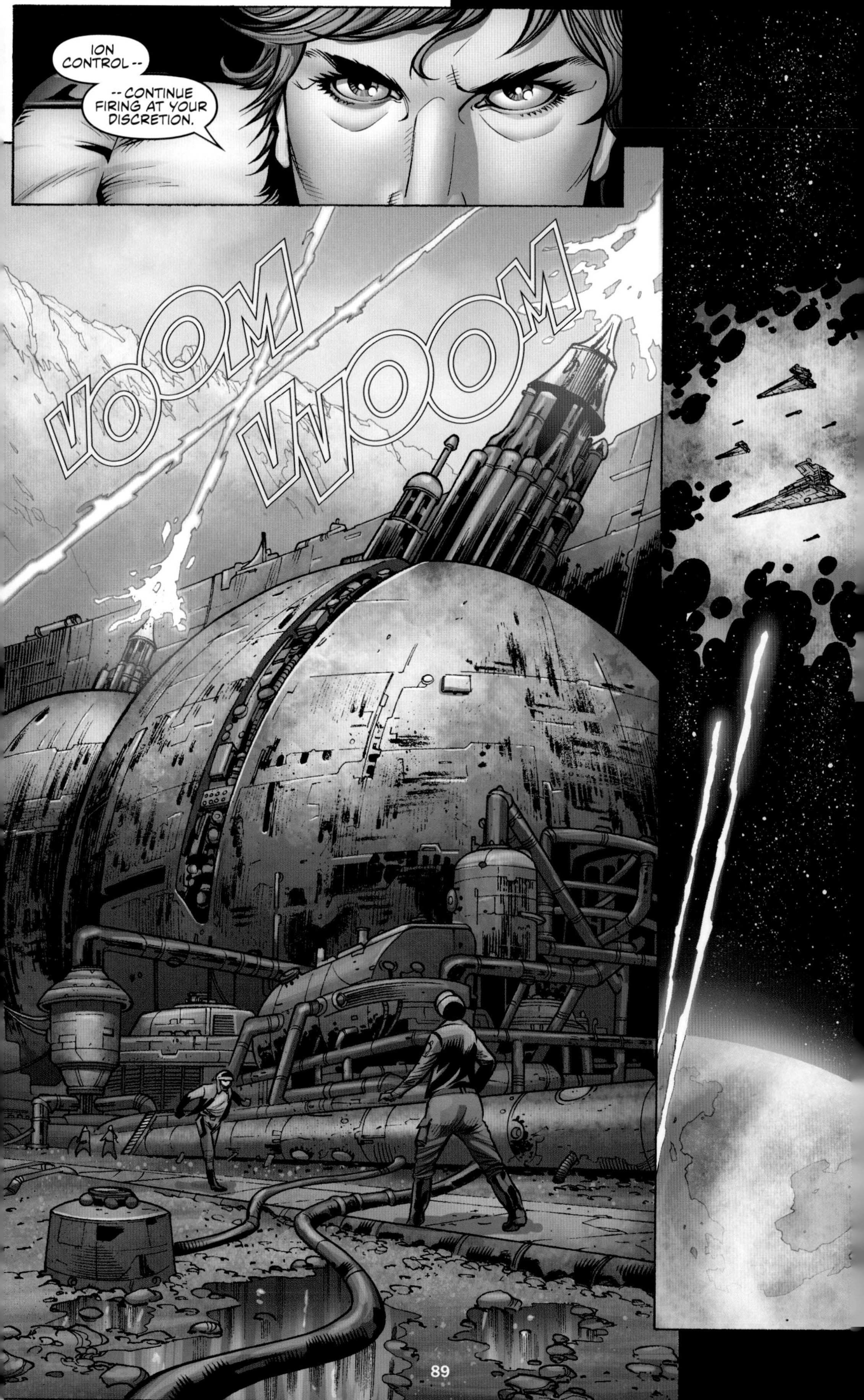
ION CONTROL --
-- CONTINUE FIRING AT YOUR DISCRETION.
VOOM
VVOOM

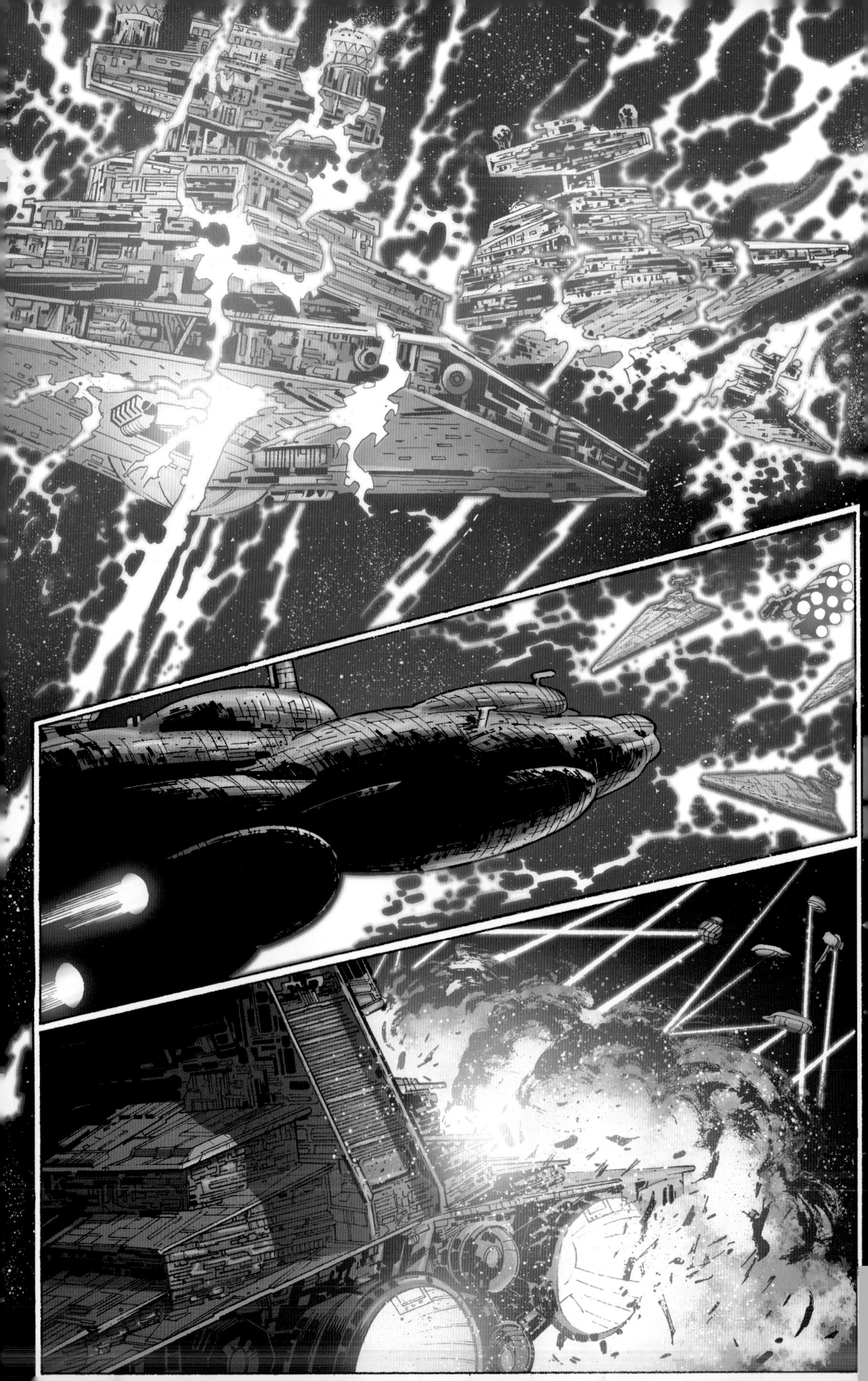

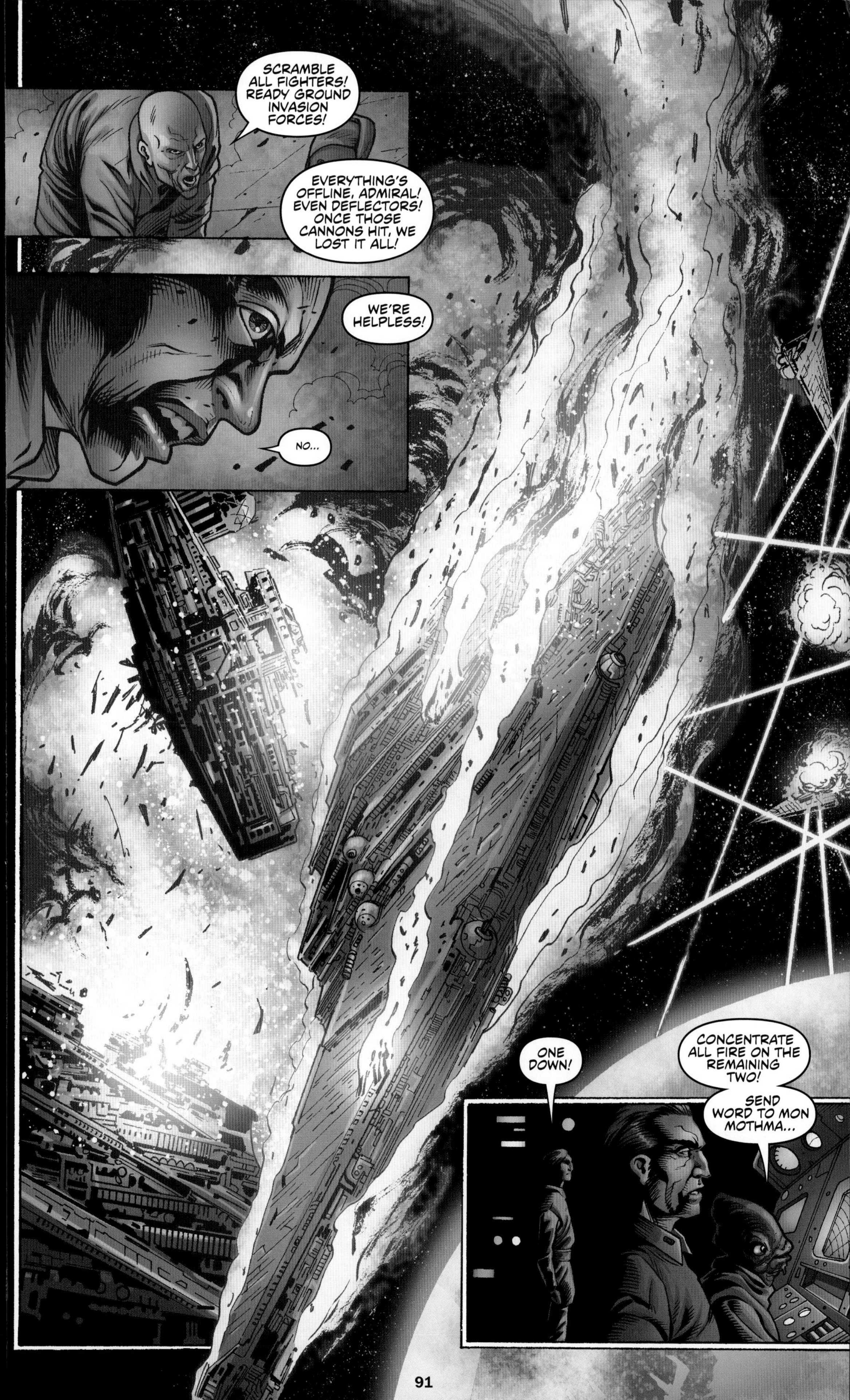
SCRAMBLE ALL FIGHTERS! READY GROUND INVASION FORCES!
EVERYTHING'S OFFLINE, ADMIRAL! EVEN DEFLECTORS! ONCE THOSE CANNONS HIT, WE LOST IT ALL!
WE'RE HELPLESS!
NO...
ONE DOWN!
CONCENTRATE ALL FIRE ON THE REMAINING TWO!
SEND WORD TO MON MOTHMA...

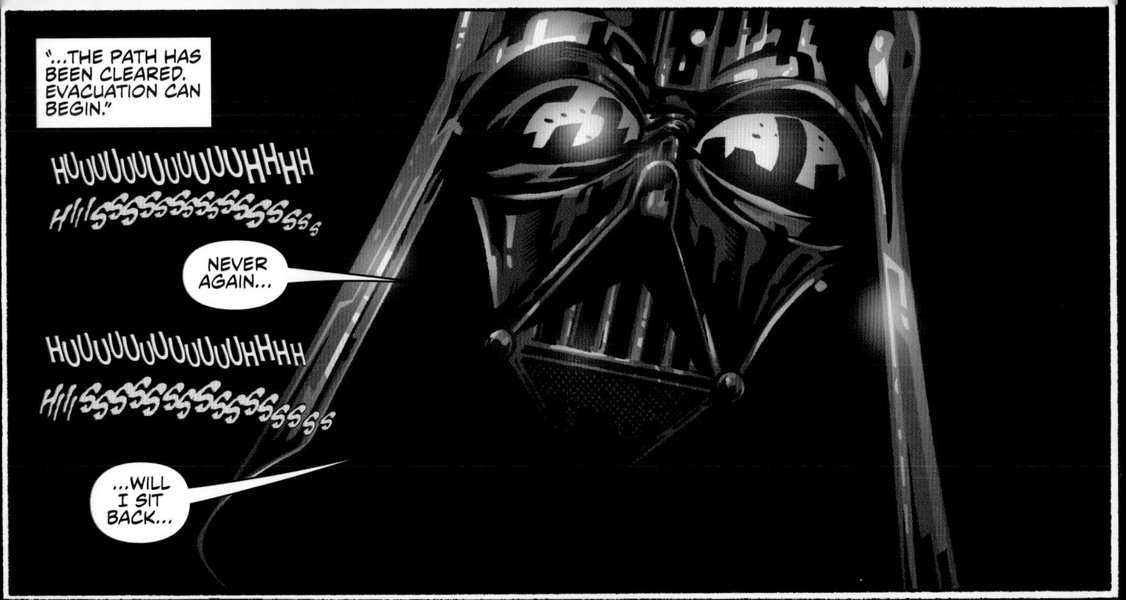
"...THE PATH HAS BEEN CLEARED. EVACUATION CAN BEGIN."
HUUUUUUUUUUUUHHHH
HIIISSSSSSSSSSSSSSS
NEVER AGAIN...
HUUUUUUUUUUUUUHHHH
HIIISSSSSSSSSSSSSSSS
...WILL I SIT BACK...

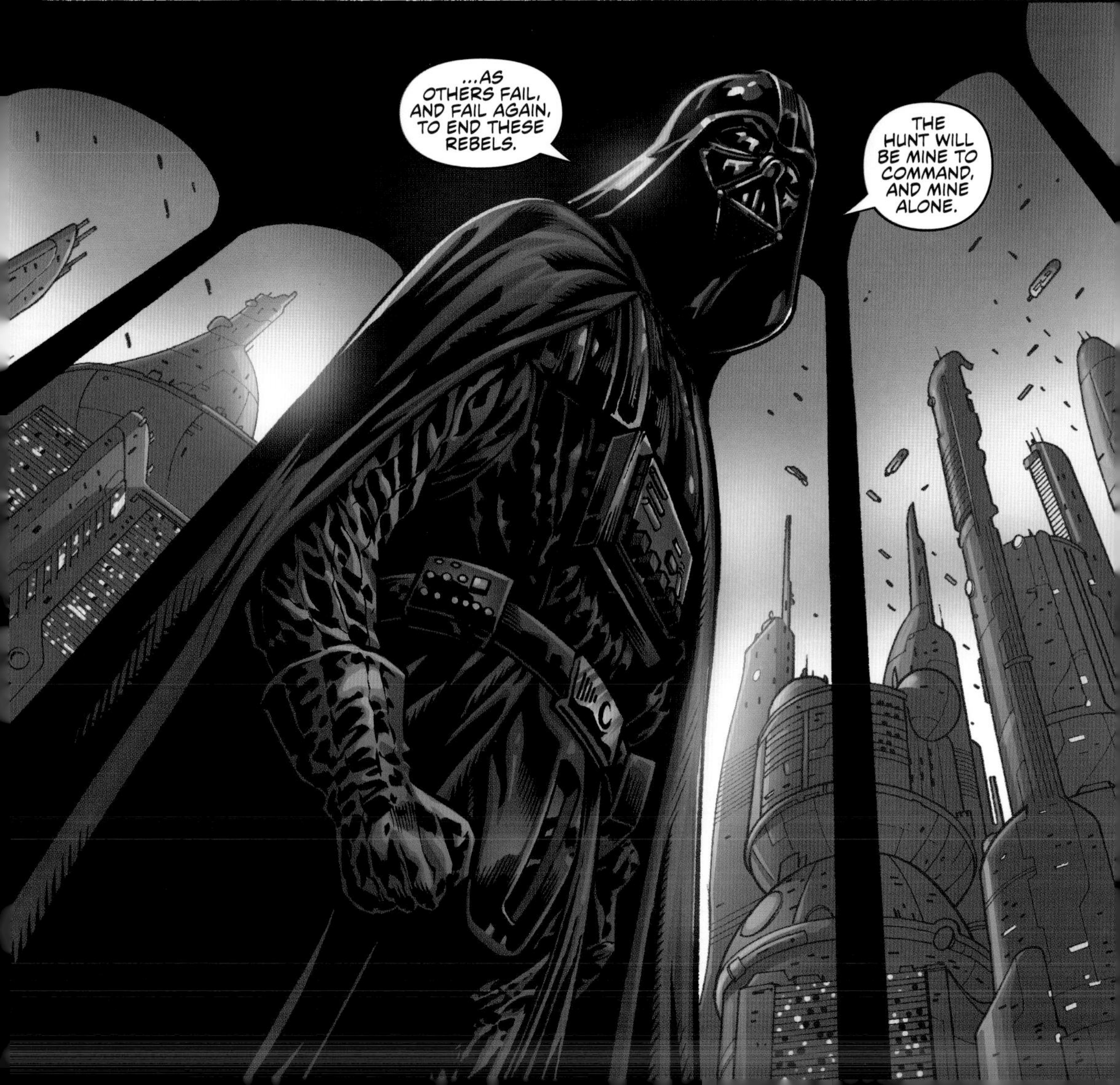
...AS OTHERS FAIL, AND FAIL AGAIN, TO END THESE REBELS.
THE HUNT WILL BE MINE TO COMMAND, AND MINE ALONE.

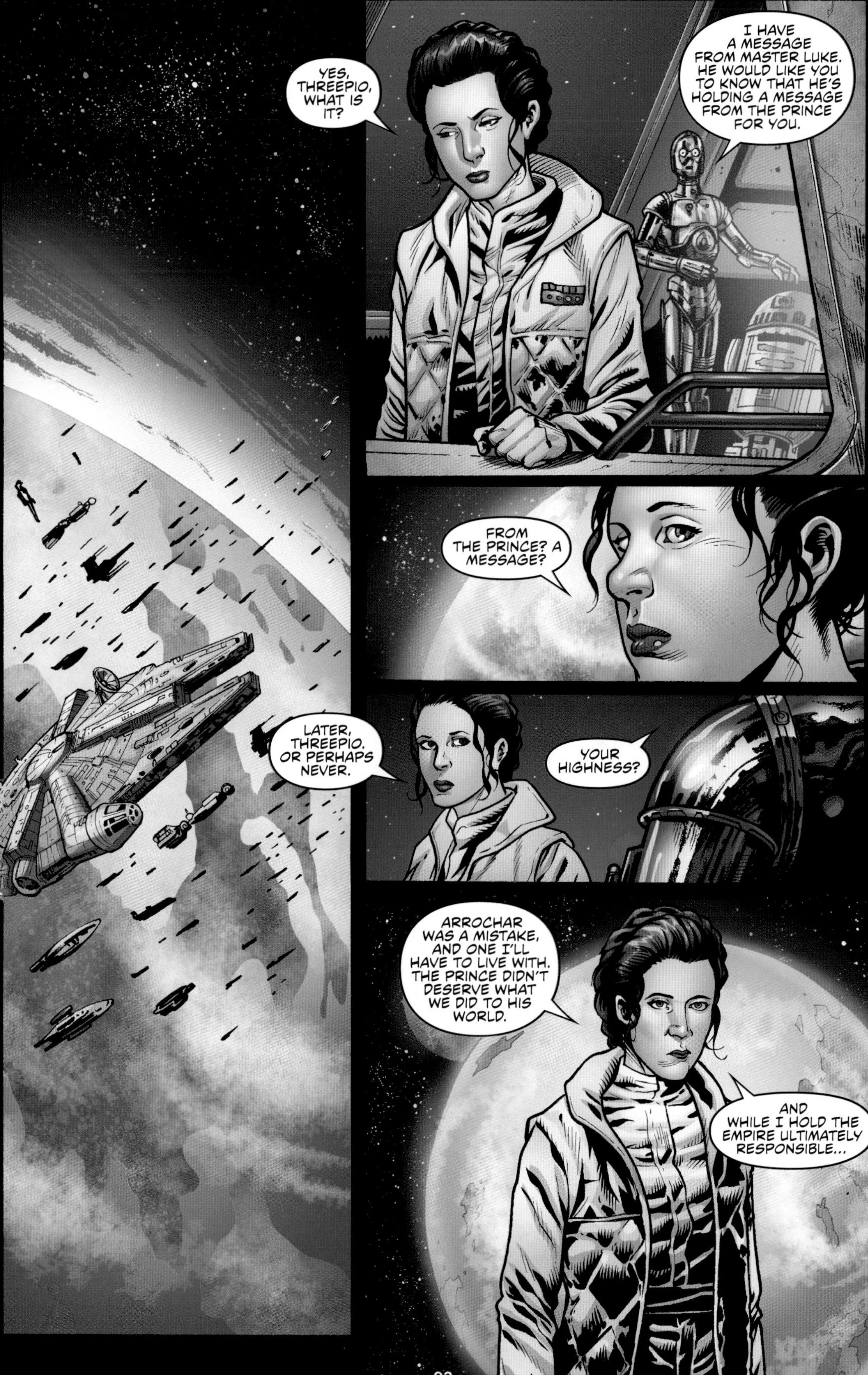
YES, THREEPIO, WHAT IS IT?
I HAVE A MESSAGE FROM MASTER LUKE. HE WOULD LIKE YOU TO KNOW THAT HE'S HOLDING A MESSAGE FROM THE PRINCE FOR YOU.
FROM THE PRINCE? A MESSAGE?
YOUR HIGHNESS?
LATER, THREEPIO. OR PERHAPS NEVER.
ARROCHAR WAS A MISTAKE, AND ONE I'LL HAVE TO LIVE WITH. THE PRINCE DIDN'T DESERVE WHAT WE DID TO HIS WORLD.
AND WHILE I HOLD THE EMPIRE ULTIMATELY RESPONSIBLE...

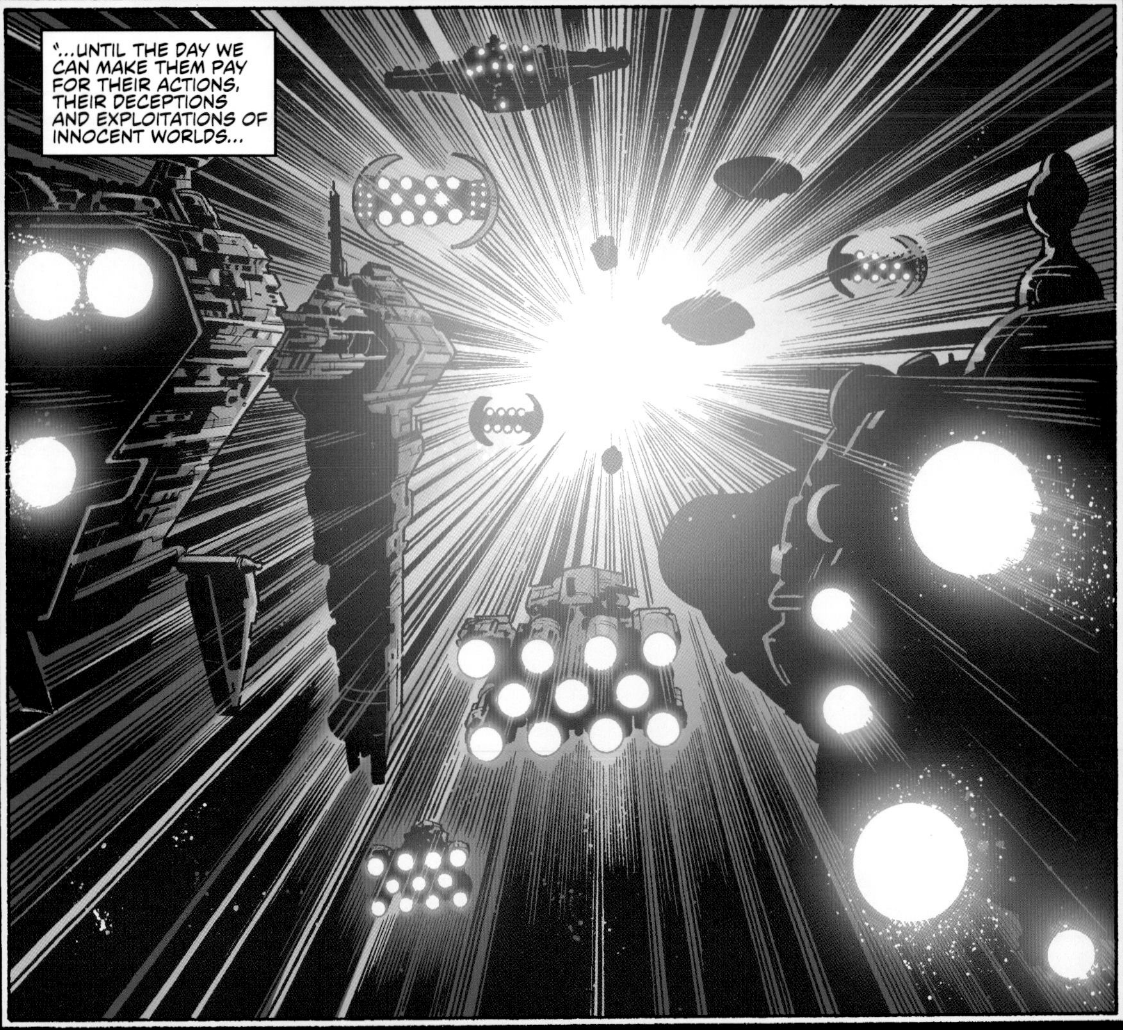
"...UNTIL THE DAY WE CAN MAKE THEM PAY FOR THEIR ACTIONS, THEIR DECEPTIONS AND EXPLOITATIONS OF INNOCENT WORLDS...

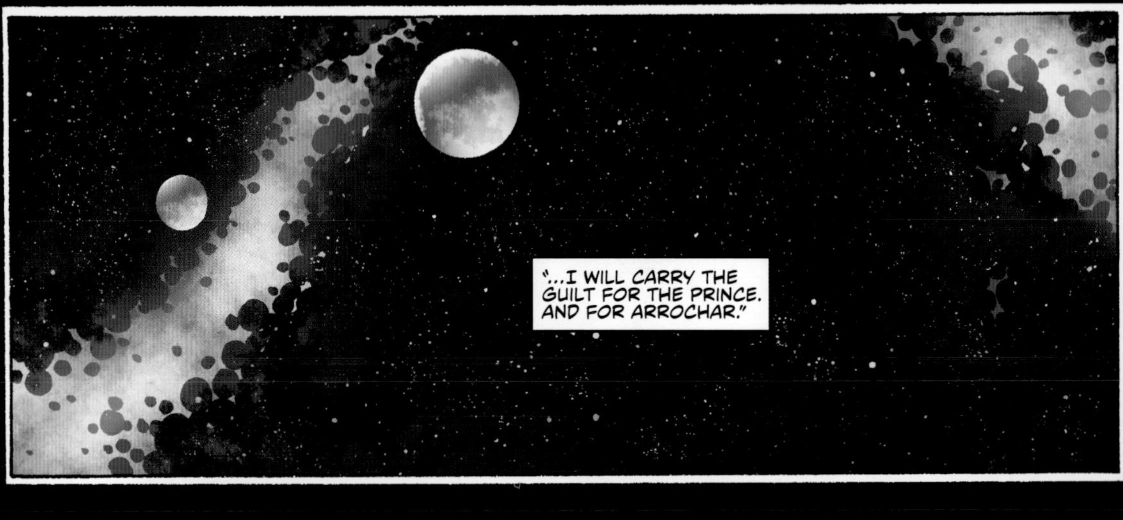
"...I WILL CARRY THE GUILT FOR THE PRINCE. AND FOR ARROCHAR."

THE END

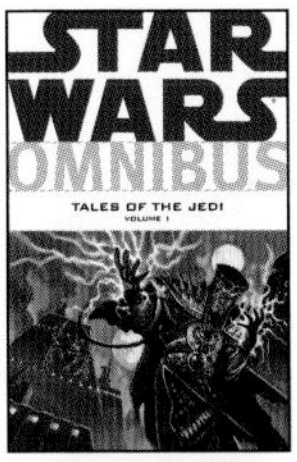
STAR WARS
OMNIBUS
TALES OF THE JEDI
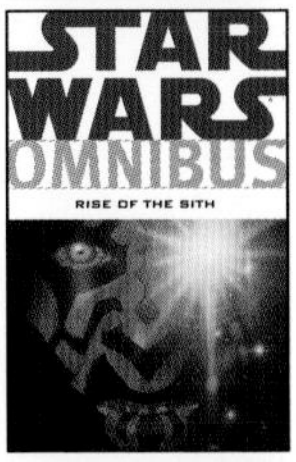
STAR WARS
OMNIBUS
RISE OF THE SITH
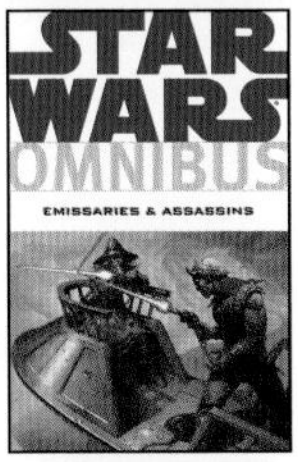
STAR WARS
OMNIBUS
EMISSARIES & ASSASSINS
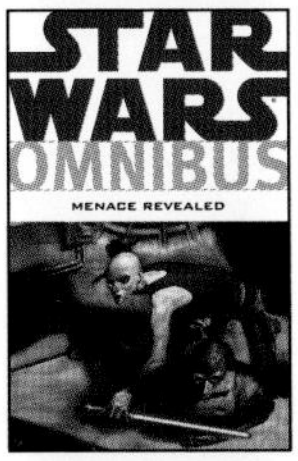
STAR WARS
OMNIBUS
MENACE REVEALED
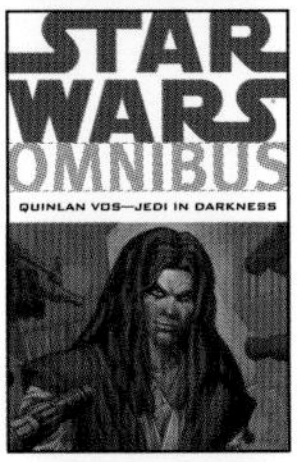
STAR WARS
OMNIBUS
QUINLAN VOS—JEDI IN DARKNESS
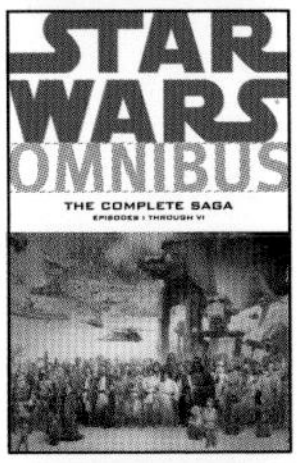
STAR WARS
OMNIBUS
THE COMPLETE SAGA
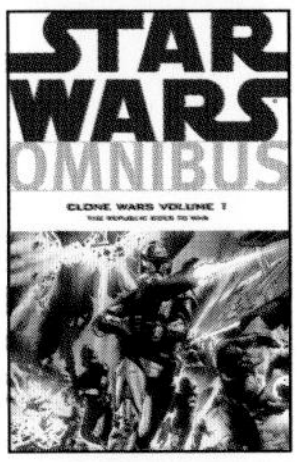
STAR WARS
OMNIBUS
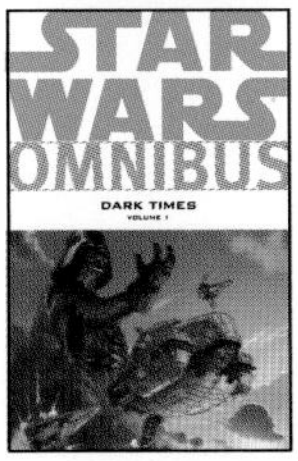
STAR WARS
OMNIBUS
DARK TIMES

STAR WARS OMNIBUS COLLECTIONS

STAR WARS: TALES OF THE JEDI

Including the *Tales of the Jedi* stories "The Golden Age of the Sith," "The Freedon Nadd Uprising," and "Knights of the Old Republic," these huge omnibus editions are the ultimate introduction to the ancient history of the *Star Wars* universe!

Volume 1: ISBN 978-1-59307-830-0 | $24.99 Volume 2: ISBN 978-1-59307-911-6 | $24.99

STAR WARS: KNIGHTS OF THE OLD REPUBLIC

Padawan Zayne Carrick is suddenly a fugitive framed for the murder of his fellow Jedi-in-training. Little does the galaxy know, Zayne's own Masters are behind the massacre and dead set on recovering him before he can reveal the truth.

Volume 1: ISBN 978-1-61655-206-0 | $24.99 Volume 3: ISBN 978-1-61655-227-5 | $24.99
Volume 2: ISBN 978-1-61655-213-8 | $24.99

STAR WARS: RISE OF THE SITH

These thrilling tales illustrate the events leading up to *Episode I: The Phantom Menace*, when the Jedi Knights preserved peace and justice . . . as well as prevented the return of the Sith.

ISBN 978-1-59582-228-4 | $24.99

STAR WARS: EMISSARIES AND ASSASSINS

Discover more stories featuring Anakin Skywalker, Amidala, Obi-Wan, and Qui-Gon set during the time of *Episode I: The Phantom Menace*!

ISBN 978-1-59582-229-1 | $24.99

STAR WARS: MENACE REVEALED

Included here are one-shot adventures, short story arcs, specialty issues, and early *Dark Horse Extra* comic strips! All of these tales take place after *Episode I: The Phantom Menace*, and lead up to *Episode II: Attack of the Clones*.

ISBN 978-1-59582-273-4 | $24.99

STAR WARS: QUINLAN VOS—JEDI IN DARKNESS

From his first appearance as a mind-wiped amnesiac to his triumphant passage to the rank of Jedi Master, few Jedi had more brushes with the powers of the dark side and the evil of the underworld than Quinlan Vos.

ISBN 978-1-59582-555-1 | $24.99

STAR WARS: THE COMPLETE SAGA—EPISODES I THROUGH VI

The comics adaptations of the complete *Star Wars* film saga—in one volume! From the first fateful encounter with Darth Maul to Luke Skywalker's victory over the Sith and Darth Vader's redemption, it's all here.

ISBN 978-1-59582-832-3 | $24.99

STAR WARS: CLONE WARS

The Jedi Knights who were once protectors of the peace must become generals, leading the clone armies of the Republic to war! These stories follow *Attack of the Clones* and feature Jedi heroes Obi-Wan Kenobi, Anakin Skywalker, Mace Windu, and Quinlan Vos.

Volume 1: The Republic Goes to War ISBN 978-1-59582-927-6 | $24.99
Volume 2: The Enemy on All Sides ISBN 978-1-59582-958-0 | $24.99
Volume 3: The Republic Falls ISBN 978-1-59582-980-1 | $24.99

STAR WARS: DARK TIMES

The struggles of the Jedi intertwine with those of others now living in fear, including the diverse crew of a smuggling ship, the *Uhumele*, and a Nosaurian whose troubles begin when the Clone Wars end.

Volume 1: ISBN 978-1-61655-251-0 | $24.99 Volume 2: ISBN 978-1-61655-252-7 | $24.99

DARK HORSE BOOKS

AVAILABLE AT YOUR LOCAL COMICS SHOP OR BOOKSTORE!

To find a comics shop in your area, call 1-888-266-4226

For more information or to order direct: • On the web: DarkHorse.com • E-mail: mailorder@darkhorse.com • Phone: 1-800-862-0052 Mon.–Fri. 9 AM to 5 PM Pacific Time

STAR WARS OMNIBUS
BOBA FETT

STAR WARS OMNIBUS
A LONG TIME AGO . . .

STAR WARS OMNIBUS
EARLY VICTORIES

STAR WARS OMNIBUS
AT WAR WITH THE EMPIRE

STAR WARS OMNIBUS
THE OTHER SONS OF TATOOINE

STAR WARS OMNIBUS
SHADOWS OF THE EMPIRE

STAR WARS OMNIBUS
X-WING ROGUE SQUADRON

STAR WARS OMNIBUS COLLECTIONS

STAR WARS: BOBA FETT

Boba Fett, the most feared, most respected, and most loved bounty hunter in the galaxy, now has all of his comics stories collected into one massive volume!

ISBN 978-1-59582-418-9 | $24.99

STAR WARS: INFINITIES

Three different tales where *one thing* happens differently than it did in the original trilogy of *Star Wars* films. Luke Skywalker, Princess Leia, Han Solo, and Darth Vader are launched onto new trajectories!

ISBN 978-1-61655-078-3 | $24.99

STAR WARS: A LONG TIME AGO. . . .

Star Wars: A Long Time Ago. . . . omnibus volumes feature classic *Star Wars* stories not seen in over twenty years! Originally printed by Marvel Comics, these recolored stories are sure to please Star Wars fans both new and old.

Volume 1: ISBN 978-1-59582-486-8 | $24.99
Volume 2: ISBN 978-1-59582-554-4 | $24.99
Volume 3: ISBN 978-1-59582-639-8 | $24.99
Volume 4: ISBN 978-1-59582-640-4 | $24.99
Volume 5: ISBN 978-1-59582-801-9 | $24.99

STAR WARS: WILD SPACE

Rare and previously uncollected stories! Contains work from some of comics' most famous writers and artists (including Alan Moore, Chris Claremont, Archie Goodwin, Walt Simonson, and Alan Davis), plus stories featuring the greatest heroes and villains of *Star Wars*!

Volume 1: ISBN 978-1-61655-146-9 | $24.99
Volume 2: ISBN 978-1-61655-147-6 | $24.99

STAR WARS: EARLY VICTORIES

Following the destruction of the first Death Star, Luke Skywalker and Princess Leia find there are many more battles to be fought against the Empire and Darth Vader!

ISBN 978-1-59582-172-0 | $24.99

STAR WARS: AT WAR WITH THE EMPIRE

Stories of the early days of the Rebel Alliance and the beginnings of its war with the Empire—tales of the *Star Wars* galaxy set before, during, and after the events in *Star Wars: A New Hope!*

Volume 1: ISBN 978-1-59582-699-2 | $24.99
Volume 2: ISBN 978-1-59582-777-7 | $24.99

STAR WARS: THE OTHER SONS OF TATOOINE

Luke's story has been told time and again, but what about the journeys of his boyhood friends, Biggs Darklighter and Janek "Tank" Sunber? Both are led to be heroes in their own right: one of the Rebellion, the other of the Empire . . .

ISBN 978-1-59582-866-8 | $24.99

STAR WARS: SHADOWS OF THE EMPIRE

Featuring all your favorite characters from the *Star Wars* trilogy—Luke Skywalker, Princess Leia, and Han Solo—this volume includes stories written by acclaimed novelists Timothy Zahn and Steve Perry!

ISBN 978-1-59582-434-9 | $24.99

STAR WARS: X-WING ROGUE SQUADRON

The starfighters of the Rebel Alliance become the defenders of a new Republic in these stories featuring Wedge Antilles and his team of ace pilots known throughout the galaxy as Rogue Squadron.

Volume 1: ISBN 978-1-59307-572-9 | $24.99
Volume 2: ISBN 978-1-59307-619-1 | $24.99
Volume 3: ISBN 978-1-59307-776-1 | $24.99

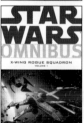

AVAILABLE AT YOUR LOCAL COMICS SHOP OR BOOKSTORE!

To find a comics shop in your area, call 1-888-266-4226

For more information or to order direct: • On the web: DarkHorse.com • E-mail: mailorder@darkhorse.com • Phone: 1-800-862-0052 Mon.–Fri. 9 AM to 5 PM Pacific Time •